THE DECODING OF EDWIN DROOD

No. III.]   JUNE, 1870.   [Price One Shilling.

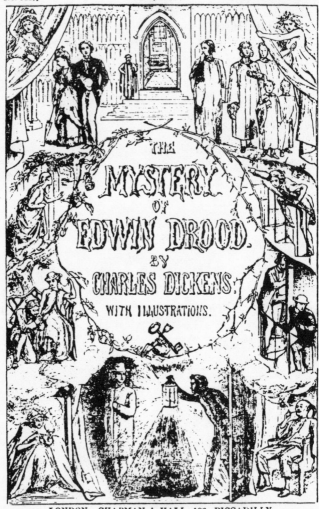

THE
MYSTERY
OF
EDWIN DROOD
BY
CHARLES DICKENS
WITH ILLUSTRATIONS.

LONDON: CHAPMAN & HALL, 193, PICCADILLY.

Advertisements to be sent to the Publishers, and ADAMS & FRANCIS, 59, Fleet Street, E.C.
[The right of Translation is reserved.]

Cover design by Luke Fildes for the wrapper of monthly parts.
Reproduced from a copy at Dickens House.

THE DECODING OF EDWIN DROOD

by

CHARLES FORSYTE

LONDON
VICTOR GOLLANCZ LTD
1980

ISBN 0 575 02789 4

MADE AND PRINTED IN GREAT BRITAIN BY
THE GARDEN CITY PRESS LIMITED
LETCHWORTH, HERTFORDSHIRE
SG6 1JS

CONTENTS

Frontispiece
Cover design for the wrapper of monthly parts of *The Mystery of
    Edwin Drood*

PREFACE

A CREDIBLE SOLUTION to Dickens's unfinished novel *The Mystery of Edwin Drood* should, I believe, meet two requirements. First, it should rest on a reasoned case. Part One of the book that follows is my personal attempt at detective work on Dickens's intentions, with my deductions. Secondly, a solution should be capable of presentation in a fictional form that will provide a satisfactory ending for the reader. This I have tried to do in Part Two.

Any writer on Dickens, even a layman, works within a tradition and owes too much to his predecessors to be able to acknowledge all his debts individually. Yet I do not think I would have written this book without the particular stimulus of Humphry House, kindest of Common Room colleagues, who showed me that Dickens was a serious author, and of Felix Aylmer, whose book *The Drood Case* focused my attention on Dickens's last work. I am also very grateful to Dr Margaret Cardwell, who read Part One in draft form and saved me from many pitfalls; the arguments and remaining errors are my own.

Part One does contain an outline of Dickens's story, but it is still better for the reader to have a prior knowledge of Dickens's text. There are many editions of *Edwin Drood*. The Clarendon Press and Penguin editions both provide an Introduction and notes, as well as reproducing Dickens's own notes for his book, and the so-called 'Sapsea Fragment', which is incorporated in my Part Two. For chapter numbering I have followed the traditional arrangement given in the Clarendon Press edition.

September 1979   C.F.

ACKNOWLEDGEMENTS

I am grateful to the publishers for permission to quote from the following: to Faber and Faber Ltd for *Opium and the Romantic Imagination* by Alethea Hayter (1968); to Granada Publishing Ltd for *The Drood Case* by Felix Aylmer (1964); to Methuen and Co Ltd for 'Dickens: The Two Scrooges' by Edmund Wilson, published in *The Wound and the Bow* (University Paperbacks, 1961); to Oxford University Press for the Pilgrim Edition of *The Letters of Charles Dickens*, edited by Madeline House and Graham Storey (1965-   ) and for the Clarendon Press edition of *The Mystery of Edwin Drood*, edited by Margaret Cardwell (1972); to Martin Secker and Warburg Ltd for *The World of Charles Dickens* by Angus Wilson (1970); to Thames and Hudson Ltd for *A Reader's Guide to Charles Dickens* by Philip Hobsbaum (1973); and to A. Wheaton and Co Ltd for *Magician's Magic* by Paul Curry (1966).

PART ONE

A PERSONAL INVESTIGATION

And in my father's grave lies buried the secret of his story.

—Kate Perugini

My poor friend's face had suddenly assumed the most dreadful expression. His eyes rolled upwards, his features writhed in agony, and with a suppressed groan he dropped on his face upon the ground. Horrified at the suddenness and severity of the attack, we carried him into the kitchen, where he lay back in a large chair and breathed heavily for some minutes. Finally, with a shame-faced apology for his weakness, he rose once more.

"Watson would tell you that I have only just recovered from a severe illness," he explained. "I am liable to these sudden nervous attacks."

—'The Adventure of the Reigate Squire', A. Conan Doyle, in *The Memoirs of Sherlock Holmes*

1

The Mystery of Edwin Drood is the most successful mystery story ever written. When Dickens died on 9 June 1870 he had reached almost exactly the half-way point, and over a century later there is no generally accepted solution to its problems.

Yet Dickens might easily not have lived to write even half of *Edwin Drood.* On 9 June 1865—five years to the day before his death—he was caught in the carnage of a mid-Victorian railway accident. He was returning from a visit to France with his mistress Ellen Ternan, and near Staplehurst in Kent the repair gang had muddled the time of the boat train and removed part of the track, with the result that some of the wooden coaches ran down the embankment and were shattered. Dickens's coach just failed to do the same. It was as though destiny had relented at the last moment and allowed him precisely five more years of creative activity—at a price. He behaved with coolness at the time, seeing his companions to safety, scrambling over the wreckage and giving help to the dying, but the shock to a sensitive and already overworked and overstrained nervous system was lasting. To the end of his life a dread was liable to come over him in any sort of conveyance. His daughter Mamie recorded how once when they were returning from London to his house at Gad's Hill, 'father suddenly clutched the arms of the railway carriage seat, while his face grew ashy pale, and great drops of perspiration stood upon his forehead, and though he tried hard to master the dread, it was so strong that he had to leave the train at the next station.'*

He did not use his five-year reprieve to write another complete novel. At Staplehurst part of the manuscript of *Our Mutual Friend* was in the carriage, to which he had to return to recover it, and this book was duly finished, but in addition to editing his weekly, *All the Year Round*, he was engaged in the public readings of his own work which dominated his later years. Readings is perhaps a misnomer. Dickens had always loved the theatre, and

* Mary Dickens, *My Father as I Recall Him* (1897), pp. 111–12.

his readings were nothing less than a one-man performance in which he was at once dramatist, producer, and a complete cast; as Carlyle had told him after a reading of The Trial from *Pickwick*, 'Charley, you carry a whole company under your own hat.' These readings, in direct contact with his public, met a deep emotional need in him, and they were a natural development of the desire to sense the reactions of his readers, and to respond to them, which underlay his preference for publishing his books in monthly or in weekly parts.

The financial rewards of this public entertainment were also considerably greater than from writing, and as he was under steady financial pressure from his family he eventually succumbed to the temptation to take his readings to America, despite the advice of some of his friends and the long railway journeys involved. Between December 1867 and 20 April 1868 he gave some seventy-five performances in the United States. As was to be expected, he became terribly exhausted under the physical and emotional strain. Yet he rallied on the Atlantic voyage home to such good effect that he was able to embark on a farewell English tour the same autumn, at the same time planning to add to his repertoire a version of the murder of Nancy by Bill Sikes. His readings had hitherto leaned heavily on the sentimental and comic aspects of his writings; this was an even more demanding excursion into the field of horror. Dickens himself had some reservations about performing it, so he tried it out on an invited audience on 14 November 1868 before giving the first public performance in January 1869. This piece came to take a curious hold over him. The desire to repeat it became obsessive. Re-enacting the murder of Nancy by Sikes created in him such a mood of excitement, according to his manager Dolby, that the shocks to the nerves invariably recurred later on in the evening after the audience had left, 'either in the form of great hilarity or a desire to be once more on the platform, or in a craving to do the work again'.* The cumulative strain of the readings took their inevitable toll of Dickens in April 1869, when he was performing in Lancashire. He had appeared some seventy-two times since his return to England, and his health now broke down. The doctors feared paralysis or a

* G. Dolby, *Charles Dickens As I Knew Him* (1885), p. 386.

14

stroke, and made him stop. He was eventually to be allowed to do a further twelve farewell performances, provided they were postponed to the following year, 1870—and no railway journeys.

As he could no longer perform, Dickens's thoughts returned to novel-writing, and in May he was starting to consider the subject for his next book. His old friend and collaborator, Wilkie Collins, had demonstrated the public liking for the sensation novel with the success of his best-seller mystery *The Moonstone* the previous year. Perhaps Sikes and Nancy put the idea of a murder into his head. But he still needed an original plot. By early August he had a 'very curious and new idea', and by the 20th of the same month was already trying out titles for his new book and discussing in a letter to his publisher Chapman whether it should come out in monthly or weekly parts. Despite the attractions of weekly contact with his readers, Dickens wisely decided to write it in monthly parts. There were to be only twelve parts—or strictly eleven, since the last number would be a double one. This would be a short book for Dickens, but a better length for a mystery story than his more usual twenty-part novel.

On Sunday 24 October 1869 the American publisher James T. Fields, who was staying at Gad's Hill with Dickens, was summoned to his small library to hear him read the first part of *The Mystery of Edwin Drood*, 'of which the ink on the last page was scarcely dry'.* So the American was almost certainly the first man to hear the impressionistic opening chapter: John Jasper is coming round from an exotic dream in an East End opium den. He hurries back to his duties as choir-master in the sleepy cathedral town of Cloisterham just in time for the evening service. Jasper is unwell during the service, but recovers and returns to his quarters in the Gate House before the arrival of his nephew and ward Edwin Drood. The twenty-year-old Drood is a student of engineering, who is shortly to go out to Egypt and join the family firm there, a frank easy-going young man of a recognisable public school stamp. He is very different from his uncle, who is only some six years older. The complexity of the dark-haired, dark-whiskered and generally sombre Jasper is made apparent from the start. Edwin Drood sees him as a round peg in a round hole, the

* Quoted Edgar Johnson, *Charles Dickens: His Tragedy and Triumph* (1953), p. 1114.

efficient and respected choir-master and music-teacher, and Jasper's own deep and even jealous affection for his nephew is underlined. Yet in the same scene he confesses to Drood his boredom and frustration in Cloisterham, and even seems threatening in his attitude to the young man. The reason for the latter is apparently Rosa Bud, a very attractive orphan who is at Miss Twinkleton's academy for young ladies, and receives music lessons from Jasper. Under the terms of his father's will Edwin is expected to marry her. A meeting between Edwin and Rosa, still half-child, half-woman, shows the friction between them created by this arranged marriage, although Edwin characteristically accepts it without serious thought.

The auctioneer (and later Mayor) of Cloisterham is Mr Sapsea, a pompous Tory figure of fun, more clerical in manner than the Dean of Cloisterham for whom he likes to be taken. Sapsea invites Jasper to his house to hear the egregious epitaph he has composed for his late wife's tomb. Wanting to get Sapsea's goodwill, Jasper flatters him. Durdles, the Cathedral's drunken and cantankerous stone-mason, who is to execute the epitaph, is also summoned and is given the key of the tomb by Sapsea, putting it in his dinner bundle. After some by-play with Jasper examining the other keys Durdles carries in his capacious pockets, the dusty mason leaves. Returning alone at the end of his evening with the tedious Sapsea, Jasper encounters a hideous ragged street urchin, known as Deputy, throwing stones at the drunken Durdles, who pays him a small retainer to shepherd him home in this way when he is in his cups. Jasper accompanies Durdles, asking him about his ability to find old bodies buried in the Cathedral, and carrying his dinner bundle for him. The number ended with Jasper back in his Gate House, looking down at his peacefully sleeping nephew before lighting up his opium pipe.

The second number introduced a sympathetic Minor Canon of Cloisterham, the athletic Septimus Crisparkle. He receives from their guardian responsibility for the education of two young people, Neville and Helena Landless from Ceylon, where these twins have suffered under a cruel stepfather. There is a strong hint of native blood in them that makes Neville Landless wild and hot-tempered, while his more disciplined sister Helena has become courageous and determined. She is quick to protect Rosa

16

when she faints in the Crisparkle drawing room as her music-master Jasper accompanies her at the piano. (Is he trying to mesmerise Rosa?) Later in the privacy of Miss Twinkleton's establishment, the Nuns' House, Rosa confesses to Helena her fear of Jasper. The two girls become close friends.

However, when Edwin Drood meets the fiery and sensitive Neville he is irritated by Neville's references to his engagement to Rosa. Egged on by Jasper and the strangely potent drink he has mixed while ostensibly trying to reconcile them, the two young men quarrel. Edwin insults Neville with a veiled reference to his dark skin, and Neville throws his drink at him. Jasper loses no time in telling Crisparkle and warning him that he has a dangerous charge. At this time Rosa is paid a visit by her guardian. He is an awkward, arid-looking, but kind-hearted lawyer, Mr Grewgious, who in his youth had been in love with Rosa's mother. He explains to Rosa the terms of her father's will, but because of her reticence fails to realise she has doubts about marrying Edwin Drood, so he undertakes to return at Christmas to settle the details of the marriage.

In the opening of the next monthly number Neville Landless admits to his tutor Canon Crisparkle, whom he likes and respects, that he has fallen in love with Rosa. He is finally persuaded by Crisparkle, and his own sister Helena—as twins they have a special affinity and a telepathic understanding—that he should make up his quarrel with Edwin, providing Drood makes the first move. The Minor Canon passes his decision to Jasper, who, after a strange initial reaction, professes to be convinced and arranges a dinner of reconciliation at his Gate House on Christmas Eve. Edwin meanwhile calls on Mr Grewgious in his Staple Inn chambers in Holborn. After meeting the lawyer's sullen clerk, Bazzard, he is quietly lectured by Grewgious on the importance of knowing his mind about marrying Rosa, and is entrusted with her mother's ring of rubies and diamonds to be put on Rosa's finger only if he is certain that he should marry her, Bazzard being witness to this transaction.

In Cloisterham, at the beginning of the Christmas week, John Jasper goes on a mysterious night expedition round the Cathedral with the mason Durdles as guide. After mounting the tower Durdles is overcome by the drink Jasper has been lavishly providing, and eventually falls asleep with his keys in the crypt. It is two in the morning before he awakes and they start to go home. Outside the Cathedral they are fusilladed with stones by the urchin Deputy, much to the fury of Jasper, who suspects him of spying on them and seizes him by the throat. The number ended with the conclusion of this 'unaccountable expedition'.

After the girls at Miss Twinkleton's academy have broken up for Christmas, Rosa and Edwin meet again. As they walk by the river and the Cathedral, the diminutive Rosa shows more character than Edwin and takes the initiative in discussing their future; they agree to break off the engagement that neither really wants. Sadly, but good friends now, they kiss goodbye, while Jasper, who is watching, sees only the kiss and knows nothing of their decision. Edwin decides not to upset his doting uncle by telling him of his changed plans. On Christmas Eve in Cloisterham Drood encounters the Opium Woman who runs the den in London visited by Jasper. She warns him that 'Ned'—the name Jasper calls him by—is threatened, but he goes on to the dinner with Jasper and Neville Landless. A terrible storm strikes Cloisterham that night, and in the morning Jasper rouses Crisparkle with the news that his nephew went off with Neville Landless the previous night and is missing.

Landless had started on a walking tour with Crisparkle's blessing early that morning. He is brought back by a search party and accused before Mayor Sapsea in spite of his protestations of innocence: he maintains that he walked with Edwin Drood down to the river to look at the effects of the storm and that they returned and parted outside Crisparkle's house. Jasper organises an intensive search for Drood along the river and coast without success. When the lawyer Grewgious arrives, as planned, and tells him of the broken engagement, Jasper faints with a terrible cry. On his recovery he puts forward the suggestion that Drood may after all have left Cloisterham voluntarily in order to avoid the embarrassment his broken engagement would cause. Crisparkle, who had joined Grewgious and Jasper and informed them that Neville was in love with Rosa, is drawn to the local weir on his way home; returning to it early the following morning he dives in and finds Drood's watch and shirt-pin. For lack of any further evidence to incriminate him Neville Landless is released, but though Crisparkle remains convinced of his innocence Neville is forced to leave Cloisterham. Jasper records in his diary both his conviction that his 'dear boy' has been murdered, and his oath to devote himself to the destruction of his murderer.

When the fifth number opens, six months have elapsed since the disappearance of Edwin and there is still no news of him. Neville Landless is living in a dusty garret in Staple Inn found for him by Mr Grewgious, studying hard under the general supervision of Crisparkle. But on a visit to his pupil in London, Crisparkle learns from Grewgious that Jasper is haunting Staple Inn keeping a watch on Neville. Meanwhile a stranger calling himself Datchery, a retired diplomat, appears in Cloisterham, taking lodgings with the Cathedral verger Tope under Jasper's Gate House; he seems to have a considerable interest in Jasper and to be wearing a wig to which he is not accustomed. Taking advantage of the school summer holidays, Jasper himself calls on Rosa at Miss Twinkleton's, and in a dramatic scene by the sun-dial in the garden openly avows his love for her, declaring that he is even prepared to abandon his fidelity to his nephew and his pursuit of Neville Landless for her sake, and threatening to hound Neville to the gallows if she refuses him. After fainting, Rosa flees to her guardian Mr Grewgious in London.

Grewgious soothes and diverts Rosa by telling her about his clerk Bazzard, the author of an unstaged play *The Thorn of Anxiety*, before listening to her story and then lodging her safely for the night at a hotel in Furnival's Inn opposite. The following morning Crisparkle arrives and is recognised by a powerful, sunburned young man; he had been Crisparkle's fag at school and had saved him from drowning. This is Lieutenant Tartar, who has retired from the Navy on inheriting an estate, and is adjusting himself to life on dry land by occupying nautical-style rooms in the set next to Neville Landless. Tartar offers his services, and Rosa is taken up to his rooms so that she can talk through the beanstalks he is growing on his roof garden to her friend Helena Landless, safe from the eyes of Jasper or his agents.

In the following number Rosa and Grewgious are taken on a boat trip up the river by Tartar, to whom Rosa's affections are evidently turning, before she is securely—if boringly—housed by her guardian with Miss Twinkleton as chaperone in rooms let by his clerk's relative Mrs Billickin. The Billickin (last of a line of Dickensian landladies) comes off much the better in the brisk guerrilla war she conducts with the genteel schoolmistress. On his side, Jasper returns to the opium den in London for the first time since Drood's disappearance, and under the influence of the Opium Woman's drug relives 'the journey' and 'the deed', as he always does in his dream before his exotic visions start. By carefully adjusting the opium mixture the woman tries to get more out of him, without success, but she does manage to follow him back to his Gate House in Cloisterham, where Datchery spots her, telling her Jasper's name and how to see him at the service next morning in the Cathedral. She in her turn tells him of her encounter and conversation with Drood on the day of his disappearance. The imp Deputy, now a firm ally of Datchery, undertakes to find out for him where she lives. The next morning the Opium Woman goes to the service, hides behind a pillar, recognises Jasper and shakes her fist at him. Returning to his breakfast, Datchery records his satisfaction by adding a large chalk mark to the tally he is keeping inside his cupboard door.

Having finished at this point on 8 June 1870—it was the end of a chapter but not of the number—Dickens wrote some letters. During dinner with his sister-in-law Georgina he had a stroke; he died the following day.

The mystery story that Dickens left unresolved has been debated ever since. For *Edwin Drood* raises not one problem but a series of connected problems, and the great difficulty for all would-be solvers is to find a solution that offers a satisfactory answer to all the problems in the text. Indeed, the first question to be asked is whether Dickens himself had a solution to these problems. This might seem unduly sceptical; but the looseness of structure in some of the earlier novels has raised doubts whether Dickens was capable of the detailed planning needed for this type of book. There is no evidence of such planning in his notes. In accordance with his usual practice, these were mere jottings, one sheet of paper to a number, and the notes for the fifth and sixth parts contain little more than the numbers and titles of the chapters. There is nothing to indicate the future shape of the book. The assistant editor of his magazine *All the Year Round*, Wills, was later quoted as saying that Dickens had got into a muddle over his plot, the worry about extricating himself being a contributory cause of his fatal stroke. Was Wills right?

Certainly Dickens did encounter difficulties when writing *Drood*. When the proofs of the first two parts came back from the printers on 1 December, he found to his horror that they were 'twelve printed pages too short!!!'. As each number was thirty-two pages long in print, this was a considerable deficit, showing how out of practice he had become in writing monthly parts. What made the problem particularly difficult was that he had stopped writing *Edwin Drood* in order to practise his final twelve readings, due to take place between 11 January and 15 March 1870. But he got down to it with his usual efficiency. The first part was made up to length by writing some more dialogue between Edwin and Rosa, and by transposing the last chapter of the second part, in which Jasper meets Deputy stoning Durdles home, to become the last chapter of the first part. To fill the gap this created in the second part, Dickens wrote a new chapter introducing Mr Grewgious, who should not have appeared until the third number. He was already starting to use up his material too quickly.

The farewell readings began on 11 January and attracted large audiences. No item was performed more often than the horrific and exhausting murder of Nancy by Bill Sikes, yet Dickens still managed to complete his third and fourth numbers. At the same time the warning signs for his health were clear, as Forster recorded when he read the latest number privately to his friends: '. . . on 21 March, when he read admirably his fourth number, he told us that as he came along, walking up the length of Oxford Street . . . he had not been able to read, all the way, more than the right-hand half of the names over the shops.'[*] He gave his last public reading on 15 March, when he told his audience, 'In but two short weeks from this time I hope that you may enter, in your own homes, on a new series of readings at which my assistance will be indispensable; but from these garish lights I now vanish for evermore, with a heartfelt, grateful, respectful, affectionate farewell.'[†] In two weeks the first number of *The Mystery of*

[*] John Forster, *The Life of Charles Dickens* (1872–4; Everyman edn, 1969), vol II, p. 411.
[†] ibid. p. 410.

Edwin Drood appeared on sale as he had promised. (Even in 1870 there were more pages of advertisement than text, the inside of the green paper cover offering Chappell's Twenty Guinea Pianoforte with check action in a mahogany or Canadian walnut case.) The new story seemed set to be as popular as the readings, and the most successful of all his books. The first printing was sold out and a second available by 9 April. In the middle of the month he was able to write, 'We have been doing wonders with No. 1 of Edwin Drood. *It has very, very far outstripped every one of its predecessors.'*

Yet only about a week later he was struggling with the next number. 'For the last week I have been most perseveringly and ding-dong-doggedly at work, making headway but slowly,' he admitted.† There was more than one cause for his difficulties. No doubt a sense of anticlimax had set in after the heady excitements of the public readings, that reaction into which he had been plunged in the past after his amateur theatricals. Dickens had also reached the point, familiar to a mystery writer, when the author has set his scene and his problem, and then has to face a long hard graft through the middle of the book before he reaches his dénouement. In his case this was compounded by the fact that he had gone on using his material up too fast. His notes show that he had originally planned the disappearance of Drood for the fifth number, whereas it had all happened in the previous number, leaving him still two-thirds of the book to write. His notes also show that he intended to put Jasper's declaration of love to Rosa in the garden of the Nuns' House before the arrival of Datchery in Cloisterham; he may well have reversed this order to avoid any appearance of cause and effect between these two events in his original plan. He ended up by considerably over-writing the number, and having to cut out no less than 154 lines.

From 30 May he was working on the sixth part at Gad's Hill, doing much of his writing during the pleasant summer weather in the Swiss chalet, a present from the actor Fechter. Dickens seemed to be getting his second wind in *Edwin Drood*, and then he was struck down.

* Quoted, *The Mystery of Edwin Drood* (Clarendon Press, 1972), ed. Margaret Cardwell p. xxv.
† ibid.

Although his health was failing during the time he was writing the book, there is no reason to think that the clarity of Dickens's mind was affected. His daughter Kate even maintained that he was more lucid than usual. 'That my father's brain was more than usually clear and bright during the writing of *Edwin Drood*, no one who lived with him could possibly doubt; and the extraordinary interest he took in the development of this story was apparent in all that he said or did, and was often the subject of conversation between those who anxiously watched him as he wrote, and feared that he was trying his strength too far,' she recorded.*

The difficulties he encountered in the writing appear to have been those of narration—using his material sooner than he had planned, keeping the story moving, and getting each number the right length—not of plot. And this would have been in character at this stage of his life. While the brash young author could write *Pickwick* off the cuff with the careless fluency of youth, the more mature Dickens had learned to plan his work with much greater care, even if the plans were in his head rather than on paper. At the end of his previous novel, *Our Mutual Friend*, he wrote of that book and the problems of monthly publication that 'it would be very unreasonable to expect that many readers, pursuing a story in portions from month to month through nineteen months, will, until they have it before them complete, perceive the relations of its finer threads to the whole pattern which is always before the eyes of the story weaver at his loom'. It would have been even more unreasonable if the same story weaver had embarked on a complex mystery story in monthly parts without having before his eyes 'the whole pattern'. And there is some evidence to support this. The illustrated cover that appeared on each monthly part (*see frontispiece*) includes a dramatic scene with a man holding a lantern that does not correspond with anything in the existing text. This scene must be from the later, unwritten part of the novel, probably the dénouement. The first sketch for the cover, made by his son-in-law, Charles Allston Collins, was approved by Dickens on 29 October 1869, only five days after he had read the first number of *Edwin Drood* to Fields. The timing shows that Dickens must have visualised this scene from the later part of the

* Kate Perugini, in *Pall Mall Magazine*, no. 158 (June 1906), p. 648.

book and given his instructions to Collins while he was engaged on the beginning of his story.

So it may be taken that Dickens did have 'the whole pattern' in his mind's eye when he embarked on *The Mystery of Edwin Drood*. This is not to say that he had worked out every last detail; but he had in his head the solution to his mystery, that would have been revealed had he lived just six more months.

How is it then that there is no general agreement on this solution? After all, *Edwin Drood* was written eighteen years before the first appearance of Sherlock Holmes, and there have been generations of increasingly sophisticated readers of mystery and detective stories since then. The real problem lies in the richness of the text of *Edwin Drood*, which cannot be conveyed in a summary. Much is hinted, much is left unsaid, and it is possible to see many different patterns. This is at once the fascination and frustration of the book. One modern critic considers that this quality now makes it impossible to penetrate Dickens's intentions, since 'every attempt to finish the trajectory which Dickens left uncompleted will indicate only the way in which the interpreter views what we already have of that trajectory'.* So his conclusion is that 'The critics should confess themselves baffled'.†

There is no better illustration of the variety of patterns in the kaleidoscope of *Edwin Drood* than a new grouping which was not perceived until 1930. In that year an American, Howard Duffield, pointed out the many parallels between the presumed murder of Drood and the practices of the Thugs, Hindu devotees of the goddess Kali, who strangled unsuspecting travellers. He concluded that the dark-skinned Jasper with his black hair and whiskers was a Thug who carried out a strangulation of Drood. This theory was espoused and further elaborated by Edmund Wilson during the Second World War in his essay 'Dickens: The Two Scrooges'. Wilson put forward the thesis that both Dickens and Jasper were divided personalities, that in Jasper the novelist was fictionalising himself. In this way Wilson both endorsed and gave a deeper significance to Duffield's idea.

* Philip Hobsbaum, *A Reader's Guide to Charles Dickens* (1973), p. 280.
† ibid. p. 279.

Mr Jasper is, like Dickens, an artist: he is a musician, he has a beautiful voice. He smokes opium, and so, like Dickens, leads a life of the imagination apart from the life of men. Like Dickens, he is a skilful magician, whose power over his fellows may be dangerous. Like Dickens, he is an alien from another world; yet, like Dickens, he has made himself respected in the conventional English community. Is he a villain? From the point of view of the cathedral congregation of Cloisterham, who have admired his ability as an artist, he will have been playing a diabolic role. All that sentiment, all those edifying high spirits, which Dickens has been dispensing so long, which he is still making the effort to dispense—has all this now grown as false as those hymns to the glory of the Christian God which are performed by the worshipper of Kali?*

It is characteristic of Droodian solutions that this view of Jasper/Dickens should have been totally contradicted by Felix Aylmer in the postwar period with an argument that may be regarded as the Agatha Christie solution to *Edwin Drood*. For it had become accepted by most students of *Drood* that Jasper had murdered his nephew, when, in true Christie style, Aylmer turned the whole structure on its head with the assertion that Jasper was not the villain of the piece but the hero. He took as his starting point the paragraph in the second chapter where Edwin Drood arrives at his uncle's Gate House, and

Mr Jasper stands still, and looks on intently at the young fellow, divesting himself of his outer coat, hat, gloves, and so forth. Once for all, a look of intentness and intensity—a look of hungry, exacting, watchful, and yet devoted affection—is always, now and ever afterwards, on the Jasper face whenever the Jasper face is addressed in this direction. And whenever it is so addressed, it is never, on this occasion or on any other, dividedly addressed; it is always concentrated. (p. 7).†

* Edmund Wilson, *The Wound and the Bow* (1941; University Paperbacks, 1961), pp. 91–2.
† Page references throughout for quotations from *The Mystery of Edwin Drood* are to the 1972 Clarendon Press edition.

Aylmer showed that Dickens intended to make this emphatic statement, and had made it even more categoric by adding to his original draft the phrases 'once for all' and 'now and ever afterwards', and turning 'when' into 'whenever'.* So Aylmer argued that if such a look of devotion invariably appeared on Jasper's face whenever he looked at Edwin Drood—and this quite literally is what Dickens said in the most uncompromising words—then it is inconceivable that he could have murdered him, and that what Dickens was really doing was to portray an ostensibly sinister figure, 'a hero who would pass for a villain'.† Jasper's true role must be that of protector, guarding young Edwin against some outside threat. (*A Kinsman's Devotion* was a possible title Dickens considered.) Such a threat could come from Egypt, where his father had worked as a civil engineer and where Drood is destined to join the family firm, a vendetta arising from some action by the elder Drood that has started a blood feud. It is suggested by Aylmer that one would-be assassin had fallen from the tower the previous year; that an attempt is made on Drood at Christmas from which he escapes, but, since he finds Jasper's scarf, he believes Jasper to be involved in the attempt and goes into hiding. (*In Hiding* was another possible title Dickens rejected.) It is an ingenious solution supported by considerable research.

Wilson and Aylmer cannot both be right; and examination shows flaws in both cases. The Thugs did not normally, if ever, attack Europeans. Their victims were chosen from travellers passing through an area where their disappearance would not attract attention, and so the very existence of Thuggee was for years unrecognised by the British in India. Thugs did not operate outside India, they worked in groups, and their main motive was robbery. For all these reasons Edwin Drood was a most unlikely victim for a Thug. And there is an even greater objection. How on earth would Edwin Drood, a typical young English public school boy, have acquired as uncle and guardian a Kali-worshipping Hindu Indian? The Landless twins come from Ceylon, and appear to have mixed blood, yet there is no hint in the text to connect Drood with India in any way. If there is an exotic mystery in *Edwin Drood*, it must surely lie in Egypt as Aylmer proposed.

* Felix Aylmer, *The Drood Case* (1964), pp. 6–7.
† ibid., p. 20.

However Aylmer's scenario is fragile too. He is driven to various implausible explanations in the attempt to maintain the sinister figure of Jasper as hero and protector of his nephew. In short, both theories fail when set against the text of the book as a whole, while at the same time leaving us with an uncomfortable dilemma. If Jasper did not kill Drood, how do we account convincingly for Jasper's actions and for the disappearance of Drood? If Jasper did kill Drood, how do we dispose of Aylmer's argument? So where do we go from here?

2

AT THIS POINT I should declare my interest. As the author of several mystery stories, I have been fascinated by *Edwin Drood* for a number of years. It seemed a standing challenge to the ingenuity of modern mystery writers to provide an ending. When I spoke to other people about *Drood*, I was surprised to find how few of them had actually read it, the old-fashioned truth being that most readers like a story to have an ending. Here was another reason for attempting the task. *Edwin Drood* is both a Dickens novel and a mystery story. Only the author's hand could have completed his novel; but an ending could still be written providing a solution to his mystery. The result would be a complete book to read containing some neglected Dickens. So I decided to make the attempt. I deliberately did not read any previous continuations. The only sound approach seemed to be to start with an open mind, to investigate Dickens's text, together with what was known of his intentions, and make my own deductions. Having some experience of constructing mystery stories, I should then be able to devise an appropriate ending. At worst the result should be a workmanlike conclusion to the book, and at best something close to the solution Dickens himself would have given had he lived.

On this basis I set to work. First, I decided to examine his intentions. There was not a great deal to go on. His own working notes for *Edwin Drood* did not indicate the future development of the story. Dickens held the cards very close to his chest, except on one occasion refusing to discuss the book with members of his own family. There were three lines of investigation that might be helpful: the little he did tell his contemporaries; his experience in mystification as an amateur conjurer; and the influence of Wilkie Collins and his mystery novel *The Moonstone*.

The most important contemporary witness was his friend, confidant, and eventual executor and biographer John Forster, who gave this account in his life of Dickens:

His first fancy for the tale was expressed in a letter in the middle of July. 'What should you think of the idea of a story beginning in this way?—Two people, boy and girl, or very young, going apart from one another, pledged to be married after many years—at the end of the book. The interest to arise out of the tracing of their separate ways, and the impossibility of telling what will be done with that impending fate.' This was laid aside; but it left a marked trace on the story as afterwards designed, in the position of Edwin Drood and his betrothed.

I first heard of the later design in a letter dated 'Friday the 6th of August 1869', in which after speaking, with the usual unstinted praise he bestowed always on what moved him in others, of a little tale he had received for his journal, he spoke of the change that had occurred to him for the new tale by himself. 'I laid aside the fancy I told you of, and have a very curious and new idea for my new story. Not a communicable idea (or the interest of the book would be gone), but a very strong one, though difficult to work.' The story, I learnt immediately afterward, was to be that of the murder of a nephew by his uncle; the originality of which was to consist in the review of the murderer's career by himself at the close, when its temptations were to be dwelt upon as if, not he the culprit, but some other man, were the tempted. The last chapters were to be written in the condemned cell, to which his wickedness, all elaborately elicited from him as if told of another, had brought him. Discovery by the murderer of the utter needlessness of the murder for its object, was to follow hard upon commission of the deed; but all discovery of the murderer was to be baffled till towards the close, when, by means of a gold ring which had resisted the corrosive effects of the lime into which he had thrown the body, not only the person murdered was to be identified but the locality of the crime and the man who committed it. So much was told to me before any of the book was written; and it will be recollected that the ring, taken by Drood to be given to his betrothed only if their engagement went on, was brought away with him from their last interview. Rosa was to marry Tartar, and Crisparkle the sister of Landless, who was himself, I think, to have perished in assisting Tartar finally to unmask and seize the murderer.

Nothing had been written, however, of the main parts of the design excepting what is found in the published numbers; there was no hint or preparation for the sequel in any notes of chapters in advance; and there remained not even what he had himself so sadly written of the book by Thackeray also interrupted by death. The evidence of matured designs never to be accomplished, intentions planned never to be executed, roads of thought marked out never to be traversed, goals shining in the distance never to be reached, was wanting here. It was all a blank.*

Despite this 'blank', Forster says a good deal. Unfortunately his reliability is in question. The publicly ponderous Forster with his 'rhinoceros laugh' was not the most attractive figure in the Dickens circle, and Dickens had even parodied some of his mannerisms as Podsnap in *Our Mutual Friend*. This itself was an indication that the two men were not so close in later life as they had been when younger; and as a result Forster was not so well informed about the later books. Since he believed the essential Dickens was shown in the novels, this put him in a quandary when he came to write about this period in his life of Dickens, so he tried to cover up the situation. The editors of the Pilgrim Edition of Dickens's letters have shown that Forster was not too scrupulous, at least by modern standards of scholarship, in quoting and editing his material, implying that letters written to others were to himself, falsifying dates, and 'improving' texts. The passage Forster quoted from 'a letter in the middle of July' was taken almost verbatim from Dickens's Book of Memoranda, in which

* Forster, op. cit. vol. II, p. 366.

between 1855 and 1865 he noted down ideas and names for his novels. The passage could not have been written in a letter of July 1869, except on the highly unlikely assumption that Dickens copied it from his book of notes. This spurious letter inevitably throws doubt on the rest of Forster's account of the genesis of *Edwin Drood*, particularly as the details of the plot were not quoted from any Dickens text but 'learnt immediately afterward'. It has been suggested that the development of the novel as given by Forster could have been inferred from an intelligent reading of the book.

Some have totally rejected Forster's account of *Edwin Drood*. Such a view ignores the essential integrity of Forster and his solid relationship with Dickens. The editors of the Pilgrim Edition point out that he had Dickens 'remarkably in perspective', and that paradoxically the numerous small distortions of fact in the *Life* 'were in the interest of a larger, or ideal, truth'.* Forster was no mere fabricator, he was putting the record straight, as he saw it, from an unequalled knowledge of Dickens and his affairs. In private he was a much more sympathetic figure than he was liable to cut in company, and a number of his friends testified to his warmth and helpfulness. So too with Dickens. If younger companions on Dickens's side, and marriage on Forster's, had to some extent taken them apart, he still had qualities of dependability and understanding that made Dickens turn to him throughout his life. He remained a friend, Dickens's executor, and the man to whom Dickens left his manuscripts. Even at this period, as Forster is careful to record, they met fairly often. Dickens spent his last birthday with the Forsters, they dined together on 22 May, and Dickens wrote to Forster on 29 May, only days before his death. Dickens also read to Forster every one of the five completed numbers of *Edwin Drood*.

Given these circumstances, it is difficult to see how Dickens could have avoided saying *something* to Forster about *Drood*. The very least he could have done was to explain that he could not give Forster any details as that would spoil the plot for him—which is virtually what Dickens did say in the letter dated Friday 6 August. But this would hardly be enough to satisfy the

* *The Letters of Charles Dickens*, ed. Madeline House and Graham Storey (Pilgrim Edition, 1965–   ), vol. I, p. xi.

touchy Forster, and Dickens would in all probability have felt himself obliged to elaborate further, vaguely outlining the story without giving away the real secret of his mystery. Again this is what Forster said he 'learnt immediately afterward'. For even if Forster intended to imply that the incommunicable idea was revealed to him subsequently, it is manifest that it was not. Dickens told Forster the necessary minimum and no more: the 'very curious and new idea' was not included. So Forster's account is quite plausible, assuming that Dickens intended to tell no one his real secret. It is less credible that Dickens told his old confidant nothing about the book, than that he did tell him roughly what Forster recorded in the *Life*. This does not imply that every detail in Forster's account was accurate, or was given to him by Dickens personally. He may well have done a little embellishing, as he did for the 'letter in the middle of July'. It is also possible that he learned of the scene in the condemned cell from Luke Fildes.

Luke Fildes was removed from his parents' house at the age of eleven and brought up by an extraordinary radical grandmother, Mary Fildes, who is alleged to have received a sabre slash from a hussar at Peterloo, and recovered to become a Chartist in the 1840s. Against her wishes, her grandson became an artist, and was in turn an illustrator, a painter, and then a fashionable portrait-painter with a grand studio house in Kensington, painting King Edward VII and King George V. He was at the start of this career, twenty-six years old, when a crisis arose at the end of 1869 over the illustrations for *Drood*, the original artist Charles Collins being too unwell to continue. Millais saw an illustration Fildes had published in the new magazine *The Graphic* and recommended him to Dickens, who liked his work and employed him. Fildes did the final version of the cover and twelve illustrations for *Drood*. He was also preparing, at the time of Dickens's death, to do a further illustration of which William Hughes in 1891 gave the following account:

> . . . Mr Luke Fildes R.A. . . . with whom we have had the pleasure of an interview . . . is convinced that Dickens intended that Edwin Drood should be killed by his uncle; and this opinion is supported by the fact of the introduction of a 'large

black scarf of strong close-woven silk', which Jasper wears for the first time in the fourteenth chapter of the story, and which was likely to have been the means of death, i.e. by strangulation. Mr Fildes said that Dickens seemed much surprised when he called his attention to this change of dress—very noticeable and embarrassing to an artist who had studied the character—and appeared as though he had unintentionally disclosed the secret. He further stated that it was Dickens's intention to take him to a condemned cell in Maidstone or some other gaol, in order 'that he might make a drawing', 'and', said Dickens, 'do something better than Cruikshank'; in allusion, of course, to the famous drawing of 'Fagin in the condemned cell'. 'Surely this,' remarked our informant, 'points to our witnessing the condemned culprit Jasper in his cell before he met his fate.'*

Another interview with Fildes, given to Harry How, was published two years later in the *Strand Magazine* for August 1893. The details reported here were slightly different. The drawing of the cell was to be the twenty-fourth, in other words the key one for the final number; the cell was said to be in Rochester gaol; and it was definitely stated that Dickens wanted Fildes 'to do Jasper in the condemned cell'. Fildes also added the detail that he had already packed to leave that day for Gad's Hill when he picked up a newspaper and read of the death of Dickens. In the event Fildes was asked by the family to come down to Gad's Hill, where he drew a picture of Dickens's study entitled 'The Empty Chair' which achieved great popularity—like Dickens himself he had a shrewd feel for the taste of the day. (He also decided to colour his drawing and so started on his painting career.) As executor Forster would also have visited Gad's Hill; he could well have heard of the proposed expedition to the condemned cell from Fildes at this time.

The article in the *Strand* contained nothing further about the death of Drood. However, in 1895 an issue of *The Art Annual* was devoted to Fildes, in which he was quoted as saying: 'He [Dickens] did, at my solicitation, occasionally tell me something—at first charily—for he said it was essential to carefully

* William R. Hughes, *A Week's Tramp in Dickens-Land* (1891), p. 140.

32

preserve the "mystery" from general knowledge to sustain the interest of the book, and later, he appeared to have complete confidence in my discretion.' * Fildes did not explain his discreet allusions until ten years later, and might never have done so if the *Times Literary Supplement* had not reviewed two books about *Edwin Drood* in its issue of 27 October 1905. The reviewer, apart from pronouncing the identity of Datchery to be the 'real mystery of the book', declared: 'Nor do we attach much importance to any of the hints that Dickens dropped, whether to John Forster, to any member of his family, or to either of his illustrators. He was very anxious that his secret should not be guessed, and the hints which he dropped may well have been intentionally misleading.' Fildes was provoked into an immediate reply that appeared in the next issue of the *Supplement*. After stating that Collins had no knowledge of the significance of the sketches he had made, and that Dickens was 'very anxious that his secret should not be guessed', he continued:

. . . these 'hints' to me were the outcome of a request of mine that he would explain some matters, the meaning of which I could not comprehend and which were for me, his illustrator, embarrassingly hidden.

I instanced in the printer's rough proof of the monthly part sent to me to illustrate where he particularly described John Jasper as wearing a neckerchief of such dimensions as to go twice around his neck; I called his attention to the circumstance that I had previously dressed Jasper as wearing a little black tie once round the neck, and I asked him if he had any special reasons for the alteration of Jasper's attire, and, if so, I submitted I ought to know. He, Dickens, appeared for a moment to be disconcerted by my remark, and said something meaning he was afraid he was 'getting on too fast' and revealing more than he meant at that early stage, and, after a short silence, cogitating, he suddenly said, 'Can you keep a secret?' I assured him he could rely on me. He then said, 'I must have the double necktie! It is necessary, for Jasper strangles Edwin Drood with it.'

I was impressed by his earnestness, as, indeed, I was at all my
* David Croal Thomson, in *The Art Annual*, 1895, p. 27.

interviews with him—also by the confidence which he said he reposed in me, trusting that I would not in any way refer to it, as he feared even a chance remark might find its way into the 'papers' and thus anticipate his 'mystery'; and it is a little startling, after more than 35 years of profound belief in the nobility of character and sincerity of Charles Dickens, to be told now he was probably more or less of a humbug on such occasions.*

Fildes has been attacked as inaccurate and inconsistent. In fairness to him, he was being reported on every occasion except in his letter, so it is impossible to know how far any discrepancies were due to Fildes or to the journalists concerned. In his letter Fildes did use the terms 'neckerchief' and 'double necktie' for Jasper's long silk scarf, but if either his terms or his memory were not precise, does it matter? The essential point remains: that Dickens changed the neckwear in which Fildes had previously depicted Jasper, that he raised the question with Dickens and got an answer. It was not inconsistent that Fildes had kept silent on Dickens's reply until 1905. He had not made any promise to Dickens on the planned visit to the condemned cell, and he evidently felt free to talk about it; he had made a promise to Dickens about the murder of Drood with Jasper's scarf that he did observe honourably, and did not reveal in full until the lapse of time and the imputations in the *Times Literary Supplement* called for a public statement. The note of pomposity in the letter may raise in the reader's mind a doubt whether the moral outrage on Dickens's behalf was not re-enforced by an irritant suggestion that a successful R.A. had had the wool pulled over his eyes as a young man. Perhaps Fildes was not entirely altruistic in his defence of Dickens, but this does not invalidate his testimony.

The third witness is the most dubious: Charles Culliford Boz Dickens, the author's eldest son. He appears to have collaborated with Joseph Hatton in a stage version of *Edwin Drood*, never put on, in which Jasper ends not in the condemned cell, but in the opium den where he poisons himself and 'dies with a defiant confession'.† In the words of his sister Kate, 'my eldest brother, Charles, positively declared that he had heard from his father's

* *Times Literary Supplement*, 3 November 1905, p. 373.

† *The Mystery of Edwin Drood*, Clarendon Press edn., p. 253.

lips that Edwin Drood was dead.'* William Hughes added a footnote to his interview with Fildes saying, 'Mr Charles Dickens informs me that Mr Fildes is right, and that Edwin Drood was dead. His (Mr Dickens's) father told him so himself.'† Charles Dickens junr. died in 1896, and it was not until 1923 that his own account was published in the Introduction to a Macmillan edition of *Edwin Drood*:

It was during the last walk I ever had with him at Gadshill, and our talk, which had been principally concerned with literary matters connected with *All the Year Round*, presently drifting to *Edwin Drood*, my father asked me if I did not think that he had let out too much of his story too soon. I assented, and added, 'Of course, Edwin Drood was murdered?' Whereupon he turned upon me with an expression of astonishment at my having asked such an unnecessary question, and said: 'Of course; what else do you suppose?'‡

In her turn the daughter of Charles junr., Mary Angela Dickens, gave a different version in a letter written in 1929:

My father told me more than once that when *Edwin Drood* was being written he went with his father for a country walk. After walking for a long time in dead silence my grandfather suddenly began to talk of the book with which he was evidently completely preoccupied. Almost as if he were talking to himself, my father said, he described the murder, standing still and going through the scene in rapid action. Then he mapped out the means by which the murderer was to be identified.

All that my grandfather thus told my father is embodied in the play in which my father collaborated with Mr Hatton.§

After this dramatic account, all that can be safely concluded is that Charles Dickens junr. was told by his father that Edwin Drood was murdered.

* Kate Perugini, op. cit., p. 646.
† W. R. Hughes, op. cit., p. 140.
‡ Quoted Clarendon Press edn., pp. xxvi–xxvii.
§ ibid., p. 253.

None of these three witnesses, Forster, Fildes or Dickens junr., was ideal. Forster manipulated to suit his purposes, Fildes was partly reported, and the only account by Charles Dickens junr. appeared long after his own death. Yet individually and collectively their testimony had to carry weight. Three men, all close to Dickens in different ways at the time he was writing the book, all maintained that Dickens had told them personally that Edwin Drood was murdered. It was highly improbable that Dickens would not have told them the truth; it was not the whole truth, but what he told them would not have been untrue. So it seemed to me at this stage that the murder of Drood by Jasper had to be accepted, and that there was no reason to doubt Forster and Fildes (even if Forster's version was possibly derived from Fildes) that the final scenes would be of Jasper in the condemned cell. Whether the other details produced by Forster in his account were accurate or not remained less certain. They might be, again they might not. I decided to leave them in suspense. What these witnesses did not provide was reliable guidance on the detailed working out of the plot. Nor did they suggest any solution to the motives of Jasper and the objection posed by Aylmer. Would the other lines of enquiry help here?

3

DICKENS SET OUT to mystify audiences long before he wrote *The Mystery of Edwin Drood*. He took up conjuring in 1842—curiously the very year in which some have argued that the events of the story were placed.

At the end of June Dickens and his wife returned from their travels in North America, and during July 'he was engaged to carry a whole bevy of young people to see the conjurer'.* This was Döbler, a magician of Viennese origin, who spoke no English but scored a success with his polished style and array of glittering and elaborate apparatus. In December Dickens was emulating Döbler, and was hard at work preparing a conjuring show for Twelfth Night, the sixth birthday of his son Charley (the same

* *Letters*, vol. III, p. 277.

Charles Dickens junr.), as he recounted to his closest American friend Cornelius Felton:

> But the best of it, is, that Forster and I have purchased between us the entire stock in trade of a conjurer, the practice and display whereof is entrusted to me. And oh my dear eyes, Felton, if you could see me conjuring the company's watches into impossible tea caddies, and causing pieces of money to fly, and burning pocket handkerchiefs without hurting 'em,—and practising in my own room, without anybody to admire—you would never forget it as long as you live.*

The show went so well that Dickens was asked to perform again in February, by which time he had some new tricks, and had made 'a most splendid trick of that apparatus which Hamley couldn't manage' so it was 'as good as Doebler'.†

On Boxing Day, 1843, Dickens celebrated the publication of *A Christmas Carol* the previous week with some energetic conjuring at a birthday party for one of the children of Macready, the famous Shakespearian actor. Jane Carlyle, who went to the party reluctantly and then thoroughly enjoyed herself, left the best description of Dickens as a conjurer:

> Dickens and Forster above all exerted themselves till the perspiration was pouring down and they seemed *drunk* with their efforts! Only think of that excellent Dickens playing the *conjurer* for one whole hour—the *best* conjurer I ever saw—(and I have paid money to see several)—and Forster acting as his servant. This part of the entertainment concluded with a plum pudding made out of raw flour, raw eggs—all the usual ingredients—boiled in a gentleman's hat—and tumbled out reeking—all in one minute before the eyes of the astonished children and astonished grown people! that trick—and his other of changing ladies' pocket handkerchiefs into comfits—and a box full of bran into a box full of—a live guinea-pig! would enable him to make a handsome subsistence let the bookseller trade go as it please—!‡

* ibid., p. 416. † ibid., p. 439.
‡ *Letters of Jane Carlyle*, ed. Leonard Huxley (1924), pp. 169–70.

These performances set a pattern, at least during the 1840s, for conjuring by Dickens on holidays and at Twelfth Night. This was not just in winter. In the summer of 1849, when the family were with him on holiday at Bonchurch in the Isle of Wight and he was working on *David Copperfield*, he suddenly decided to give a mighty conjuring performance for all the children in Bonchurch. Forster sent him the apparatus and the show 'went off in a tumult of wild delight'.* Fortunately Forster also preserved what appears to have been the bill of this performance by 'The Unparalleled Necromancer RHIA RHAMA RHOOS, educated cabalistically in the Orange Groves of Salamanca and the Ocean Caves of Alum Bay', and reproduced the description of six of the magical feats, The Leaping Card Wonder, The Pyramid Wonder, The Conflagration Wonder, The Loaf of Bread Wonder, The Travelling Doll and the Pudding Wonder.

Despite the showman's hyperbole, the descriptions of these tricks are sufficiently precise to enable them to be identified. What is more, Rhia Rhama Rhoos was specific enough to enable most of the apparatus he used to bring about these effects to be recognised in the classic nineteenth-century work on conjuring, *Modern Magic* by Professor Hoffmann. This was the pen name of Angelo John Lewis, a lawyer and magic enthusiast whose book, though not published until after the death of Dickens, reflected the practice and equipment of magicians earlier in the century. The identification of Dickens's apparatus shows that in five out of the six tricks he used a faked container of some sort. In The Pyramid Wonder a shilling vanished from 'a brazen box' and reappeared in the smallest of a nest of boxes, usually half a dozen, so constructed that while they could all be closed simultaneously once the coin was secretly placed inside the smallest box, each one had to be opened individually. The pyramid effect is achieved by standing each box as it is removed on the lid of the larger box from which it has just been taken. (It was this trick Dickens had in mind in *Bleak House* when describing the lawyer Tulkinghorn 'who has the honour of acting as legal adviser of the Dedlocks, and has as many cast-iron boxes in his office with that name outside, as if the present baronet were the coin of the conjurer's trick, and were constantly being juggled through the whole set.') Counting the

* Forster, op. cit. vol. II, p. 51.

usual number of six boxes in the nest, this adds up to a total of no less than eleven special boxes or containers for the five tricks!

Even with all this apparatus, Dickens would still have needed some adroitness. He would have had to obtain the shilling from the brazen box and transfer it to the nest of boxes undetected (or pass it to his assistant to load the boxes behind the scene), and the same would apply to the watch trick. Dickens may have acquired the ability to 'palm', that is, to hold an article by a contraction of the muscles in the palm of the hand, but this would not have been necessary as long as he could hold an object concealed while the hand remained looking natural, so the audience would not suspect its presence. A certain dexterity was called for rather than true sleight of hand. So the picture that emerges of Dickens as a conjurer is of a performer depending heavily on mechanical devices, and probably on the help of his assistant and confederates, rather than on legerdemain to produce his effects.

This view is confirmed by Dickens's reactions to a French conjurer he saw performing in Boulogne in 1854. He was immensely impressed by this man's skill in handling cards, but what really amazed him was when the Frenchman went down among his audience and without any apparent conjurer's apparatus performed feats of what we would call mental magic: written predictions, spirit writing on slates, and seeing through a blindfold. Parapsychological phenomena, such as the hypnotism which he hints Jasper employs, in *Edwin Drood*, fascinated Dickens through his life, and this kind of magic came as a revelation to him. He went away astonished—and baffled. 'I never saw anything in the least like this; or at all approaching to the absolute certainty, the familiarity, quickness, absence of all machinery, and actual face-to-face, hand-to-hand fairness between the conjurer and the audience, with which it was done. I have not the slightest idea of the secret.'*

Forster summed it up in his usual sensible way when he said that Dickens was 'with his tools at hand, a capital conjurer'.† Yet this raises the question: why was Dickens with such limited technical skills a capital conjurer? Part of the answer must be that Dickens was a natural actor. A conjurer has been well defined as an actor persuading an audience that he is a magician. For this Dickens was

* Forster, op. cit., vol. II, pp. 154–5.   † ibid., p. 153.

perfectly equipped. His conjuring, indeed, can be seen as part of his turning to amateur theatricals, and it is significant that at the time of two of his very successful performances he had other things on his mind: when Jane Carlyle saw him at the Macready party he was concerned with the problems and poor sales of *Nicholas Nickleby,* while Bonchurch he found so enervating and depressing that he never went back. Conjuring seems to have served him as an outlet, just as he was to plunge into stage acting as a relief from his domestic tensions.

His acting ability would have had plenty of scope in the presentation of The Travelling Doll Wonder, the only trick in the Bonchurch programme that did not depend on a special container. It was the one that his daughter Mamie particularly recalled later in life: 'One of these conjuring tricks comprised the disappearance and reappearance of a tiny doll, which would announce most unexpected pieces of news and messages to different children in the audience; this doll was a particular favourite, and its arrival eagerly awaited and welcomed.'* The Bonus Genius, as it was also known, had long been a favourite, and a conjuring pamphlet, *Hocus Pocus Junior,* published nearly two centuries earlier in 1658, had a conjurer showing this trick on the title page. The secret was simple. The wooden doll had a detachable head. It was covered by a long cloak, with just the head appearing through the opening. Inside the cloak was a hidden patch pocket big enough to take the head. Under the pretext of getting money for the doll's travels, the performer removed the doll's body and left it in his pocket, while the head remained visible. Professor Hoffmann explains the next stage:

> The performer has, meanwhile, again put the right hand under the cloak, and with two fingers holds the little pocket open for the reception of the head. As he says the last words, he gives the head a sharp downward rap with the fingers of the left hand, and lets it fall into the little pocket, the effect being as if the figure had suddenly vanished. The performer shakes the cloak, and turns it inside out to show that it is empty, taking care always to grasp it by that part which contains the head, when all other portions of the cloak may be shown freely; and as the

* Mary Dickens, op. cit., p. 34.

40

audience are not aware that the figure is divisible, and supposing it to be indivisible, . . . there is nothing to lead them to guess the secret.*

By reversing the procedure the doll messenger can be made to reappear. Dickens's imagination would have produced much amusing by-play with this doll and exciting messages for the young members of his audience, and with its mysterious comings and goings it is hardly surprising that it was the most popular of his feats with his children.

Paul Curry chose to open his book *Magician's Magic* with a description of the Travelling Doll in order to illustrate the importance of misdirection in magic. After describing the mechanics, he comments: 'Simple? Obvious? Simple, perhaps—most tricks are—but certainly not obvious. For in this explanation, one important ingredient is missing: the ability of a skilled magician to *misdirect* the attention of his audience so that they see and remember only those things he *wants* them to see and remember. In the hands of a clever, glib performer The Little Messenger was both baffling and entertaining.'† And as an example of such an entertainer he cites Dickens. Curry makes the point that if the performer had just removed the doll's body and put his hand in his pocket to dispose of it, the action would have been suspicious and could have been noticed. The play over the money needed for the doll's journey could be entertaining in itself, but—more important—it provides the reason why his hand should go to his pocket, so the move is not suspected. Such misdirection is the essence of good magic. It is not used just to distract attention from a physical move, as in the example of the doll. Misdirection is constantly employed by a conjurer to send the mind of his audience away from his secret and in a direction that is helpful to him. So it becomes almost second nature to the magician to use misdirection, and his art would be far less effective without this psychological element: it is generally recognised that children are more difficult to deceive than grown-ups, precisely because it is easier to misdirect the more sophisticated adult mind.

Here then was another element in the success of Dickens as a

* Professor Hoffmann, *Modern Magic* (1876), pp. 321–3.
† Paul Curry, *Magician's Magic* (1966), p. 25.

conjuror, despite his limited technical skill: the art of misdirection. He had already put it to very effective literary use in 1846 with the first novel for which he planned each instalment on paper before he started to write. The title, *Dombey and Son*, was calculated to give the reader the impression that the story was largely about the relations between Mr Dombey and his son Paul, so enabling Dickens to spring the bombshell of young Paul Dombey's death in the fifth number. The question remained whether—and how—he had used the art of misdirection that he had learned as a magician when he set out to mystify his wider audience in *The Mystery of Edwin Drood*.

4

Two brothers, William Wilkie Collins and Charles Allston Collins, both had a role in the creation of *Edwin Drood*. Their father, William Collins, R.A., was known to Dickens. Born before the French Revolution, he remained a man in an eighteenth-century mould, pious, strict, and with aristocratic patrons including King George IV; such patronage enabled him to leave his family in relative comfort. It was the younger son, named after Washington Allston, the American painter, who took more after his father in character. He grew up to be a serious young man, red-headed, pale, not very robust, in whom the piety inherited from his father at one time took the form of a religious asceticism which his friends thought damaging to his health. He was a particular friend of J. E. Millais, with whom he studied art at the Academy Schools. He acted as a mediator between Ruskin and Millais, who wrote him a letter expressing his qualms on the very day he married Effie, Ruskin's former wife. Millais proposed Charles Collins as a member of the Pre-Raphaelite Brotherhood, but he was black-balled by Holman Hunt and Rossetti. He remained on the fringes of the movement, and had one picture hung in the Academy in 1852; he was such a perfectionist that he finished few paintings, and after a time gave up painting for writing. When he was thirty-one he was accepted by Kate Dickens, too much like her father in temperament to live comfortably in the Dickens household under her aunt Georgina.

Dickens agreed to the match reluctantly—not without reason, for after a long period of deteriorating health Charles Collins outlived him by only three years.

Collins was already a sick man when Dickens entrusted him with the illustrations for *Edwin Drood*. He managed to produce a sketch for the cover which gained Dickens's approval, and at least half a dozen other sketches for early scenes in the novel, before he had to give up and hand over to Luke Fildes. Fildes would have questioned him with interest on taking over, it is fair to assume, for he later asserted more than once that Collins did not know the significance of the scenes he had drawn on Dickens's instructions, and 'had not the faintest notion what they meant'.* Collins's wife Kate had the same impression. 'The same reasons that prevented me from teasing my father with questions respecting his story made me refrain from asking any of Mr Collins; but from what he said I certainly gathered that he was not in possession of my father's secret, although he had made his designs from my father's directions.'† So it is somewhat surprising that when Augustin Daly, then considering a stage version, wrote to find out what he knew, Collins wrote a reply on 4 May 1871 containing these statements:

The late Mr Dickens communicated to me some general outlines for his scheme of 'Edwin Drood', but it was at a very early stage in the development of the idea, and what he said bore mainly upon the earlier portions of the tale.

Edwin Drood *was never to reappear*, he having been murdered by Jasper. The girl Rosa not having been really attached to Edwin, was not to lament his loss very long, and was, I believe, to admit the sailor Mr Tartar to supply his place. It was intended that Jasper himself should urge on the search after Edwin Drood and the pursuit of his murderer, thus endeavoring to direct suspicion from himself, the real murderer. This is indicated in the design, on the right side of the cover, of the figures hurrying up the spiral staircase emblematical of a pursuit. They are led on by Jasper who points unconsciously to his own figure in the drawing at the head of the title. The female

* *The Art Annual*, 1895, p. 27.
† Kate Perugini, op. cit., p. 650.

43

figure at the left of the cover reading the placard 'Lost' is only intended to illustrate the doubt entertained by Rosa Budd [*sic*] as to the fate of her lover Drood. The group beneath it indicates the acceptance of another suitor.

As to any theory further it must be purely conjectural.*

What Charles Collins had to say about the significance of Jasper pointing at himself in his cover sketch could have been of great interest. Unfortunately the figure of Jasper on the stair *appears* to be pointing not at the other Jasper figure, but at Edwin Drood.† So in the light of the comments of Fildes and of Collins's own wife Kate, it seemed that the interpretation of this sick and quirky artist was not to be relied on.

His brother Wilkie Collins played a different role. Named after the painter Sir David Wilkie, he too moved among the Pre-Raphaelites and had a picture hung in the Academy Exhibition of 1849, without making art his profession. Millais painted his portrait in 1850 at the age of twenty-six. It still survives in the annex of the National Portrait Gallery showing Wilkie Collins as he was just before he met Dickens: a small, studious-looking young man, only five feet six with tiny hands and a large forehead. In spite of his demure look, he was a hedonist who took naturally to a bohemian style of living—he never married but lived with two mistresses. An interest in the theatre led to his introduction to Dickens in 1851 as suitable for a part in an amateur production, and so he started by playing valet to Dickens's lord. It was a relationship that was slowly to change over the years. Collins acted well, and Dickens found him a congenial companion to distract him from his increasing marital problems. At the same time Collins was serious in his approach to writing, so Dickens began to use his contributions and to encourage him. By 1856 he had become so useful a contributor that Dickens proposed he should be taken on to the staff of *Household Words* at five guineas a week. Collins, always shrewd over money, was not keen since he was earning almost as much as an outside contributor, and if he

* Quoted *The Mystery of Edwin Drood*, Clarendon Press edn., pp. 238–9.

† The sketch is reproduced in the Clarendon Press edition opposite p. 242.

joined the staff his contributions would be unsigned; he also seems to have suggested that readers might confuse his work with that of Dickens. Dickens commented somewhat sharply to Wills: 'I think him wrong in his objection, and have not the slightest doubt that such a confusion of authorship (which I don't believe to obtain in half-a-dozen minds out of half-a-dozen hundred) would be a far greater service than dis-service to him. This I clearly see.'* A compromise was reached over Collins's next story and he joined *Household Words,* making his working collaboration with Dickens even closer.

When Dickens launched into his own magazine *All the Year Round* he started with his *A Tale of Two Cities* as the serial, following it with Collins's story *The Woman in White.* Dickens was generous in his praise—'a very great advance on all your former writing'—but he did also offer the criticism that 'the three people who write the narratives in these proofs have a DISSECTIVE property in common, which is essentially not theirs but yours'. The public was less critical than his editor and Wilkie Collins enjoyed a great success, giving him for the first time a measure of financial independence, so in 1861 he resigned from *All the Year Round,* after five years working on Dickens's journals. Dickens was sorry to lose him, but he continued to take a close interest in his next book *No Name,* suggesting improvements, and no less than 27 possible titles, generously offering to help Wilkie out when he was taken ill before finishing it. In the event they did not collaborate again until 1867.

At the beginning of that year Wilkie Collins was planning *The Moonstone*—unlike Dickens he planned his work on paper in great detail. It was agreed that it would be serialised in *All the Year Round,* and at the end of June Dickens wrote to Wills:

I have heard read the first three numbers of Wilkie's story this morning and have gone minutely through the plot of the rest to the last line. It gives a series of 'narratives', but it is a very curious story, wild, yet domestic, with excellent character in it, and great mystery. It is prepared with extraordinary care, and has every chance of being a hit. It is in many respects much better than anything he has done.†

* Quoted Kenneth Robinson, *Life of Wilkie Collins* (1952), pp. 98–9.
† Quoted ibid., p. 184.

Collins also agreed to collaborate again with Dickens in a special Christmas story of forty-eight pages, *No Thoroughfare*, and they worked closely together to finish it before Dickens sailed on the S.S. *Cuba* on 9 November for his long reading tour in America.

While Dickens was away Wilkie Collins had to adapt *No Thoroughfare* for a stage production, help the assistant editor Wills with the running of *All the Year Round,* and catch up on writing *The Moonstone*, due to start serialisation on 4 January 1868. *No Thoroughfare* was successfully opened at the Adelphi Theatre on Boxing Day, with Dickens's friend Fechter in the main role. *The Moonstone* ran into problems. Collins's much-loved mother became seriously ill in the New Year and he realised she was dying. He was prostrated by an attack of rheumatic gout which particularly affected his eyes; he was in this helpless condition when the news came in March that she was dead. Not more than a third of the story had been written when publication began, so he had to keep going through all this, unable to write himself and forced to dictate *The Moonstone* in such bouts of agony that his cries of pain were too much for his male secretaries and only a woman was able to stand it. The heavy doses of opium he took left him afterwards with no recollection of the ending of the story.

He was only recovering in May, when Dickens returned from his exhausting American tour to find fault with Collins and Fechter over the production still successfully running at the Adelphi. Then Dickens dashed off to Paris to have a hand in a French production. He wrote to Collins on 4 June, as the latter was still unfit to travel, that the Paris production was a great success. At the end of the next month, in a letter to Wills dated 26 July, Dickens criticised *The Moonstone*, which was approaching the end of its weekly serialisation in *All the Year Round*: 'I quite agree with you about *The Moonstone*. The construction is wearisome beyond endurance, and there is a vein of obstinate conceit in it that makes enemies of readers.'*

Dickens had changed his tune since his earlier comment. Yet his criticism did pick up a general point about Wilkie Collins's writing that he had made at the time of *The Woman in White*: '. . . I always contest your disposition to give an audience credit for nothing, which necessarily involves the forcing of points on

* Quoted ibid., p. 197.

their attention, and which I have always observed them to resent when they find out—as they always will and do.'* No doubt Dickens felt that, as with the stage production of *No Thoroughfare,* his editorial hand could have improved the book a good deal if he had not been away. He could not really complain of a loss of readers, though, for despite the circumstances under which it had been written *The Moonstone* was proving another success for Wilkie Collins, with great interest being aroused in its outcome. The evidence is that *The Moonstone* was improving the sales of *All the Year Round.* Here, perhaps, was the heart of the offence, the source of the ill-tempered note in Dickens's observation. For notwithstanding the great success of his readings, Dickens had not published a novel for nearly three years, *Our Mutual Friend* having finished appearing in November 1865, and he had nothing on the stocks, while Wilkie Collins, who was hardly more than a good craftsman, was eclipsing his master in popularity with the reading public. It was not a state of affairs that could be to the liking of The Inimitable.

There are a number of obvious similarities between *The Moonstone* and *The Mystery of Edwin Drood.* There is the exotic, Oriental element of India in *The Moonstone,* and of Egypt and Ceylon in *Drood.* In both opium plays an important part, the whole of Collins's book turning on the unconscious theft of the Indian gem by the hero, Franklin Blake, while under the influence of a dose of opium administered to him secretly; and John Jasper is an opium addict pursued by the Opium Woman. In both books there are remarks stressing the beneficent effects of opium as counterbalancing the bad. There is a considerable resemblance between the two urchins who help the detectives. Gooseberry, who watches the transfer of the Moonstone when it finally reappears, is so called on account of 'the extraordinary prominence of his eyes. They projected so far, and they rolled about so loosely, that you wondered uneasily why they remained in their sockets.'† (Was this fancy, one wonders, prompted by Collins's own bloodshot and bandaged eyes as he dictated?) Deputy, the ragamuffin who assists Datchery, is described when imitating the

* ibid., p. 132.

† W. Collins, *The Moonstone* (Oxford World's Classics edn., 1928), p. 481

Opium Woman as with 'his eyes rolling very much out of their places' (p. 214). Both Gooseberry and Deputy are early members of the tribe of sharp young detective's assistants continued by Conan Doyle in Sherlock Holmes's Baker Street Irregulars.

Such parallels between the two books could be merely coincidental or reflecting the taste of the time; but Dickens put two allusions in a single chapter of the opening number of *Edwin Drood* that exclude any possibility but premeditation. Wilkie Collins had ended his first weekly number of *The Moonstone* with a scene where three mysterious Indians appear outside a country house and pour ink into the hand of a small English waif, who sees in this ink mirror Franklin Blake coming to the house with the Moonstone in his possession. In exactly the same place, at the end of the third chapter of *Edwin Drood*, Dickens wrote the following dialogue between Edwin and Rosa:

> "Eddy, no! I'm too stickey to be kissed. But give me your hand, and I'll blow a kiss into that."
> He does so. She breathes a light breath into it, and asks, retaining it and looking into it:
> "Now say, what do you see?"
> "See, Rosa?"
> "Why, I thought you Egyptian boys could look into a hand and see all sorts of phantoms? Can't you see a happy Future?"
>
> (p.23)

Whether or not Dickens intended by the 'Egyptian boy' to twit Wilkie Collins for using a blond English boy with the Indians, the position of the scenes each at the end of the third chapter of the book cannot be chance. To make it beyond all doubt, Dickens put in the same chapter another reference to *The Moonstone*, where the original reads:

> " . . . The book in your hand is Dr Elliotson's *Human Physiology*; and the case which the doctor cites rests on the well-known authority of Mr Combe."
> The passage pointed out to me was expressed in these terms:
> "Dr Abel informed me," says Mr Combe, "of an Irish porter to a warehouse, who forgot, when sober, what he had done

when drunk; but, being drunk, again recollected the transactions of his former state of intoxication. On one occasion, being drunk, he had lost a parcel of some value, and in his sober moments could give no account of it. Next time he was intoxicated, he recollected that he had left the parcel at a certain house, and there being no address on it, it had remained there safely, and was got on his calling for it."*

Elliotson was a well-known doctor and practitioner of mesmerism—or animal magnetism as it was then known—and was the family physician to both Dickens and Wilkie Collins. Dickens alludes to this passage in his description of the principal of the young ladies' seminary, Miss Twinkleton:

As, in some cases of drunkenness, and in others of animal magnetism, there are two states of consciousness which never clash, but each of which pursues its separate course as though it were continuous instead of broken (thus if I hide my watch when I am drunk, I must be drunk again before I can remember where), so Miss Twinkleton has two distinct and separate phases of being. Every night, the moment the young ladies have retired to rest, does Miss Twinkleton smarten up her curls a little, brighten up her eyes a little, and become a sprightly Miss Twinkleton whom the young ladies have never seen.

(p. 15)

Again, in linking it to Miss Twinkleton, Dickens introduced a slightly mocking note in his second allusion in this chapter to *The Moonstone*. It is difficult to resist the conclusion that Dickens was having a little fun at Wilkie Collins's expense in the first number of *Edwin Drood*, and intimating that he was proposing to do something better in his own book.

After the death of Dickens, it was often assumed that Wilkie

* *The Moonstone*, p. 433. This principle still seems to work, and not only for drunken Irishmen. The *Sunday Times* of 10 April 1977 carried the following item: 'Students who drink beer while studying should have a few more drinks before taking their exams, a scientist told a conference on experimental biology in Chicago. Dr Ronald Peterson said tests on soldiers showed that material learned under the influence of some drugs or alcohol is best remembered under the same influence.'

Collins would finish *Edwin Drood*. He had to make a public disclaimer, as well as dealing with an American continuation that claimed to be by Charles Dickens and Wilkie Collins. Understandably, his private opinion of *Edwin Drood* was low. He never uttered his criticisms in public, but in a pencilled comment in his copy of Forster's *Life of Dickens* he called it 'Dickens's last laboured effort, the melancholy work of a worn-out brain'. Such was Wilkie Collins's epitaph for this book.

5

MY SEARCH FOR clues to the solution of *Edwin Drood* left me with two conclusions and a hunch. The hunch amounted to no more than a feeling that in setting out to write a mystery story the old conjurer would have drawn on his experience in deceiving an audience—legitimate deception, not fraud. Just how he might exercise his magician's craft I did not know. A reasonable guess, though, would be the use of some strong misdirection to distract the attention of his audience from his real purposes, just as a conjurer does. The first of my conclusions was that Dickens intended to reveal Jasper as the murderer of his nephew, eventually ending up in the condemned cell, where he would probably make clear his past, his personality and his motivations. No light had been shed on the problems that this development of the story would raise, such as how the different facets of Jasper's character were to be reconciled, or whether Dickens's uncompromising description of Jasper in the second chapter did not make this scenario impossible without downright dishonesty on the author's part. Despite these difficulties, I considered that the testimony of men to whom Dickens would not have lied could not be rejected. I decided to work on the basis that Jasper killed Edwin Drood. The second conclusion was that Dickens was consciously setting out with his last novel to write a book that would outclass *The Moonstone*. His third chapter virtually announced his intention. He wanted to show the world that he could outdo his former protégé in Wilkie Collins's particular and highly successful field of the sensation novel.

If this last conclusion were correct, one thing must follow: the plot of *Edwin Drood* could *not* turn on the effects of opium. To base the story on that drug would be to produce an imitation *Moonstone*, the very last effect Dickens would wish to make. Yet the opium theme is present from the first page of *Drood* and continues to the last chapter Dickens ever wrote, in which Jasper made tantalising admissions to the Opium Woman under the influence of the drug. Dickens seems to be taking the story to an eventual full confession by Jasper when the Opium Woman has found the right mixture to make him talk, as she threatens. Yet this would be *The Moonstone* over again, where Franklin Blake under the influence of another dose of opium re-enacts the events of the first occasion when he removed the gem. ('If I hide my watch when I am drunk, I must be drunk again before I can remember where.'). Dickens had to have another explanation for *Edwin Drood*; so the strong emphasis he put on opium merited a critical look.

Edwin Drood opens with a striking paragraph describing Jasper's return to consciousness from an opium dream:

An ancient English Cathedral Town? How can the ancient English Cathedral town be here! The well-known massive grey square tower of its old Cathedral? How can that be here! There is no spike of rusty iron in the air, between the eye and it, from any point of the real prospect. What is the spike that intervenes, and who has set it up? Maybe, it is set up by the Sultan's orders for the impaling of a horde of Turkish robbers, one by one. It is so, for cymbals clash, and the Sultan goes by to his palace in long procession. Ten thousand scimitars flash in the sunlight, and thrice ten thousand dancing-girls strew flowers. Then, follow white elephants caparisoned in countless gorgeous colours, and infinite in number and attendants. Still, the Cathedral tower rises in the background, where it cannot be, and still no writhing figure is on the grim spike. Stay! Is the spike so low a thing as the rusty spike on the top of a post of an old bedstead that has tumbled all awry? Some vague period of drowsy laughter must be devoted to the consideration of this possibility.

(p. 1)

Jasper finds that he is lying across a broken-down bed with a Chinaman, a Lascar, and the Opium Woman in a squalid den in the East End of London.

Dickens had done his homework on the opium den. He probably paid more than one visit to the den of 'Opium Sal' in Shadwell. On one visit the American publisher James T. Fields who accompanied him saw Opium Sal, the Chinamen and Lascars, and the opium pipes made from penny ink bottles as Dickens was to describe them; he also heard fragments of speech later put into the mouth of the Opium Woman. In addition Dickens consulted Sir John Bowring, who had served as Consul in Canton and as Governor of Hong Kong, on opium-smoking in the Far East. Yet Dickens had one handicap in writing about the drug: he could depict its effects only as an external observer. Unlike Wilkie Collins, whose addiction became so great that he consumed quantities of laudanum—opium dissolved in alcohol —sufficient to kill an ordinary man, Dickens did not know at first hand the dreams and terrors that beset the addict. He himself seems to have taken opium on few occasions and merely in medicinal doses. He would not have experienced the characteristic dreams of voyaging through immensities of time and space, with gigantic, sinister architectural structures. This could explain why his description of Jasper's opium vision has been found implausible:

> The opium scenes in *Edwin Drood* are brilliantly convincing when they describe the dialogue and movements of the drugged man, but sound factitious when they depict his visions of processions, flashing scimitars, and dancing girls. An American doctor who had himself experimented with opium-smoking criticised the visions which Dickens bestowed on John Jasper as more like those of a hashish-smoker than an opium-smoker.*

I believe Dickens derived the ingredients of Jasper's vision from neither opium nor hashish, but from a literary source dealing with an entirely different kind of vision. Edward Lane's monumental work *The Manners and Customs of the Modern Egyptians*

* Alethea Hayter, *Opium and the Romantic Imagination* (1968), pp. 295–6.

described Egypt in the earlier part of the century. When he was living there Lane had been particularly interested in the feats performed by Egyptian sorcerers using the ink mirror, and with some difficulty he had organised a demonstration, using a boy he chose personally in the street. The sorcerer had drawn a magic square in the palm of the boy's hand and poured a little ink in the centre. After he had written an invocation to 'the prince and his troops', he caused the boy to see in the ink mirror a man sweeping the ground with a broom. The sorcerer told the boy to give a series of instructions, which the boy then saw carried out in his ink mirror. The man who had been sweeping fetched a total of seven flags, red, black, white, green and blue in colour. Men came and pitched the Sultan's large green tent. A considerable number of soldiers appeared, pitched their tents, and fell in on parade. Similarly, on the boy's orders, a red bull was dragged in by some men, beaten, killed, cooked, and then eaten by the soldiers; the Sultan wearing a high red cap rode on a bay horse to his tent; and his court formed up round him. After these preliminaries, at Lane's request the boy was able to describe Lord Nelson, whom he had never heard of, complete with missing arm.* Dickens was always interested in paranormal phenomena, and Lane's account, only briefly summarised here, would certainly have attracted his attention. It contains almost all the principal elements of Jasper's vision. The Sultan riding by, the parade, the soldiers, the attendants, the variety of bright colours, and the sinister killing are all there. Dickens has elaborated them, magnified the tent into a palace, and transmuted the red bull into white elephants—perhaps the phrase was less common in his day? He would not have had to invent the dancing girls, who do not appear in the boy's vision, as Lane devoted a complete chapter of his book to the public dancers of Egypt. All the ingredients were there, wanting only a further touch of the author's imagination.

So for all the accuracy of Dickens's description of the opium den and the behaviour of opium addicts, there is something borrowed and wrong in Jasper's opium vision. It makes an impressive opening to the book on first reading; on closer examination it begins to look stagey. This paragraph made me wonder

* Edward Lane, *The Manners and Customs of the Modern Egyptians* (1834; Everyman edn., 1954), pp. 274–82.

again why Dickens put so much stress on opium. Admittedly opium dens were a relatively new feature in England, and they provided the author with an exotic contrast to the staid cathedral city of Cloisterham. Yet such emphasis on opium merely as local colour hardly seemed reason enough. Or could it be, I wondered, that opium was being used as a colourful piece of misdirection of the very kind I was half expecting? If this were the case, the opium interest would be there not so much for its own sake as to attract attention away from some crucial part of the story that might appear suspicious in isolation. I asked myself what might be vulnerable if opium were lifted right out of the story. One possible answer was the Opium Woman, Princess Puffer as Deputy calls her. Opium provides a reason for her contact with Jasper, for finding out his secrets, and even for pursuing him to discover more; it could camouflage a deeper relationship that some have suspected between her and Jasper. While this would be very convenient for the story-teller, if there is such a relationship, this hardly seemed an adequate explanation. For assuming that my first conclusion was correct that Jasper is the murderer of Edwin Drood, it is Jasper's personality that is the central problem of the novel. If opium was a piece of major misdirection, Dickens would be likely to employ it only to distract the reader from the key secret to Jasper himself. And there is one feature of Jasper that is presented as linked with opium: his periodic fits. I decided to examine them more closely.

The best description of one of Jasper's attacks is in the second chapter. The fit takes place in the middle of the conversation between Drood and Jasper, as his nephew is telling him he is fortunate that his life has not been planned for him.

"Good Heaven, Jack, you look frightfully ill! There's a strange film come over your eyes."

Mr Jasper, with a forced smile, stretches out his right hand, as if at once to disarm apprehension and gain time to get better. After a while he says faintly:

"I have been taking opium for a pain—an agony—that sometimes overcomes me. The effects of the medicine steal over me like a blight or a cloud, and pass. You see them in the act of passing; they will be gone directly. Look away from me. They will go all the sooner."

With a scared face, the younger man complies, by casting his eyes downward at the ashes on the hearth. Not relaxing his own gaze at the fire, but rather strengthening it with a fierce, firm grip upon his elbow-chair, the elder sits for a few moments rigid, and then, with thick drops standing on his forehead, and a sharp catch of his breath, becomes as he was before. On his so subsiding in his chair, his nephew gently and assiduously tends him while he quite recovers. When Jasper is restored, he lays a tender hand upon his nephew's shoulder, and, in a tone of voice less troubled than the purport of his words—indeed with something of raillery or banter in it—thus addresses him:

"There is said to be a hidden skeleton in every house; but you thought there was none in mine, dear Ned."

(pp. 10–11)

Later in the story, on the very day of his disappearance, Drood meets the Opium Woman in Cloisterham, and is reminded of his uncle's attack.

. . . he sees that the woman is of a haggard appearance, and that her weazen chin is resting on her hands, and that her eyes are staring—with an unwinking, blind sort of steadfastness—before her.

Always kindly, but moved to be unusually kind this evening, and having bestowed kind words on most of the children and aged people he has met, he at once bends down, and speaks to this woman.

"Are you ill?"

"No, deary," she answers, without looking at him, and with no departure from her strange blind stare.

"Are you blind?"

"No, deary."

"Are you lost, homeless, faint? What is the matter, that you stay here in the cold so long, without moving?"

By slow and stiff efforts, she appears to contract her vision until it can rest upon him; and then a curious film passes over her, and she begins to shake.

He straightens himself, recoils a step, and looks down at her in a dread amazement; for he seems to know her.

"Good heaven!" he thinks, next moment. "Like Jack that night!"

(p. 126)

Some have seen in this passage the recognition by Drood of a family likeness between Jasper and the Opium Woman. In my reading of it, Drood's first impression of recognising her is immediately followed, 'next moment', by the thought that the woman is having the same kind of fit as his uncle. He questions her, and she admits that she smokes opium and begs money from him for this purpose. In this way Drood and the reader are left with the idea that Jasper and the woman have both suffered a similar, opium-induced attack. As this description occurs in the fourth number, Dickens's original readers would not be likely to recall that Jasper's attack, which they would have read about three months earlier in the second chapter of the first number, was really of quite a different character. His attack came on suddenly and was of short duration, but was extremely unpleasant while it lasted, with symptoms of acute distress in the gripping fingers, perspiration on the forehead, and sudden relaxation at the end as the crisis passed. The Opium Woman was quite another case. She was already in her dream-like state when Drood found her. There is no agonising paroxysm with gripping fingers and perspiration. Whereas Jasper went rigid, the woman shakes. She does not make a recovery and return to an outwardly normal appearance. The Opium Woman manages to focus on Edwin with some difficulty and then conduct a conversation with the young man, on one occasion 'trailing off into a drowsy repetition'. The differences between her condition and that of Jasper are far greater than any apparent similarities.

There is another crucial difference. We do not see the Opium Woman before Edwin speaks to her, but there is no hint that she has herself changed in any way as a result of her opium trance. She does warn Edwin that Ned (which Jasper alone calls him) is 'A threatened name. A dangerous name', yet there is no personal malevolence towards Drood in her warning—rather the reverse. Jasper, on the other hand, seems strangely affected by his attack.

56

Before it takes place he is the welcoming, molly-coddling uncle, with his look of 'hungry, exacting, watchful and yet devoted affection', even if an element of tension does come in when the subject of Rosa is raised. After his fit Jasper speaks in a new spirit of disillusion:

". . . How does our service sound to you?"
"Beautiful! Quite celestial."
"It often sounds to me quite devilish. I am so weary of it! The echoes of my own voice among the arches seem to mock me with my daily drudging round. No wretched monk who droned his life away in that gloomy place, before me, can have been more tired of it than I am. He could take for relief (and did take) to carving demons out of the stalls and seats and desks. What shall I do? Must I take to carving them out of my heart?"
(p. 11)

A new warning note enters his conversation too. ' "You know now, don't you, that even a poor monotonous chorister and grinder of music—in his niche—may be troubled with some stray sort of ambition, aspiration, restlessness, dissatisfaction, what shall we call it?" ' He gives a triple warning to his nephew: ' "Take it as a warning, then.". . . "You won't be warned, then?" . . . "You can't be warned, then?" ' (*'You won't take warning then?'*—is underlined in Dickens's notes.) The import of these warnings is obscure. Edwin Drood takes them to be the friendly concern of his uncle. We cannot be so sure. The loving uncle has become rather sinister, with more than a hint of insincerity in the phrases that Dickens chose to use to describe him after his recovery. He 'remains in that attitude . . .' 'Mr Jasper dissolves his attitude' (pp. 12, 13). Jasper is certainly in an odd mood after his seizure.

Jasper's seizure with Edwin Drood gives the fullest account of his symptoms, but his first attack occurs after his return to consciousness in the opium den.

He rises unsteadily from the bed, lays the pipe upon the hearthstone, draws back the ragged curtain, and looks with repugnance at his three companions. He notices that the woman has opium-smoked herself into a strange likeness of the Chinaman. His form of cheek, eye, and temple, and his colour, are repeated in her. As he lies on his back, the said Chinaman convulsively wrestles with one of his many Gods, or Devils, perhaps, and snarls horribly. The Lascar laughs and dribbles at the mouth. The hostess is still.

"What visions can *she* have?" the waking man muses, as he turns her face towards him, and stands looking down at it. "Visions of many butchers' shops, and public houses, and much credit? Of an increase of hideous customers, and this horrible bedstead set upright again, and this horrible court swept clean? What can she rise to, under any quantity of opium, higher than that!—Eh?"

He bends down his ear, to listen to her mutterings.

"Unintelligible!"

As he watches the spasmodic shoots and darts that break out of her face and limbs, like fitful lightning out of a dark sky, some contagion in them seizes upon him: insomuch that he has to withdraw himself to a lean arm-chair by the hearth—placed there, perhaps, for such emergencies—and to sit in it, holding tight, until he has got the better of this unclean spirit of imitation.

(pp. 2–3)

The description of this fit is much shorter than the Drood seizure. All the same, most of the characteristics of the later one are there, implicitly or explicitly: the sudden onset, the sharpness of the paroxysm, the gripping of the arms of the chair by the fire, and the recovery. Only the glazing of the eyes and the perspiration on the forehead are not recorded. Once again the fit is linked with the Opium Woman, in this case by 'some contagion' and an 'unclean spirit of imitation'. There is also a subtle suggestion that such attacks are not unknown among opium-smokers in the 'arm-chair by the hearth—placed there perhaps for such emergencies'. Are we being gently conned into accepting that Jasper's symptoms in his fits are the product of opium, distracting our attention from the fact that he does not behave in the same way as the Opium Woman or her other clients, and that their symptoms are described while they are sleeping off the drug, whereas he has fully regained consciousness before he has his seizure?

Even more striking in this fit is the difference between Jasper Before and Jasper After. Jasper Before looks at his surroundings in a mood of philosophical disgust. ' "What visions can *she* have?" ' he reflects: what images can opium conjure up in such a slum-dweller's mind? He bends down to listen and see whether her mutterings give any clue. ' "Unintelligible!" ' is his conclusion. Jasper After behaves like another man.

> Then be comes back, pounces on the Chinaman, and seizing him with both hands by the throat, turns him violently on the bed. The Chinaman clutches the aggressive hands, resists, gasps, and protests.
>
> "What do you say?"
>
> A watchful pause.
>
> "Unintelligible!"
>
> Slowly loosening his grasp as he listens to the incoherent jargon with an attentive frown, he turns to the Lascar and fairly drags him forth upon the floor. As he falls, the Lascar starts into a half-risen attitude, glares with his eyes, lashes about him fiercely with his arms, and draws a phantom knife.
>
> (p. 3)

There is no mistaking the change from his previous questioning mood to one of suspicious violence. After his fit Jasper behaves like a homicidal maniac, half strangling the Chinaman and dragging the Lascar off the bed to the ground: he acts 'violently' with 'aggressive hands'. While Dickens described the violence, he did attempt to camouflage it in two ways. The Chinaman himself was depicted as violent before Jasper's attack on him: '. . . the said Chinaman convulsively wrestles with one of his many Gods, or Devils, perhaps, and snarls horribly.' In this way Jasper's action is made to appear no more than another example of the 'unclean spirit of imitation' or the normal behaviour of an opium-smoker. The second device, the use of ' "Unintelligible!" ' before and after the fit provides an impression of continuity, that Jasper is continuing from the same point and with the same purpose as before the fit. It is even used a third time to re-enforce this idea.

59

'When any distinct word has been flung into the air, it has had no sense or sequence. Wherefore "unintelligible!" is again the comment of the watcher, made with some reassured nodding of his head, and a gloomy smile.' Was this conjurer's misdirection at work? It might be. The important fact not to lose sight of was that Jasper had emerged from this fit not just in a more sinister mood, but exhibiting uncontrolled violence.

I then recalled that Dickens had written an earlier version of Jasper's seizure with Edwin Drood, and that he had then pasted a slip of paper over it on which he had written the final, published version. The obliterated passage in his first version, which started with Jasper's explanation, ran as follows:

> "(I have been taking) opium for a pain—an agony—[I] sometimes have. Its effects steal over me like a blight or a cloud, and pass. (There is no cause for alarm) You see them in the act of passing. Put those knives out at the door—both of them!"
>
> "My dear Jack, why?"
>
> "It's going to lighten; they may attract the lightning; put them (away) in the dark."
>
> With a scared and confounded face, the younger man complies. No (lightning) flash ensues, nor was there, for a moment, any passing likelihood of a thunder storm. He gently and assiduously tends his kinsman who by slow degrees recovers and clears away that cloud or blight. When he, (Jasper)—is quite himself and is as it were once more all resolved into that concentrated look, he lays a tender hand upon his nephew's shoulder and thus addresses him.
>
> (pp. 10–11.)*

In the second version of this passage, Dickens cut out all reference to the knives and lightning (see above, pp. 54–5). The clear implication of the first version being that Jasper is subject to an almost overpowering urge to use the knives on somebody, Dickens must have considered on reflection that he was showing too much of his hand too soon. The significance of this first draft

* Words in brackets are deleted in the manuscript, except (Jasper).

is that in Dickens's original conception of the scene the affectionate and loving uncle emerged from his fit not merely moody, but positively murderous.

So my examination of the two Jasper fits led me to the conclusion that they were not the same in kind as those of the Opium Woman. Jasper's crises were short, sharp and agonising, and followed by recovery once the paroxysm was over. But while the physical effects were short-lived, there was a more lasting psychological effect. Moreover it was a change very much for the worse. Jasper Before was the efficient choir-master and affectionate uncle known to Cloisterham; Jasper After was dissatisfied, cynical, insincere, threatening, and above all a man of violence, whether the violence was overt or suppressed. In short, Jasper After had just the qualities to be expected in the murderer of Edwin Drood. As a convenient shorthand I called this vicious personality The Murderer.

Jasper's fits now took on a very different look. Dickens had been at pains to suggest from the opening pages of *Edwin Drood* that they were the effect of opium. I now saw that what we are witnessing in these anguished moments does not require a physical explanation. Jasper's symptoms appear as the bodily signs of a profound psychological upheaval. The fit signals a complete change of personality, marking a rapid transition from the doting uncle to the man of violence capable of murdering his nephew. The physical agony reflects the internal revolution that is going on as The Murderer subdues the other Jasper and assumes complete control.

This is not to deny that Jasper is addicted to opium and suffers from its effects. He is subject to day reveries, those waking dreams characteristic of opium addiction that have been seen in the Opium Woman. One of the first confidences made by Rosa to Helena is that a glaze sometimes comes over Jasper's eyes and 'he seems to wander away into a frightful sort of dream—' (p. 54). But it is significant that Dickens never gives a direct description of Jasper in one of these day-dreams, with the possible and brief exception of the time when Crisparkle goes to see Jasper, who 'sprang from the couch in a delirious state between sleeping and waking, crying out: "What is the matter? Who did it?" ' (p. 85). For if Dickens had given as full a description of Jasper's waking

61

dreams as he did of the very different change-of-personality fits, he would have made the contrast obvious to his readers.

If my hypothesis were correct, Jasper's special fits had no connection with opium, but were the outward signs of a change-over between two totally different personalities: one the doting, affectionate uncle, the other the violent murderer. On this reading of his intentions, Dickens had set himself a daunting task of concealing the true character of the change-of-personality fits and the separate nature of the two Jasper personalities without arousing the suspicion of his readers. To accomplish such a feat of camouflage would demand immense professional skill, with a constant balance on a knife-edge. If successfully maintained it would certainly be a tour de force that would eclipse Wilkie Collins and *The Moonstone*. This scenario could well be described as 'Not a communicable idea (or the interest of the book would be gone) but a very strong one, though difficult to work', as Dickens had told Forster. My theory looked plausible—but so had many other Drood theories. Would it stand up to the acid test of the whole of Dickens's text? And if this was indeed Dickens's real secret, his 'very curious and new idea', what means had he used to conceal his purpose and yet make it acceptable to his readers when he finally unveiled his solution? With these questions in mind, I began to scrutinise carefully all that Dickens had written in *The Mystery of Edwin Drood*.

6

ON MY INTERPRETATION of his fits, it is Jasper who awakens in the opium den at the beginning of *Edwin Drood*, and it is The Murderer who leaves the den. (I am using Jasper in the sense of Jasper Before, the 'normal' man, and The Murderer to signify the violent personality that emerges after a fit.) The Murderer hurries back to Cloisterham Cathedral just in time for the evening service, and the first chapter ends significantly when 'the intoned words, "WHEN THE WICKED MAN—" rise among groins of arches and beams of roof, awakening muttered thunder'.

The words 'WHEN THE WICKED MAN' held a particular significance for Dickens, as his notes show. He followed his usual plan of making working notes during the writing of *Edwin Drood*, taking a single sheet of paper for each number of the book, folding it in half, and writing general memoranda on the left-hand page so formed, and chapter headings with items for inclusion in the chapter on the right-hand page. The memoranda on the left-hand page start:

> Opium-Smoking
> Touch the Key note
> 'When the Wicked Man'—

So Dickens's notes gave the crucial information that in the opening of *Edwin Drood* he would be sounding the key note of the story. After *The Moonstone*, the key note he had in mind could hardly be 'Opium-Smoking'. To what else could he be referring other than the phrase standing out in capital letters in his text 'WHEN THE WICKED MAN'?

The implications of this phrase, his key note, merit close attention. For the ordinary reader the heavy hint in capitals at the end of the first chapter would leave a general impression that the choir-master just returned from the opium den was an evil man. On the interpretation of Jasper's fits that I had made, 'THE WICKED MAN' would have a more specific sense, indicating that the personality singing in the Cathedral choir that afternoon was The Murderer. It fitted my interpretation exactly. Yet the layers of meaning did not end here, for the church-going Victorian reader would have been familiar with the rest of the words from the Prayer Book at the opening of Morning and Evening Prayer: 'When the wicked man turneth away from his wickedness that he hath committed, and doeth that which is lawful and right, he shall save his soul alive.' This quotation from the prophet Ezekiel would often have been in the reader's ears in church—and should have provided the vital clue, for the whole sentence deals with the transformation of the wicked man into the just man. This is the 'key note' of *Edwin Drood*: the change of one personality into another.

This key note applies to the whole work. At the same time it is especially relevant to the immediate context. For Dickens wanted to go on in his next chapter to show Jasper in his normal affectionate and fussy relationship with his nephew Edwin, and in order to do this he had to make Jasper replace the wicked man, The Murderer, before Drood arrived the same evening. So the words 'WHEN THE WICKED MAN' are also a signal that the transformation from the wicked man is about to take place. And sure enough it does—in the Cathedral. It is the only example in the book of what may be called the reverse fit, in which the Jasper personality returns and takes over from The Murderer. Dickens did not describe it directly and used the classic device of the messenger, in the person of Mr Tope the verger, to report Jasper's 'kind of fit'.

"Mr Jasper was that, Tope?"

"Yes, Mr Dean."

"He has stayed late."

"Yes, Mr Dean. I have stayed for him, your Reverence. He has been took a little poorly."

"Say 'taken', Tope—to the Dean," the younger rook interposes in a low tone with this touch of correction, as who should say: "You may offer bad grammar to the laity, or the humbler clergy; not to the Dean."

Mr Tope, Chief Verger and Showman, and accustomed to be high with excursion parties, declines with a silent loftiness to perceive that any suggestion has been tendered to him.

"And when and how has Mr Jasper been taken—for, as Mr Crisparkle has remarked, it is better to say taken—taken—" repeats the Dean; "when and how has Mr Jasper been Taken——"

"Taken, sir," Tope deferentially murmurs.

"——Poorly, Tope?"

"Why, sir, Mr Jasper was that breathed——"

"I wouldn't say 'That breathed', Tope," Mr Crisparkle interposes, with the same touch as before. "Not English—to the Dean."

"Breathed to that extent would be preferable," the Dean (not unflattered by this indirect homage), condescendingly remarks; "would be preferable."

"Mr Jasper's breathing was so remarkably short"; thus discreetly does Mr Tope work his way round the sunken rock, "when he came in, that it distressed him mightily to get his notes out: which was perhaps the cause of his having a kind of fit on him after a little. His memory grew DAZED." Mr Tope, with his eyes on the Reverend Mr Crisparkle, shoots this word out, as defying him to improve upon it: "and a dimness and giddiness crept over him as strange as ever I saw: though he didn't seem to mind it particularly, himself. However, a little time and a little water brought him out of his DAZE." Mr Tope repeats the word and its emphasis, with the air of saying: "As I *have* made a success, I'll make it again."

"And Mr Jasper has gone home quite himself, has he?" asks the Dean.

"Your Reverence, he has gone home quite himself. And I'm glad to see he's having his fire kindled up, for it's chilly after the wet, and the Cathedral had both a damp feel and a damp touch this afternoon, and he was very shivery."

(pp. 4–5)

Since this seizure was being reported by Mr Tope, the description of it is not precise. Nevertheless, it is called 'a kind of fit'. Jasper's breathing was difficult, he was 'distressed' and suffered from 'giddiness', and, after being unable to concentrate on anything else for a time, made a fairly quick recovery that left him a little shaky. All these were symptoms of his change-of-personality fit in the presence of Edwin Drood. If this fit in the Cathedral as described by Tope seems less severe, it may also be because Jasper on this occasion is returning to his 'normal' personality. At the same time Dickens uses the words 'DAZED' and 'DAZE'—emphasised by capital letters and by Mr Tope himself—which give the reader the impression that Jasper was suffering from the effects of his recent visit to the opium den.

In this sequence of events Dickens had set himself a difficult problem: Jasper has three of his fits in the first two chapters. Small wonder that Dickens told Forster that his idea was 'difficult to work'! It was a feat of virtuosity on his part to compress these fits into the space of ten pages without making them obvious. His technique in doing this was interesting. The first change-of-personality fit in the den was described almost in passing, attracting no special notice in the flow of the narrative. The second, in the Cathedral, was camouflaged by the social comedy between the two clergy and the verger Tope, so that Dickens was able to give the full treatment to the third fit in the main scene between Jasper and Edwin Drood. In each instance Dickens also appeared to employ the misdirection of suggesting that opium was the cause of the fit.

The attack in the Cathedral having restored Jasper to his everyday self, Dickens described him in the paragraph on which Aylmer took his stand.

> With the check upon him of being unsympathetically restrained in a genial outburst of enthusiasm, Mr Jasper stands still, and looks on intently at the young fellow, divesting himself of his outer coat, hat, gloves, and so forth. Once for all, a look of intentness and intensity—a look of hungry, exacting, watchful, and yet devoted affection—is always, now and ever afterwards, on the Jasper face whenever the Jasper face is addressed in this direction. And whenever it is so addressed, it is never, on this occasion or on any other, dividedly addressed; it is always concentrated.

Everything that Dickens wrote here applies to Jasper, not to The Murderer. But was Aylmer justified in claiming that Dickens had made his statements so categorical that they would admit of only one interpretation, with the consequence that 'He [Jasper] may be possessed by seven devils, but this will make no difference'?* I do not think so. For Dickens is careful to refer not to Jasper's face, but to 'the Jasper face', and moreover to emphasise the point by immediate repetition. It is a curious turn of phrase, half suggesting in itself that there could be another face, and it should have carried a danger signal. It serves as a reminder that we are listening to the persuasive spiel of the old magician, and that Scot had warned his Elizabethan contemporaries that 'a part of this art, which is called naturall or witching magicke, consisteth as well in the deceipt of words, as in the sleight of hand: wherein plain lieing is avoided with a figurative speech, in the which, either the words themselves, or their interpretation have a double or doubtful meaning. . . .'.† For here Dickens is performing a literary conjuring

* F. Aylmer, op. cit., pp. 14–15.

† Reginald Scot, *The Discoverie of Witchcraft* (1584; Centaur Press edn., 1964), B. XIII, ch. XI, pp. 257–8.

trick. Jasper, who went on his sinister journey before committing the murder in his opium dreams, is the novelist's counterpart of the Travelling Doll, who went on her journeys for the amusement of Mamie and the other Dickens children. The audience saw the face of the travelling doll and assumed it was the whole figure. As Hoffmann put it, 'the audience are not aware that the figure is divisible, and supposing it to be indivisible . . . there is nothing to lead them to guess the secret.' So it is with the Jasper face. This is Dickens performing for his wider audience the old trick of the Bonus Genius.

Just as Dickens was fair to his readers in the warning he inserted in this paragraph, so he continued to give clues after the fit with Drood had brought the return of The Murderer personality. Indeed, in his first, deleted, version of the fit there is an echo of 'the Jasper face' paragraph which itself contains another warning: 'When he, (Jasper)—is quite himself and is as it were once more all resolved into that concentrated look, he lays a tender hand upon his nephew's shoulder and thus addresses him' (p. 11 n.). That qualification of three small words slipped in, 'as it were', would have warned the perceptive reader that this time the concentrated look, with all that it entails, is not reality but appearance. In the event, this sentence was deleted when Dickens cut out the knives passage, yet it illustrates the care with which he chose his words, and other pointers remained in the published text. There is the irony of Drood telling The Murderer of 'the disinterestedness of your painfully laying your inner self bare', and Dickens gets very close to the bone when Jasper seems to stop breathing and then becomes 'a breathing man again without the smallest stage of transition between the two extreme states' (p. 12). Finally the sinister side of The Murderer is brought out. 'Mr Jasper, with his hand to his chin, and with an expression of musing benevolence on his face', after delivering his warnings to Drood without effect, asks 'Shall we go and walk in the churchyard?'

The reference to the churchyard was not accidental, as the notes make clear. The memoranda on the left-hand side contain:

Uncle and Nephew
Gloves for the Nuns' House
Churchyard

The word 'Churchyard' is partially underlined. Even more explicitly, under the notes for Chapter II on the right-hand side Dickens wrote:

> Uncle and Nephew.
> Murder very far off

So by the end of the second chapter Dickens had already demonstrated the operation of the Jasper personalities, and had hinted at the consequence for Edwin Drood. In the next chapter Dickens was to throw more light on the nature of Jasper.

On the left-hand page of general notes, 'Churchyard' is followed by:

> Cathedral town running throughout

This has double underlining for its importance in setting the scene. The next items are somewhat surprising:

> Inside the Nuns' House
> Miss Twinkleton and her double existence

Miss Twinkleton and her 'states of existence' have already been met in the context of *The Moonstone*. Dickens's notes show that her role was more than poking fun at the earlier mystery story: there was a serious point to be made, or else her 'double existence' would not have merited recording in his brief jottings. This is the paragraph into which he expanded his note in the third chapter:

> As, in some cases of drunkenness, and in others of animal magnetism, there are two states of consciousness which never clash, but each of which pursues its separate course as though it were continuous instead of broken (thus if I hide my watch when I am drunk, I must be drunk again before I can remember where), so Miss Twinkleton has two distinct and separate phases of being. Every night, the moment the young ladies have retired to rest, does Miss Twinkleton smarten up her curls a little, brighten up her eyes a little, and become a sprightly Miss Twinkleton whom the young ladies have never seen. Every night, at the same hour, does Miss Twinkleton resume the topics of the previous night, comprehending the tenderer scandal of Cloisterham of which she has no knowledge what-

ever by day, and references to a certain season at Tunbridge Wells (airily called by Miss Twinkleton in this state of her existence "The Wells"), notably the season wherein a certain finished gentleman (compassionately called by Miss Twinkleton in this state of her existence, "Foolish Mr Porters") revealed a homage of the heart, whereof Miss Twinkleton, in her scholastic state of existence, is as ignorant as a granite pillar. Miss Twinkleton's companion in both states of existence, and equally adaptable to either, is one Mrs Tisher: a deferential widow with a weak back, a chronic sigh, and a suppressed voice, who looks after the young ladies' wardrobes, and leads them to infer that she has seen better days. Perhaps this is the reason why it is an article of faith with the servants, handed down from race to race, that the departed Tisher was a hairdresser.

(pp. 15–16)

Nowhere in this paragraph has Dickens brought in the expression 'double existence' used in his notes—doubtless it would have been too revealing. Instead he employed more ambiguous phrases, 'phases of being' and 'state of existence', that could be camouflaged with spinster schoolmistress comedy. The serious message was none the less spelled out for the reader in the first sentence before the diversionary activities of Miss Twinkleton, Mr Porters and Mrs Tisher. For this sentence widened the principle underlying *The Moonstone* from states produced by a drug—alcohol or opium—to abnormal conditions of the mind without drugs. 'As, in some cases of drunkenness, *and in others of animal magnetism*. . .' It was done in an apparently unimportant parenthesis, yet effectively it stated the principle underlying the case of Jasper on which the mystery of *Edwin Drood* was based. Miss Twinkleton is the comic exemplar of this principle. She is neither drugged nor drunk, yet she has a double existence and separate states of consciousness. Through her Dickens was able to flesh out his principle in another character and illustrate that Jasper did not have to be under the influence of any kind of drug to suffer from separate states of consciousness, and that he could have one state of consciousness as The Murderer of whose activities he would be totally unaware in his normal state as Jasper.

69

Dickens stated the ground rules of *Edwin Drood* under the double diversion of the comedy schoolmistress and of cocking a snook at *The Moonstone*.

Between Jasper's change-of-personality fit in the presence of his nephew and Drood's disappearance there are no further attacks of this kind described by Dickens. This can be explained by the needs of the story. The Murderer has to keep appearing to carry out the various steps that lead to the murder. It has to be The Murderer who cultivates Sapsea and Durdles for his purposes; who deliberately fans the quarrel between Neville Landless and Edwin Drood; who after some initial reluctance agrees to their reconciliation and is instrumental in arranging the final dinner party; who goes with Durdles on the mysterious night expedition to the Cathedral when the mason falls into a drugged sleep; and who goes to the dinner party with a 'great black scarf' round his neck and a face that is for the moment 'knitted and stern'. Dickens's working notes confirm, if confirmation be needed, what The Murderer is up to:

> <u>Mr Sapsea</u> Connect Jasper with him. (He will want a solemn donkey bye and bye.) . . . The Keys. Stony Durdles . . . <u>Quarrel</u> (Fomented by Jasper) . . . <u>Jasper lays his ground</u> . . . <u>Chapter X Smoothing the Way</u> That is, for Jasper's plan, through Mr Crisparkle; . . . <u>Chapter XII. A Night with Durdles</u> Lay the ground for the manner of the murder, to come out at last. Keep the boy suspended.

The last note draws attention to the trait of The Murderer that has already been noted, the barely suppressed violence, for which Deputy is an especial target: ' "Hold your hand and don't throw while I stand so near him, or I'll kill you!" ' he cries at their first encounter. After the night expedition Durdles and Jasper emerge from the Cathedral to find Deputy, who Jasper imagines has been spying on his activities. ' "What! Is that baby-devil on the watch there!" cries Jasper in a fury: so quickly roused, and so violent, that he seems an older devil himself.' He seizes Deputy by the throat and is forced to release him when Deputy craftily curls up his legs, leaving himself suspended, and simulates strangulation—acting the fate of Edwin Drood. Another target for this violence is Neville Landless. At the start of the same Cathedral expedition Jasper watches 'Neville, as though his eye were at the trigger of a loaded rifle, and he had covered him, and were going to fire. A sense of destructive power is so expressed in his face, that even Durdles pauses in his munching. . . .'

The Murderer also shows another very different quality that seems to appear when his plans are going ahead: he sings beautifully. As he leads Neville and Edwin to their quarrel he 'beautifully turns the refrain of a drinking song . . .'. Before setting out on the night expedition in the Cathedral 'he sits chanting choir-music in a low and beautiful voice, for two or three hours . . .'. On the day of the murder his voice is perfection. 'Mr Jasper is in beautiful voice this day. In the pathetic supplication to have his heart inclined to keep this law, he quite astonishes his fellows by his melodious power. He has never sung difficult music with such skill and harmony, as in this day's Anthem. His nervous temperament is occasionally prone to take difficult music a little too quickly; today, his time is perfect.'

All these varied signs mark The Murderer as he makes his moves towards Drood's death.

The predominance of The Murderer in this section of the book raises the question whether Jasper appears at all in his normal personality. Did Jasper or The Murderer write the entries in his diary? Is it Jasper or The Murderer at the piano accompanying Rosa in the scene where she breaks down? Either is possible. There is not enough evidence to be sure, particularly as Dickens could not allow any obvious differences to show that would draw attention to the two different personalities, and used opium-smoking, hypnotic powers and pregnant remarks to make Jasper look consistently sinister. Many chapters end in such a way: chapters I, II and V in Part 1; chapters VII and IX in Part 2; chapters X and XII in Part 3; and chapter XIII in Part 4. And these include the endings of the first three numbers, ensuring that the final impression left on the mind of the reader of each part would be a threatening or sinister Jasper. Whether Jasper appears in his normal persona or not in this part of the book therefore becomes a question that cannot reasonably be answered, and no doubt Dickens meant it so.

71

7

A STRIKING CHANGE comes with the death of Drood. The morning after his disappearance a different Jasper appears, 'white, half-dressed, panting, and clinging to the rail before the Minor Canon's house'. Although he defers to Sapsea at the enquiry in a way that suggests The Murderer, his behaviour is that of the doting uncle who has lost his beloved nephew and is obsessed with finding him again. What is more, Dickens virtually says so. 'It would be difficult to determine which was the more oppressed with horror and amazement: Neville Landless, or John Jasper. But that Jasper's position forced him to be active, while Neville's forced him to be passive, there would have been nothing to choose between them. Each was bowed down and broken' (p. 135). These words could only apply to the unknowing Jasper personality. It is the near-frantic uncle who takes part in the search along the river for Drood, and whom Grewgious finds sitting exhausted in his chair on the evening of the second day of the search, when he arrives to inform Jasper that Edwin and Rosa had decided not to marry:

> "This young couple, the lost youth and Miss Rosa, my ward, though so long betrothed, and so long recognising their betrothal, and so near being married——"
> Mr Grewgious saw a staring white face, and two quivering white lips, in the easy chair, and saw two muddy hands gripping its sides. But for the hands, he might have thought he had never seen the face.
> "—This young couple came gradually to the discovery, (made on both sides pretty equally, I think), that they would be happier and better, both in their present and their future lives, as affectionate friends, or say rather as brother and sister, than as husband and wife."
> Mr Grewgious saw a lead-coloured face in the easy chair, and on its surface dreadful starting drops or bubbles, as if of steel.
> "This young couple formed at length the healthy resolution of interchanging their discoveries, openly, sensibly, and tenderly. They met for that purpose. After some innocent and

generous talk, they agreed to dissolve their existing, and their intended, relations, for ever and ever."

Mr Grewgious saw a ghastly figure rise, open-mouthed, from the easy chair, and lift its outspread hands towards its head.

"One of this young couple, and that one your nephew, fearful, however, that in the tenderness of your affection for him you would be bitterly disappointed by so wide a departure from his projected life, forbore to tell you the secret, for a few days, and left it to be disclosed by me, when I should come down to speak to you, and he would be gone. I speak to you, and he IS gone."

Mr Grewgious saw the ghastly figure throw back its head, clutch its hair with its hands, and turn with a writhing action from him.

"I have now said all I have to say: except that this young couple parted, firmly, though not without tears and sorrow, on the evening when you last saw them together."

Mr Grewgious heard a terrible shriek, and saw no ghastly figure, sitting or standing; saw nothing but a heap of torn and miry clothes upon the floor.

Not changing his action even then, he opened and shut the palms of his hands as he warmed them, and looked down at it.

(pp. 137–8)

With this ending to the chapter, Dickens focuses attention on Jasper's collapse and away from his symptoms, which carry the hallmarks of his change-of-personality fits: the sudden onset, the agony, the hands gripping the sides of the chair, the beads of sweat, and the subsequent recovery are all features of his earlier crises. It appears that The Murderer is taking over again. In terms of the story these changes of personality are logical. Once the murder of Drood has been carried out, there is no need for The Murderer, who immediately gives way to the other personality; Jasper, with his innocent activity and suspicions best serves the purposes of The Murderer when the deed has been done. But the arrival of Grewgious and his news creates a fresh situation in which The Murderer must be ready to take any necessary action. This leads to the crash change of personality that takes place under the eyes of Grewgious.

So chapter XVI opens with The Murderer back in the driving seat again. Dickens gives a hint to this effect by using the word 'fit' in his opening sentence, 'When John Jasper recovered from his fit or swoon . . .', and there is another in the way that, after previously refusing to eat, 'Jasper both ate and drank almost voraciously. Combined with the hurry in his mode of doing it, was an evident indifference to the taste of what he took, suggesting that he ate and drank to fortify himself against any other failure of the spirits, far more than to gratify his palate.' The Murderer needs his strength and his wits to cope with the new problem, and attacks his food with characteristic aggression. Eating also gives him time to think, and to realise the advantage of now arguing that Drood may have left Cloisterham of his own free will to escape the embarrassment that would follow public knowledge of the ending of his engagement to Rosa; if this view is accepted the search for Drood would be called off. He accordingly sets out this argument to Grewgious and then to Crisparkle. Dickens's first note under this chapter on the right-hand side sums it up: 'Jasper's artful use of the communication on his recovery.'

At this point the well-meaning Crisparkle has to open his mouth—and say the wrong thing—by revealing that Neville Landless is in love with Rosa. This completely changes the situation again. The mutual agreement to break the engagement meant that Rosa was not in love with Edwin, and so was good news for The Murderer; the information that he had another rival—who was perhaps the real reason for Rosa's ending her engagement—was disastrous, and 'turned him paler'. The Murderer's principal aim now must be to eliminate his rival. He can hardly change his tune again on the spot, but he seems to use his hypnotic powers to put the thought of Cloisterham weir into Crisparkle's mind. Crisparkle walks there, thinks of Drood, but sees nothing; after dreaming of the weir that night, he returns in the morning and recovers Drood's gold watch and tie-pin. This second plan of The Murderer is summed up in Dickens's chapter notes: 'Cloisterham Weir, Mr Crisparkle, and the Watch and pin. Jasper's artful turn'. Crisparkle's discovery of Drood's possessions arouses public suspicion of Neville Landless, and so although there is no evidence against him he is forced to leave Cloisterham. At this point the narrative returns to Jasper:

It was not until then that John Jasper silently resumed his place in the choir. Haggard and red-eyed, his hopes plainly had deserted him, his sanguine mood was gone, and all his worst misgivings had come back. A day or two afterwards, while unrobing, he took his Diary from a pocket of his coat, turned the leaves, and with an expressive look, and without one spoken word, handed this entry to Mr Crisparkle to read:

"My dear boy is murdered. The discovery of the watch and shirt-pin convinces me that he was murdered that night, and that his jewellery was taken from him to prevent identification by its means. All the delusive hopes I had founded on his separation from his betrothed wife, I give to the winds. They perish before this fatal discovery. I now swear, and record the oath on this page, That I nevermore will discuss this mystery with any human creature, until I hold the clue to it in my hand. That I never will relax in my secrecy or in my search. That I will fasten the crime of the murder of my dear dead boy, upon the murderer. And That I devote myself to his destruction."

(p. 146)

So the chapter—and with it the fourth number—ends. The decisive personality of The Murderer has disappeared again, for it must be the other Jasper personality who resumes his duties in the Cathedral, all unconsciously vowing in his diary his own eventual destruction. This was an important point to Dickens. The last detailed chapter note he made for the book was: 'Jasper's Diary. "I devote myself to his destruction".'

My interpretation of Jasper's collapse in front of Grewgious and these subsequent events rests on the previous analysis of Jasper's fits, on the text itself, and on Dickens's own chapter notes. But there remains one piece that does not fit into the jigsaw. This is the memorandum on the left-hand page of the notes, 'Jasper's failure in the one great object made known by Mr Grewgious', for he is told of his failure to get rid of a rival for Rosa not by Grewgious but by Crisparkle. The explanation of this apparent contradiction between Dickens's note and his text seems to lie in the nature of the notes on the left-hand page. They are more general and appear to have been written earlier than the chapter notes on the right-hand page. Thus for the next number, the fifth, the left-hand notes for Edwin's disappearance after the last meeting with Rosa were obsolete by the time the author came to write the number, and he wrote 'Done already' against them. Similarly it would seem that the 'Jasper's failure' entry was an earlier idea that Dickens modified when he came to write the chapter, producing a subtler version in which there were two informants instead of one, each in turn causing Jasper to change his plans. This double turn Dickens indicated in his crowded notes for the chapter on the right-hand page, which have already been quoted.*

When the fifth number opens six months have elapsed in the story. For the first two chapters of the number Jasper remains a shadowy figure, once spotted by Mr Grewgious keeping watch on Neville Landless in Staple Inn, and also appearing briefly in Cloisterham to vouch for the Topes as landlords to the newly arrived Datchery. It is in the chapter called 'Shadow on the Sun-Dial' that Jasper has a major scene with Rosa, when, in the garden of the Nuns' House, he declares his passion for her and his willingness to abandon his revenge and his duty for her sake; he threatens to ruin the Landlesses by having Neville condemned for the murder of Drood unless she consents to give herself to him. It is pure Victorian melodrama that is difficult for the modern reader to take seriously—indeed Aylmer suggested that Jasper was deliberately playing the role of stage villain.† The scene is so theatrical, even for Dickens, that it may be suspected he wrote it with an eye on an eventual stage adaptation of *Edwin Drood* to follow the success of *No Thoroughfare*, and with Fechter in the role of Jasper, but the Victorians would have taken it perfectly seriously. They responded to the emotional appeal of even indifferent melodrama such as *The Frozen Deep*, when the tears of Maria Ternan fell on Dickens's face as the dying Wardour, and it was in the year after *Edwin Drood*, 1871, that Henry Irving appeared in the premiere of the celebrated melodrama *The Bells*,

* The notes for the fourth number are reproduced in facsimile in the Clarendon Press edition, facing p. 219.

† See Aylmer, op. cit., 132–6.

which had several affinities with *Drood*. * Dickens certainly wrote it as a serious, dramatic scene.

Jasper makes a good stage villain in this scene as he leans insouciantly on the sun-dial, apparently the music-master chatting to his pupil while he propositions and blackmails her, although the mask slips with 'His preservation of his easy attitude rendering his working features and his convulsive hands absolutely diabolical . . .' Working features, convulsive hands? Is this another Jasper fit coming on? No, for there are no other symptoms, and, even more important, this man betrays no inkling throughout the scene of The Murderer's secret knowledge. He really does appear to believe Neville Landless to be guilty, has spent the last six months trying to prove it as he vowed to do in his diary, and it is the measure of his overwhelming passion for Rosa that he is prepared to forgo all this if he can only have her. He is prepared to abandon his duty to his nephew to find the murderer: ' "There is my fidelity to my dear boy after death. Tread upon it!" ' To allow Neville's presumption in loving Rosa to go unpunished: ' "There is the inexpiable offence against my adoration of you. Spurn it!" ' To throw away his efforts of the last six months: ' "There are my labours in the cause of a just vengeance for six toiling months. Crush them!" ' The scene reaches its climax with Jasper declaring: ' "There is my past and my present wasted life. There is the desolation of my heart and my soul. There is my peace; there is my despair. Stamp them into the dust, so that you take me, were it even mortally hating me!" ' Here is the dramatic irony of this scene. For beneath the conventional melodrama Dickens had another purpose, to show that in the moment of truth produced by the frustrated intensity of his desire for Rosa, Jasper still believes in the guilt of Neville Landless. However ungentlemanly his behaviour to Rosa may be, it demonstrates that in this personality he is innocent of murder. That is the subtlety underlying the crude melodramatics.

Dickens was nothing if not generous in the number of clues he left to his mystery, and the reader who missed the point in this chapter was given a summary in the next under the guise of Rosa's reflections and her dawning suspicions of Jasper:

* See *The Mystery of Edwin Drood*, Clarendon Press edition, p. 250 n. 4.

She ran over in her mind again, all that he had said by the sun-dial in the garden. He had persisted in treating the disappearance as murder, consistently with his whole public course since the finding of the watch and shirt-pin. If he were afraid of the crime being traced out, would he not rather encourage the idea of a voluntary disappearance? He had unnecessarily declared that if the ties between him and his nephew had been less strong, he might have swept "even him" away from her side. Was that like his having really done so? He had spoken of laying his six months' labours in the cause of a just vengeance at her feet. Would he have done that, with that violence of passion, if they were a pretence? Would he have ranged them with his desolate heart and soul, his wasted life, his peace, and his despair? The very first sacrifice that he represented himself as making for her, was his fidelity to his dear boy after death. Surely these facts were strong against a fancy that scarcely dared to hint itself. And yet he was so terrible a man! In short, the poor girl (for what could she know of the criminal intellect, which its own professed students perpetually misread, because they persist in trying to reconcile it with the average intellect of average men, instead of identifying it as a horrible wonder apart), could get by no road to any other conclusion than that he *was* a terrible man, and must be fled from.

(pp. 174–5)

Here Dickens has put the case for Jasper's ignorance of the murder during the sun-dial scene—while following it with a clear hint that the murderer is 'a horrible wonder apart'. In the opening paragraphs of his final chapter, indeed, Dickens indicates that The Murderer has *not* been in control since he reappeared before Grewgious:

Although Mr Crisparkle and John Jasper met daily under the Cathedral roof, nothing at any time passed between them bearing reference to Edwin Drood after the time, more than half a year gone by, when Jasper mutely showed the Minor Canon the conclusion and the resolution entered in his Diary. It is not likely that they ever met, though so often, without the thoughts of each reverting to the subject. . . . False pretence not being in the Minor Canon's nature, he doubtless displayed openly that he would at any time have revived the subject, and even desired to discuss it. The determined reticence of Jasper, however, was not to be so approached. Impassive, moody, solitary, resolute, concentrated on one idea, and on its attendant fixed purpose that he would share it with no fellow-creature, he lived apart from human life.

(pp. 202–3)

This was the behaviour of the unenlightened uncle.

After presenting this picture of a consistently single-minded Jasper concentrating on avenging his nephew for more than six months, Dickens set about tantalising his readers a few pages further on in the same chapter with the other side of Jasper, as revealed under opium. He returns again to the opium den—it seems for the first time since the murder of Drood—in which the story began. The Opium Woman expresses her surprise at seeing him again, and starts adjusting his mixture to make him talk, in which she has a limited degree of success only.

"It's to be hoped it was pleasant to do, deary."

"It *was* pleasant to do!"

He says this with a savage air, and a spring or start at her. Quite unmoved, she retouches or replenishes the contents of the bowl with her little spatula. Seeing her intent upon the occupation, he sinks into his former attitude.

"It was a journey, a difficult and dangerous journey. That was the subject in my mind. A hazardous and perilous journey, over abysses where a slip would be destruction. Look down, look down! You see what lies at the bottom there?"

He has darted forward to say it, and to point at the ground, as though at some imaginary object far beneath. The woman looks at him, as his spasmodic face approaches close to hers, and not at his pointing. She seems to know what the influence of her perfect quietude will be; if so, she has not miscalculated it, for he subsides again.

"Well; I have told you, I did it, here, hundreds of thousands of times. What do I say? I did it millions and billions of times. I did it so often, and through such vast expanses of time, that when it was really done, it seemed not worth the doing, it was done so soon."

"That's the journey you have been away upon?" she quietly remarks. He glares at her as he smokes; and then, his eyes becoming filmy, answers: "That's the journey."

(pp. 206–7)

With further coaxing she gets him to continue:

"Sure, sure, sure! Yes, yes, yes! Now, I go along with you. You was too quick for me. I see now. You come o' purpose to take the journey. Why, I might have known it, through its standing by you so."

He answers first with a laugh, and then with a passionate setting of his teeth: "Yes, I came on purpose. When I could not bear my life, I came to get the relief, and I got it. It WAS one! It WAS one!" This repetition with extraordinary vehemence, and the snarl of a wolf.

She observes him very cautiously, as though mentally feeling her way to her next remark. It is: "There was a fellow-traveller, deary."

"Ha ha ha!" He breaks into a ringing laugh, or rather yell.

"To think," he cries, "how often fellow-traveller, and yet not know it! To think how many times he went the journey, and never saw the road!"

The woman kneels upon the floor, with her arms crossed on the coverlet of the bed, close by him, and her chin upon them. In this crouching attitude, she watches him. The pipe is falling from his mouth. She puts it back, and laying her hand upon his chest, moves him slightly from side to side. Upon that he speaks, as if she had spoken.

"Yes! I always made the journey first, before the changes of colours and the great landscapes and glittering processions began. They couldn't begin till it was off my mind. I had no room till then for anything else."

Once more he lapses into silence. Once more she lays her hand upon his chest, and moves him slightly to and fro, as a cat might stimulate a half-slain mouse. Once more he speaks, as if she had spoken.

"What? I told you so. When it comes to be real at last, it is so short that it seems unreal for the first time. Hark!"

"Yes, deary. I'm listening."

"Time and place are both at hand."

He is on his feet, speaking in a whisper, and as if in the dark.

"Time, place, and fellow-traveller," she suggests, adopting his tone, and holding him softly by the arm.

"How could the time be at hand unless the fellow-traveller was? Hush! The journey's made. It's over."

"So soon?"

"That's what I said to you. So soon. Wait a little. This is a vision. I shall sleep it off. It has been too short and easy. I must have a better vision than this; this is the poorest of all. No struggle, no consciousness of peril, no entreaty—and yet I never saw *that* before." With a start.

"Saw what, deary?"

"Look at it! Look what a poor, mean, miserable thing it is! *That* must be real. It's over!"

He has accompanied this incoherence with some wild un-meaning gestures; but they trail off into the progressive inaction of stupor, and he lies a log upon the bed.

(pp. 207–8)

The Opium Woman can get no more out of Jasper, but he has said enough: it is evident that he has been re-living the murder. 'The journey' is used as a euphemism for the murder; yet there are clear indications that a real physical journey was involved up perilous heights from which he could look down on an object 'far beneath', and this could refer only to Cloisterham Cathedral tower. So what Jasper conveys in this scene, may, I believe, be summed up as follows:

In the past he had come to the den to experience the relief he obtained from opium. His colourful opium visions were in-variably preceded by a vision of the killing of the 'fellow-traveller', Edwin Drood. The murder took place on the Cathedral tower, where he had taken the unsuspecting victim. After the belated realisation of his plight, with ineffectual struggles and pleas for mercy, the victim's body was dropped from a height on the tower and Jasper looked down on it far beneath him. This was the vision he had experienced innumerable times under the influence of opium. But when he turned his dreams into reality by murdering Drood, it fell short of the expectations of the vision. Now even the vision has become tainted by reality and no longer satisfies. The victim failed to recognise his danger, to struggle and beg for his life, while the final appearance of the body far below was strikingly wrong and disappointing—so wrong that it is the reality and not the vision that he now sees even under the influence of the drug.

Something must have gone badly awry in the murder.

8

THIS EXAMINATION OF the text of *Edwin Drood* confirmed to my satisfaction my interpretation of Jasper and his fits. It is true that under the direct influence of opium the vicious side of his personality comes to the surface, so that in his opium dreams he enacts the murder; and in this condition he lets enough drop for the Opium Woman to have a good idea what is going on in his mind, enabling her to give her warning to Edwin and to attempt to probe Jasper further. Yet the choir-master who returns to consciousness has no memory of these visions of violence. He is the uncle devotedly and possessively attached to his nephew. In this normal, undrugged state it requires one of the change-of-personality fits, which owe nothing to opium, to effect the transition to the other personality, the man of violence plotting and carrying out Drood's destruction. The two personalities are distinct, the affectionate uncle having no inkling of the murderous plans of his counterpart. It was a remarkable piece of psychology for 1869—Sigmund Freud was still only a thirteen-year-old schoolboy.

My understanding of the nature of John Jasper made Edmund Wilson's theory that Dickens was fictionalising himself in the character appear as untenable as Aylmer's interpretation (see above, p. 24. This does not mean that Dickens did not put into Jasper some part of himself, and even of his experience in leading a double life with his mistress Ellen Ternan. In some measure all authors do this. But I found it impossible to believe that he could have identified himself with a character having such a completely divided consciousness, and moreover a murderer—for murderers are not sympathetic characters to Dickens. John Jasper was a vicious specimen of a type of criminal mind. Dickens would surely *not* have been amused at the suggestion that he and Jasper were of a kind.

On the other hand, for the purely physical symptoms of Jasper's fits, it is not necessary to look further than Dickens himself. The sudden onset of the fit, the pallid face, the great drops of perspiration on the forehead, the hands clutching at the arms of the seat, the overpowering nature of the attack: all these were Dickens's own symptoms as described by his daughter Mamie during one of his nervous crises in a train following the Staplehurst disaster (see above, p. 13).

If Dickens did not find the original for Jasper in himself, where did he get the idea? It seems likely that it came to him spontaneously, and that Jasper was yet another product of his prodigious creative imagination. Yet there is also a possible literary source. James Hogg, a shepherd from the Scottish Borders, had written in 1824 a strange story entitled *The Private Memoirs and Confessions of a Justified Sinner*. The principal character, Robert Wringhim, is persuaded by the Devil, who assumes a variety of human shapes, that since he is one of the Elect predestined to salvation any action he takes against the ungodly is a virtuous act. In this way Wringhim is persuaded to murder a Presbyterian minister and his own brother. (It is strongly hinted that Wringhim is illegitimate.) He falls into a confused state of mind, later realising that there are periods of time, one lasting as long as six months, of which he now has no recollection. He learns that during these blank periods he has been engaged in various crimes, including seduction and further murders.

Whether Dickens was aware of Hogg's work I did not know. I found from the catalogue of Dickens's Gad's Hill library sold after his death that he had owned Hogg's *Tales and Sketches by the Ettrick Shepherd*, a six-volume collection which contained a bowdlerised version of the work entitled *The Private Memoirs and Confessions of a Fanatic . . .* Despite the cuts in this version, the idea of two personalities with separate consciousness was still there, put most succinctly in the words of Robert Wringhim himself when facing the accusations of the Devil: ' "If this that you tell me be true," said I, "then is it as true that I have two souls, which take possession of my bodily frame by turns, the one being all unconscious of what the other performs; for as sure as I have at this moment a spirit within me, so sure am I utterly ignorant of the crimes you now lay to my charge." '* I cannot say whether Dickens ever read this novel. What can be said is that the central idea for the character of Jasper was contained in a book standing on the shelves of his library at Gad's Hill.

In the process of examining Dickens's text for his handling of Jasper, I had made a further discovery: examples of the same theme kept cropping up through *Edwin Drood*. These were not clues to the mystery in the classic detective-story sense, even though to the enlightened reader they could convey a great deal, but were rather variations on the theme. They were to be found in the most unlikely places, some comic, some serious, while others were that peculiarly Dickensian combination of both. Some were apparently trivial, even looking suspiciously like padding, yet they fell into place once the central idea of the work had been identified. In certain instances they were covert images of Jasper, others were variants on the motif of duality.

The prime example, of course, was Miss Twinkleton. Just as the unaware music-master is ignorant of the activities of The Murderer, so the schoolmistress 'in her scholastic state of existence, is as ignorant as a granite pillar' of the affairs of the heart that concern her in her other state of being. A more complex use of the Twinkleton image is seen in the opening paragraph of the fourth number:

Miss Twinkleton's establishment was about to undergo a serene hush. The Christmas recess was at hand. What had once, and at no remote period, been called, even by the erudite Miss Twinkleton herself, "the half"; but what was now called, as being more elegant, and more strictly collegiate, "the term"; would expire to-morrow. A noticeable relaxation of discipline had for some few days pervaded the Nuns' House. Club suppers had occurred in the bedrooms, and a dressed tongue

* James Hogg, *Tales and Sketches by the Ettrick Shepherd* (1837), vol. V, p. 162.

had been carved with a pair of scissors, and handed round with the curling-tongs. Portions of marmalade had likewise been distributed on a service of plates constructed of curlpaper; and cowslip wine had been quaffed from the small squat measuring glass in which little Rickitts (a junior of weakly constitution), took her steel drops daily. The housemaids had been bribed with various fragments of riband, and sundry pairs of shoes, more or less down at heel, to make no mention of crumbs in the beds; the airiest costumes had been worn on these festive occasions; and the daring Miss Ferdinand had even surprised the company with a sprightly solo on the comb-and-curlpaper, until suffocated in her own pillow by two flowing-haired executioners.

(pp. 111–12)

The reference to 'the erudite Miss Twinkleton' recalls that there are two halves to the schoolmistress—a suggestion immediately re-enforced by the seemingly ingenuous, yet emphasised, reference to 'the half'. Then comes the first sinister note with 'expire to-morrow'. There follow the festive meals and delicacies, served with their double objects, scissors and curling tongs, while Rickitts's steel drops look forward to the 'dreadful starting drops or bubbles, as if of steel' that mark the transition to The Murderer, and after some improvised music as the theme of the music-master, Miss Ferdinand is suffocated by the two 'flowing-haired executioners'. In this way the very first paragraph of the number in which the murder takes place prefigures the action that follows: the separation at the end of term anticipates the parting of Rosa and Edwin, the dormitory feast looks forward to the Christmas Eve dinner for Neville and Edwin, and the suffocation of Miss Ferdinand to Edwin's murder. The duality of the murderer is indicated twice, at the beginning by the reminders about Miss Twinkleton, and in the final words of the paragraph by the image of the *two* flowing-haired executioners.

Another duality pattern reflecting Jasper is provided by the Landless twins. Individually they are very different. Their early privations and lack of education have produced opposite effects on brother and sister. Neville Landless describes himself at his first meeting with Crisparkle as having had 'to suppress a deadly and bitter hatred' and having been made 'secret and revengeful' and driven in his weakness to being 'false and mean', while the same experience has tempered his sister Helena so that 'She has come out of the disadvantages of our miserable life, as much better than I am, as that Cathedral tower is higher than those chimneys' (pp. 48-9). In their attempts to escape 'the flight was always of her planning and leading. Each time she dressed as a boy, and showed the daring of a man' (p. 49). She was never subdued or made to cry. As a pair they have a strong side, and a weak or vicious side—as Jasper has. Their experiences have also engendered 'something untamed about them both; a certain air upon them of hunter and huntress; yet withal a certain air of being the objects of the chase, rather than the followers' (p. 44). The point is taken up again two chapters further on, when Neville is beginning the conversation that will end in the quarrel with Edwin 'in a watchfully advancing, and yet furtive and shy manner, very expressive of that peculiar air already noticed, of being at once hunter and hunted' (p. 55). Neville is indeed destined to be hunted by Jasper, just as brother and sister will surely in turn hunt Jasper. Here again as hunter and hunted they reflect the duality of Jasper, himself the pursuer and the pursued.

The Landlesses also have the unity of twins. From that strange affinity they possess the ability to read each other's minds, to the initial incredulity of Canon Crisparkle; but after teaching Neville for a short while he 'thought how the consciousness'—that key word in *Edwin Drood*—'had stolen upon him that in teaching one he was teaching two' (p. 78). This natural telepathy between the twins corresponds to Jasper's hypnotic ability to project thoughts into the minds of others, a power he exercises on both Rosa and Crisparkle. Yet in this respect the twins are the mirror-image of Jasper: they are two with almost a common consciousness, while he is one with a divided consciousness.

Dickens's first notes on them, on the left-hand page of his second number, run:

Neville and Olympia Heybridge—or Heyfort?
<u>Neville and Helena Landless</u>
Mixture of Oriental blood—or imperceptibly acquired nature—in them. <u>Yes</u>

Dickens did not spell this out in the text; but his description of them—'both very dark, and very rich in colour' (p. 44)—and Neville's own suspicions that he may have 'a drop of what is tigerish' in the native blood (p. 49) strongly suggest that they are Eurasian. Drood certainly thought so, judging by his taunt: ' "but you are no judge of white men" ' (p. 60). The change of name is also of interest. Modern critics have tended to look for possible significance in the final choice of 'Helena Landless' with its resemblance to that of Dickens's mistress Ellen Lawless (Ternan). No doubt it did give the novelist secret satisfaction to work this clue to his private life into his book, just as he worked in many other hidden indications of his plot, but not enough is known of this relationship to justify reading any more into the novel, and the name Landless was surely significant in itself. The twins *are* landless, without a country of their own or a culture to which they completely belong. They are *déracinés*. Following the Jasper parallel, is this perhaps a hint from Dickens that, when Jasper's background is finally revealed, he too will turn out to be another such product of mixed blood and different cultures?

Sapsea, on the other hand, is a true-blue Englishman. The monumentally pompous and stupid auctioneer, and later Mayor, of Cloisterham served Dickens as a Tory butt and as part of the mechanics of the plot; convinced as he is of the essential soundness of Jasper and un-Englishness of Neville, he is immediately disposed to suspect Neville after the disappearance of Drood. But Sapsea also has another role. His foible is to dress like the Dean and to be taken for the Dean, affecting an ecclesiastical air in his own auctioneer's pulpit. So when he unexpectedly encounters the Dean just before Jasper's night expedition with Durdles he 'is instantly stricken far more ecclesiastical than any Archbishop of York, or Canterbury' (p. 100). The Dean greets the Mayor 'with a nod of good-natured recognition of his Fetch', and Sapsea 'falls to studying his original in minute points of detail' before being persuaded by Jasper that he had suggested the idea of the night expedition. A Fetch is 'the apparition, double, or wraith of a living person', according to the *Shorter Oxford Dictionary*. The Dean, himself the representative of Church authority in *Drood*, has acquired a double in the person of Sapsea. But the duality goes further. For Sapsea sees himself as representing the civil authority as Mayor and the ecclesiastical authority in his fantasy as Dean: in his person he is both Church and State. The idea is present in *Drood*, but is most clearly expressed in the 'Sapsea Fragment',* after he believes he has been taken for the Dean. 'For I felt that I was picked out (though perhaps only through a coincidence) to a certain extent to represent what I call our glorious constitution in church and state. The phrase may be objected to by captious minds; but I own to it as mine. I threw it off in argument some little time back. I said, Our Glorious Constitution in Church and State' (p 232). Sapsea represents—if only in his own mind—the classic duality of Christian society.

Even the victim himself, Edwin Drood, has his double. In a passage that is not in the manuscript—Dickens probably wrote it later at the printers to make up the length of his first number—Rosa describes to Edwin her birthday party, at which one of the girls impersonated him: Rosa refused to dance with this fiancé, who showed a similar lack of enthusiasm for her. ' "Oh, she did it so well!" cries Rosa, in a sudden ecstasy with her counterfeit betrothed' (p. 18). Edwin is impersonated a second time when his quarrel with Neville is re-enacted by Miss Giggles and the inevitable Miss Ferdinand, who claps on a paper moustache (p. 66). This may not have been the last time Dickens intended to introduce an impersonation of Drood by a pupil of Miss Twinkleton.

Mr Grewgious makes his own small contribution to the theme when giving Edwin his lecture: 'But my picture does represent the true lover as having no existence separable from that of the beloved object of his affections, and as living at once a doubled life and a halved life' (p. 95). Grewgious also causes to be summoned the pair of comedy waiters who provide dinner from Furnival's Inn. The by-play of the flying waiter who does all the work and rushes backwards and forwards through the fog fetching everything from Furnival's, while the immovable waiter stands and does nothing, 'having sternly (not to say with indignation) looked on at the flying waiter while he set clean glasses round', at first suggests that the pair are no more than comic padding. Yet they

* This short incomplete section about Sapsea was found among Dickens's papers after his death by Forster. See Clarendon Press edition, p. xlviii and pp. 232–5, and Penguin edition, pp. 296–301.

were important enough in Dickens's mind to be put down with a line round them in his notes for the chapter. I realised belatedly that they were another figuring of Jasper: the immovable, disapproving and superior waiter is the choir-master's normal self, and the object of his disapproval, the flying waiter who comes and goes in the fog and makes all the preparations represents The Murderer making his periodic appearances and his sinister preparations. Dickens clinched the identification with his final punch line: 'And here let it be noticed, parenthetically, that the leg of this young man in its application to the door, evinced the finest sense of touch: always preceding himself and tray (with something of an angling air about it), by some seconds: and always lingering after he and the tray had disappeared, like Macbeth's leg when accompanying him off the stage with reluctance to the assassination of Duncan' (p. 93). The flying waiter finally becomes identified with Macbeth proceeding to the murder of his guest.

This is the only direct reference to Macbeth himself in *Drood*, but there are echoes of the play throughout the book, not surprisingly, as Dickens knew it well and *Macbeth* always came readily to his mind. It was one of the great roles of his friend Macready—for whose daughter Dickens and Forster had conjured—and the actor had chosen to appear as Macbeth in his final stage performance in 1851. Dickens specially included Sikes and Nancy in his reading at Cheltenham in 1869 so that the old man, still living there in retirement, could hear it; the murder of Nancy rendered him excited and speechless, until eventually paying Dickens the supreme accolade of 'Two Macbeths!'

The play was also very relevant to the story of *Edwin Drood*. Both concern the murder of a likeable, unsuspecting kinsman, an act made even more treacherous by the victim being the guest of the murderer. So the allusions to the play start as early as the opening of the second chapter with 'the rook . . . when he wings his way homeward towards nightfall' recalling 'Light thickens, and the crow/Makes wing to the rooky wood' (*Macbeth* III. ii). The fearful storm that blew down chimneys following the killing of Duncan has its counterpart in the storm in Cloisterham, where 'Chimnies topple in the streets' and the Cathedral tower itself is damaged (p. 130). Jasper in his final opium-den scene with his 'Time and place are both at hand' (p. 208) is echoing Lady

Macbeth's 'Nor time nor place/Did then adhere, and yet you would make both' (I. vii). The most obvious allusion of all is the title Dickens gave to the chapter of the final dinner party and Drood's disappearance: 'When Shall These Three Meet Again?' This variant on the witch's incantation 'When shall we three meet again?' has been seen as an argument for the survival of Edwin Drood. I do not find this convincing, but I suggest that there is a sense in which Dickens intended the three to meet again, as will be seen in my completion of the story.

There is, I believe, another example of the general theme, that is not a human character. In *Edwin Drood* opium itself has two faces, one good and one bad. Wilkie Collins had made the point through Ezra Jennings in *The Moonstone*, and the Opium Woman defends it when she asks Datchery for money to buy medicine ' "as does me good" '. ' "It's opium, deary. Neither more nor less. And it's like a human creetur so far, that you always hear what can be said against it, but seldom what can be said in its praise" ' (p. 212).

More significant than the text is perhaps the monthly cover (see frontispiece). The left-hand side of the cover seems to symbolise the Good, or perhaps Love. In the top corner is a female figure wearing a chaplet and holding flowers, and the branches enclosing the small scenes on this side of the page are covered in roses. In the scenes themselves Rosa is coming out of the Cathedral on the arm of Edwin Drood, then looking at a poster announcing his loss, and next accepting the attentions of another suitor. The final scene at the bottom on this side is of the Opium Woman sitting on her bed, pipe in hand. On the top right-hand side of the cover is a female harpy with snake-like hair and a dagger in her hand, symbolising Evil or Hatred. The scenes below are framed by bare branches with thorns that would make any gardener wince, and show Jasper and the choir coming out of the Cathedral, then the pursuit scene up the spiral stair, and finally at the bottom, balancing the Opium Woman on the other side, a Chinaman with a pig-tail sitting in a chair and smoking his pipe. Both the Chinaman and the Opium Woman are like Victorian factory chimneys, producing clouds of smoke that roll into the next scene.

The two opium-smoking figures and their positions have caused some puzzlement and speculation. Is the Opium Woman put below the Rosa scenes to hint at an unrevealed relationship between them? Is she put on the side of the Good to show that she is one of the forces ranged against Jasper? And who is the Chinaman? The most likely candidate for the Chinaman is never seen, but is mentioned by the Opium Woman: ' "Jack Chinaman t'other side the court; but he can't do it as well as me" ' (p. 2). This hardly seems to merit a place on the cover when much more important characters are omitted. My own interpretation is that Dickens had a double purpose here, as so often. The first was to draw the attention of his readers to opium with this heavy emphasis on the cover. The sight of the two figures and their rolling clouds of opium smoke would impress the reader before he had read a single word of the text. At the same time, by placing one figure on the Good side and one on the Evil side of the jacket, Dickens was symbolising the double nature of opium. Jack Chinaman, I suggest, represents the Oriental use of the drug as a harmful narcotic, a stupefier and degrader, while the Opium Woman on the side of the Good represents its beneficent aspect as a Victorian medicine, the pain-killer and tranquilliser. So opium itself becomes another dual personality in *Edwin Drood*.

Mr Honeythunder the philanthropist has not previously been mentioned, since he plays no part in the story except to introduce the Landless twins. Yet he too has his place in the pattern of *Edwin Drood*. He is an arrogant, bullying do-gooder, whose profession of love for humanity is in complete contrast with his behaviour to people: 'his philanthropy was of that gunpowderous sort that the difference between it and animosity was hard to determine'. In the chapter Dickens entitled 'Philanthropy, Professional and Unprofessional', Honeythunder is contrasted with Canon Crisparkle, and his double moral standards held up to ridicule. Symbolically he first arrives in Cloisterham 'twisting a double eye-glass by its riband, as if he were roasting it'—a nice image of his aggressiveness, his moral contortions, and his double vision.

Dickens also worked in a number of smaller touches, that might pass unnoticed without an awareness of his theme: pairs of objects are particularly in evidence. The second chapter opens with a pair of rooks who seem intent on deception, 'conveying to mere men the fancy that it is of some occult importance to the body politic,

that this artful couple should pretend to have renounced con-
nexion with it' (p. 4). Crisparkle's mother, the china shepherdess,
has a sister, 'another piece of Dresden china, and matching her so
neatly that they would have made a delightful pair of ornaments
for the two ends of any capacious old-fashioned chimneypiece,
and by right should never have been seen apart . . .' (p. 42). Miss
Twinkleton has in her parlour a pair of significant globes, one
terrestrial, the other celestial. 'These expressive machines imply (to
parents and guardians) that even when Miss Twinkleton retires
into the bosom of privacy, duty may at any moment compel her to
become a sort of Wandering Jewess, scouring the earth and
soaring through the skies in search of knowledge for her pupils'
(p. 17). This duality does not seem to be for the public eye. On
being invited to the Crisparkles' 'Miss Twinkleton did, indeed,
glance at the globes, as regretting that they were not formed to be
taken out into society; but became reconciled to leaving them
behind' (p. 42).

These many variations on the theme of duality in the book
served to confirm my analysis of Dickens's 'curious and new
idea'. I was reminded of Angus Wilson's comment: 'Not very
much that is meaningful can be said about the totality of *Edwin
Drood*, because Dickens was the sort of artist whose parts (whatever the contrary appearance) are so interrelated that only the
whole gives the key to the whole.'* Certainly we have no more
than half of *Edwin Drood*, yet the concept of duality does seem to
provide a key to many of the parts, as well as to the central mystery itself. No doubt Dickens would have revealed further hidden
relationships on the same theme if he had lived to complete his
design. This knowledge did not help directly with the concrete
details of his plot needed to complete the story. Nevertheless,
understanding of his technique in handling his theme did prove
crucial in decoding a passage that provided some further useful
clues.

* Angus Wilson, *The World of Charles Dickens* (1970; Penguin edn.,
1972), p. 291.

9

I HAVE TO confess that when I first began to re-read *Edwin Drood* in the search for a solution to the mystery, there was a passage I used to skip regularly. Dickens opened his third monthly number at chapter X with a recapitulation of the quarrel between Edwin and Neville, no doubt to refresh the memory of his readers; this summary takes the form of a conversation between Crisparkle and his mother, 'the china shepherdess'. Subsequently the Minor Canon encounters the Landless twins and persuades Neville to meet Drood half-way in a reconciliation. Sandwiched between these scenes are two lengthy, apparently irrelevant paragraphs describing the dining-room closet at Minor Canon Corner, and the room that serves as a herb closet. There seemed so much whimsy in the description of the preserves in the dining-room closet and of Crisparkle submitting himself to the herbal ministrations of the china shepherdess that, unlike Crisparkle, I could not stomach it and turned the page. I should have known better and remembered the opinion of Dickens's daughter Kate: 'After reading *Edwin Drood* many times, as most of us have read it, we must, I think, come to the conclusion that not a word of this tale was written without full consideration. . . .'* But it was only when I myself began to understand Dickens's technique in this book that I started to pay serious attention to what may be called—with apologies to Erle Stanley Gardner—The Case of the Curious Closets.

This is the first paragraph, describing the dining-room closet:

As, whenever the Reverend Septimus fell a musing his good mother took it to be an infallible sign that he "wanted support", the blooming old lady made all haste to the dining-room closet, to produce from it the support embodied in a glass of Constantia and a home-made biscuit. It was a most wonderful closet, worthy of Cloisterham and of Minor Canon Corner. Above it, a portrait of Handel in a flowing wig beamed down at the spectator, with a knowing air of being up to the contents of

* Kate Perugini, op. cit., p. 648.

the closet, and a musical air of intending to combine all its harmonies in one delicious fugue. No common closet with a vulgar door on hinges, openable all at once, and leaving nothing to be disclosed by degrees, this rare closet had a lock in mid-air, where two perpendicular slides met: the one falling down, and the other pushing up. The upper slide, on being pulled down (leaving the lower a double mystery), revealed deep shelves of pickle-jars, jam-pots, tin canisters, spice-boxes, and agreeably outlandish vessels of blue and white, the luscious lodgings of preserved tamarinds and ginger. Every benevolent inhabitant of this retreat had his name inscribed upon his stomach. The pickles, in a uniform of rich brown double-breasted buttoned coat, and yellow or sombre drab continuations, announced their portly forms, in printed capitals, as Walnut, Gherkin, Onion, Cabbage, Cauliflower, Mixed, and other members of that noble family. The jams, as being of a less masculine temperament, and as wearing curlpapers, announced themselves in feminine caligraphy, like a soft whisper, to be Raspberry, Gooseberry, Apricot, Plum, Damson, Apple, and Peach. The scene closing on these charmers, and the lower slide ascending, oranges were revealed, attended by a mighty japanned sugar-box, to temper their acerbity if unripe. Home-made biscuits waited at the Court of these Powers, accompanied by a goodly fragment of plum-cake, and various slender ladies' fingers, to be dipped into sweet wine and kissed. Lowest of all, a compact leaden vault enshrined the sweet wine and a stock of cordials: whence issued whispers of Seville Orange, Lemon, Almond, and Carraway-seed. There was a crowning air upon this closet of closets, of having been for ages hummed through by the Cathedral bell and organ, until those venerable bees had made sublimated honey of everything in store; and it was always observed that every dipper among the shelves (deep, as has been noticed, and swallowing up head, shoulders, and elbows), came forth again mellow-faced, and seeming to have undergone a saccharine transfiguration.

(p. 79)

There are several indications that this closet held a particular significance. Dickens's notes for the chapter consist of only four sentences and two of these concern the closet: 'Minor Canon Corner. The closet I remember there as a child.' The reader, who would not have the privilege of seeing the author's notes, was given a strong hint in Handel's 'knowing air of being up to the contents of the closet', and his apparent intention of showing that all its contents have a single fugal theme. As the paragraph follows Crisparkle's reflections on the Landless twins and his realisation that 'in teaching one he was teaching two', the reader was already forewarned what that theme might be. This 'closet of closets' is no ordinary cupboard and has more than mere domestic significance; it has the air of having been 'hummed through by the Cathedral bell and organ', which links it not just to the Cathedral in general but to its music in particular—in short, to Jasper.

For the dining-room closet is the most detailed and precise image of Jasper in *Edwin Drood*. There are the two halves, completely separate, only one of which can be seen at a time. When the upper half is visible, the lower half is 'a double mystery'. The upper half is normal and kindly with its portly Pickwickian pickles and female jam charmers. Here things are what they appear to be and say they are. 'Every benevolent inhabitant of this retreat had his name inscribed upon his stomach.' But when they disappear from sight, the lower half may be opened, revealing less agreeable contents: bitterness in the oranges, and a suggestion of insincerity and even conflict in 'the Court of these Powers' and the kissing of ladies' fingers, with the sweet wine and cordials confined to a 'compact leaden vault' from which only 'whispers' of the sharp flavours can emerge. There is a powerful suggestion of death, too, in this leaden vault at the lowest level. Yet these profound inner differences will not be seen in the outward man, for this strange closet has the power of making all 'mellow-faced', and The Murderer himself would emerge 'seeming to have undergone a saccharine transformation'. In this one image Dickens has given Jasper's essential character.

Yet there was one odd feature of this paragraph that I could not explain. Dickens used the word 'fugue' here in its accepted musical sense of a number of parts developing a single theme. It is completely relevant to his method in writing the closet paragraph, and moreover the word had no other meaning in the language even when the appropriate fascicle of the *Oxford English Dictionary* was published over thirty years later in 1901. It was not until the twentieth century that it acquired a technical meaning in psychiatry. Volume II of the Supplement to the *Dictionary* defines a fugue in this later sense as 'A flight from one's own identity, often involving travel to some unconsciously desired locality', adding that 'On recovery, memory of events during the state is totally repressed . . .'. The definition does not exactly fit Jasper's case, but the element of flight to the opium den in the London slums and the repression of the memory of The Murderer's activities still offer a most striking parallel. Yet this is not all. Dickens also used 'sublimate' in its primary meaning of turning from solid to vapour and back to solid again. Again this has become a term in modern psychology meaning to 'divert the energy of a primitive impulse into a culturally higher activity', and as such it seems entirely appropriate to explain the origin of The Murderer's exquisite singing as he prepares the death of Drood (see above, p. 71). Yet it had no such meaning when the *Oxford English Dictionary* was published. How are we to explain Dickens's use in 1870 of two words in a single paragraph whose twentieth-century meanings are eerily relevant to his subject? Coincidence or precognition? The question is one that would have greatly intrigued the author himself.

The dining-room closet being so pregnant with meaning, the herb-closet also merited close attention:

The Reverend Septimus yielded himself up quite as willing a victim to a nauseous medicinal herb-closet, also presided over by the china shepherdess, as to this glorious cupboard. To what amazing infusions of gentian, peppermint, gilliflower, sage, parsley, thyme, rue, rosemary, and dandelion, did his courageous stomach submit itself! In what wonderful wrappers enclosing layers of dried leaves, would he swathe his rosy and contented face, if his mother suspected him of a toothache! What botanical blotches would he cheerfully stick upon his cheek, or forehead, if the dear old lady convicted him of an imperceptible pimple there! Into this herbaceous penitentiary, situated on an upper staircase-landing: a low and narrow whitewashed cell, where bunches of dried leaves hung from rusty hooks in the ceiling, and were spread out upon shelves, in company with portentous bottles: would the Reverend Septimus submissively be led, like the highly-popular lamb who has so long and unresistingly been led to the slaughter, and there would he, unlike that lamb, bore nobody but himself. Not even doing that much, so that the old lady were busy and pleased, he would quietly swallow what was given him, merely taking a corrective dip of hands and face into one great bowl of dried rose-leaves, and into the other great bowl of dried lavender, and then would go out, as confident in the sweetening powers of Cloisterham Weir and a wholesome mind, as Lady Macbeth was hopeless of those of all the seas that roll.

(pp. 79–80)

Nauseous is indeed the right adjective! But what did the herb-closet convey? Not another Jasper image, nor even a more general duality theme, was apparent, with the exception of the final Macbeth reference.

Here the manuscript of *Edwin Drood* was suggestive. Dickens wrote it in a blue ink. Just a few alterations and two relatively short passages were written in another ink that probably started life as black, and is now brown. One of these brown ink passages starts in the middle of the conversation about Neville between Crisparkle and the china shepherdess and finishes at the conclusion of the dining-room closet paragraph, the herb-closet then reverting to the normal blue. The significance of these ink changes is not known—possibly Dickens was writing in a different place. It does suggest a break between the writing of the two closet paragraphs. The herb-closet did not appear in Dickens's notes, so it could well have been an afterthought, an idea for putting over something further in a similar paragraph that came to him after writing the dining-room closet passage. A different idea, using a different technique.

The herb-closet appeared a typical Dickens mélange of the jocular and the sinister. Then I tried underlining the sinister parts:

The Reverend Septimus yielded himself up quite as willing a victim to a nauseous medicinal herb-closet, also presided over by the china shepherdess, as to this glorious cupboard. To what amazing infusions of gentian, peppermint, gilliflower, sage,

97

parsley, thyme, rue, rosemary, and dandelion, did his courageous stomach submit itself! In what wonderful wrappers enclosing layers of dried leaves, would he swathe his rosy and contented face, if his mother <u>suspected</u> him of a toothache! What botanical blotches would he cheerfully stick upon his cheek, or forehead, if the dear old lady <u>convicted</u> him of an imperceptible pimple there! Into this herbaceous <u>penitentiary</u>, situated on an upper staircase-landing: a <u>low and narrow whitewashed cell</u>, where bunches of dried leaves <u>hung from rusty hooks in the ceiling</u>, and were spread out upon shelves, in company with portentous bottles: would the Reverend Septimus submissively be led, like the highly-popular <u>lamb</u> who has so long and unresistingly been <u>led to the slaughter</u>, and there would he, unlike that lamb, bore nobody but himself. Not even doing that much, so that the old lady were busy and pleased, he would quietly swallow what was given him, merely taking a corrective`dip of hands and face into the great bowl of dried rose-leaves, and into the other great bowl of dried lavender, and then would go out, as confident in the sweetening powers of Cloisterham Weir and a wholesome mind, as <u>Lady Macbeth</u> was <u>hopeless</u> of those of all the seas that roll.

The first six items seemed to form a progression of events:

> a victim
> suspected
> convicted
> penitentiary
> low and narrow whitewashed cell
> hung from rusty hooks in the ceiling

So a crime with a victim is followed by suspicion, a conviction, prison, and a small whitewashed cell where something is hung from rusty hooks in the ceiling. This hardly suggests an official execution on a gallows; the image it conjures up is rather suggestive of a prisoner hanging himself in his cell. Then after the lamb led to the slaughter, the paragraph ended with another Macbeth allusion. This passage is the only direct reference to Lady Macbeth in

Edwin Drood, although the quotation Dickens appeared to be thinking of comes from Macbeth himself after the murder of Duncan: 'Will all great Neptune's ocean wash this blood/ from my hand?' (II. ii). However the 'sweetening powers' of Cloisterham Weir (echoes of the dining-room closet!) and Lady Macbeth's hopelessness of being cleansed powerfully recall her sleep-walking scene: 'Here's the smell of the blood still: all the perfumes of Arabia will not sweeten this little hand' (V. i). This creates another parallel with Jasper: Lady Macbeth walking and talking in her sleep is no more aware of what she is doing than Jasper is aware of what The Murderer does. Her sleep-walking, that symptom of another sick mind, also acts as a reminder that Lady Macbeth is at the point of suicide. At the end of the play she is overwhelmed by her sense of guilt and kills herself. Thus two separate suggestions of suicide may be seen in the closet paragraph, which I take as a hint from Dickens that Jasper will ultimately hang himself in his cell. This interpretation also provides a meaning for the lamb led to the slaughter: the sacrificial lamb in this context would be the affectionate and loving uncle of Edwin Drood who pays the price for the deed of The Murderer. On finally realising the hideous truth, Jasper in his guilty despair would hang himself in his whitewashed cell, and thereby fulfil his oath to be avenged on the murderer of his 'dear dead boy'.

The two closet paragraphs, read together, seem to encapsulate the story of *Edwin Drood*. The dining-room closet presents an image of Jasper, his two distinct and separate halves, one apparently normal, the other sinister. The herb-closet adumbrates the events that will follow from this division: his crime, conviction, imprisonment, and the suicide in his cell by which the one half finally exacts retribution on his murderous alter ego. It is only a faint skeleton outline. Dickens was giving hints, not providing a synopsis.

There remains a wry footnote. Dickens spent the day of Wednesday, 8 June, working at the final chapter of *Edwin Drood* in the Swiss chalet at Gad's Hill. He returned to the main house about an hour before the time fixed for dinner, writing two letters in the library. One of the letters was a reply to a Mr J. M. Makeham who had written to him complaining about the 'lamb . . . led to the slaughter' on the grounds that 'it is drawn from a passage of Holy Writ which is greatly reverenced . . . as a prophetic description of the sufferings of Our Saviour'. Dickens replied that 'It would be quite inconceivable to me—but for your letter—that any reasonable reader could possibly attach a scriptural reference to a passage in a book of mine, reproducing a much abused social figure of speech . . . I am truly shocked to find that any reader can make the mistake.'* Dickens must have been more taken aback than he admitted in the letter to find himself under attack for this phrase from his description of the herb-closet. And the final irony he would not have known: this letter was one of the last things, possibly the very last, he was ever to pen. His fatal stroke came that same evening while he was at dinner.

10

I NOW HAD enough information about Jasper from Dickens's text to set against the evidence of contemporaries. In every case the agreement was astonishingly close, particularly as they did not all realise the significance of what they knew.

Fildes's case was uncomplicated. His information that there was to be a scene in the condemned cell was reflected in the herb-closet references to a prison and a low and narrow white-washed cell. His revelation in 1905 that Jasper would strangle Edwin Drood was also foreshadowed in the asphyxiation of Miss Ferdinand.

With hindsight it was fascinating to see how close the two Collins brothers got in their very different ways to penetrating Dickens's secret. In spite of his apparent ignorance, Charles Collins turned out to be bang on target psychologically, even if not literally, when he wrote of the pursuers of the murderer in his cover sketch being 'led on by Jasper who points unconsciously to his own figure in the drawing at the head of the title'. Jasper was indeed unconsciously pursuing himself, the hunter and the hunted. Yet how did Charles Collins, who clearly did not know the secret, come to describe the situation so aptly? It can only be

* See *The Mystery of Edwin Drood*, Penguin edition, p. 308 n.

conjectured that the artist absorbed something from Dickens, when he was describing the posture of the characters he wanted Collins to draw. Did Dickens perhaps let slip the revealing word 'unconsciously' to him? We are unlikely ever to know.

Collins's brother Wilkie was no less interesting. Although Wilkie Collins refused to write a completion of *Edwin Drood*, he did write a Christmas story in the following year, 1871, for *The Graphic*—that same magazine in which Fildes's drawings had led to his choice as the illustrator of *Edwin Drood*. This story, *Miss or Mrs?*, contains many of the same plot ingredients as *Drood*. The heroine, Natalie Graybrooke, is in love with her cousin, a young doctor Laurie Linzie. Her father wants her to marry an associate Richard Turlington, now a city merchant but formerly a ruthless and unscrupulous captain in the merchant navy under another name. Turlington has got into financial difficulties, so when he discovers that Natalie has secretly married Linzie and he has lost her dowry, he plans to murder her father who has been unwise enough to make him his sole executor. The Graybrookes are invited to his house in Somerset, which is separated from the village church by the length of the churchyard. Going to a den in the East End of London near the river, Turlington finds an old seaman accomplice from his past, now far gone in gin and opium, and hires him to murder the father as he is walking through the churchyard, to take his money and jewellery so that robbery would appear the motive, and then to destroy his own clothes in an outhouse where there is a cauldron of quick-lime. The murder is planned for Christmas Eve, and a disguised stranger (it is Linzie) appears in the village just before this. The seaman strikes down his victim and robs him as planned, but then, apparently while in the act of checking whether he is dead, has a fit; 'a sort of vision' overcomes him, enabling his victim to escape to safety. Finally the villain Turlington kills himself accidentally when his pistol misfires as he is trying to shoot Natalie and her husband.

Wilkie Collins would seem to have deliberately transposed some elements to make the parallel with *Drood* less complete. The timid heroine Natalie is tall, well-developed physically for her age, and dark, having a mixture of French and Negro blood on her mother's side, while her resolute bosom friend is minute and fair, so reversing the physical appearances of Rosa and Helena. There is also a firm with business in the Middle East, and even a branch house in Egypt at Alexandria, but it is Turlington who is the partner, not Linzie. So there were sufficient differences between the two stories to enable Collins, if necessary, to disclaim any connection. It may be worth noting that when *Miss or Mrs?* was published in book form by Bentley in 1873, together with two shorter stories, Wilkie Collins's introduction specifically mentioned his lost friend Dickens only with reference to the two shorter tales. Yet there are sufficient plot ingredients in common to indicate the kind of ending Wilkie Collins would have written to *Drood*, and to justify regarding *Miss or Mrs?* as his unofficial solution. In his scenario Jasper would have had one of his fits at a critical moment in his attempt on Edwin, enabling his victim to escape, while Jasper himself would have died in some way by his own hand. The real interest of this implied solution was that Wilkie Collins, the old collaborator of Dickens who was well acquainted with his methods, was shrewd and experienced enough to grasp the importance of the fits. A master of mechanics himself, he realised these fits had an essential part in the plot, while characteristically he lacked the imaginative insight to perceive their real significance, and so could only produce the lame notion that a fit would frustrate the murderer. Little wonder that he had a poor opinion of Dickens's last work, indicating his idea of the solution in a second-rate potboiler. Yet both the Collins brothers had in their individual ways got close to the truth. If only they could have combined their knowledge!

All the same it was Forster who provided most illumination. As the closest of all to Dickens, he had been told more than the others without fully understanding. Knowing the secret of Jasper's abrupt transitions from one personality to another, I found his account of especial interest: 'The story, I learnt immediately afterward, was to be that of the murder of a nephew by his uncle; the originality of which was to consist in the review of the murderer's career by himself at the close, when its temptations were to be dwelt upon as if, not he the culprit, but some other man, were the tempted. The last chapters were to be written in the condemned cell, to which his wickedness, all elaborately elicited from him as if told of another, had brought him.' It has been conjectured that this review of his past by Jasper, speaking as though of another

102

man, would be made while he was under some external influence, such as opium—extremely unlikely for the reasons already considered relating to Wilkie Collins and *The Moonstone*. The other possible influence being hypnosis, Helena Landless has been put forward as the candidate hypnotist. She is certainly not afraid of Jasper and possesses telepathic powers with her brother, but there is no evidence in the text that she—or any of the other characters—has the ability to mesmerise Jasper into a confession. It is Jasper himself who is the possessor of hypnotic powers, used against Rosa and even Crisparkle, and it would be stretching the reader's credulity if this powerful, sinister character could be mastered in his art by a novice at the end of the story. I now saw that no such assumptions were required to make good sense of Forster. If the personality of The Murderer decided to tell everything in prison, he would have to talk of the second personality as of 'some other man'. Only The Murderer would know the whole story, so he would be the narrator of the account in which the affectionate uncle, with his limited knowledge of what had happened, would be spoken of in the third person. Once the secret of Jasper's two separate personalities was known, Forster's account had the ring of truth. Dickens would have been planning to use his final double number to reveal his secret to his readers and to tell the history of Jasper and the murder of Edwin Drood through the mouth of The Murderer in the condemned cell—the extra length of the double number giving him the space to do this and wind up his story in the one issue.

According to Forster this information was to be 'all elaborately elicited from him'. This could be a Forster gloss to explain what he did not understand himself. Or Dickens could have used it himself if he had some particular ploy in mind to make The Murderer begin his revelations. This was a minor point. Over-all Forster's account had the stamp of authenticity. He was not in a position to comprehend the real originality of Dickens's idea, or the secret springs of the book, and yet his account was perfectly consonant with it. It illustrated again his dependability in essentials when writing of Dickens.

However the Forster version did seem to differ from the course of events implied in the herb-closet outline. According to my interpretation of that paragraph, the story would not end with

The Murderer but with the 'innocent' Jasper committing suicide. Then I saw that these two versions were not contradictory; rather they were complementary. After the revelations of The Murderer would come the final change from the violent personality back to Jasper's normal self, leaving Jasper as the occupant of the condemned cell still convinced of his innocence. The scene would be set for Dickens's last *coup de théâtre* in *Edwin Drood*, as the reader would not at first be aware of the change. Jasper would protest his innocence for the last time, before the internal barrier between the two personalities, already almost destroyed by The Murderer's admissions, collapses under some final pressure, and the memory of everything returns to the appalled Jasper. Jasper hangs himself in his cell, and with his own hands executes The Murderer. Dickens's text and Forster together had provided the logical and dramatic end to the story.

This was the final link in a chain leading to another conclusion: if Dickens had lived a few months longer, the world would never have heard of Dr Jekyll or Mr Hyde. Robert Louis Stevenson could hardly have written his story fifteen years later had Dickens completed *Edwin Drood*, which anticipates the central idea of *The Strange Case of Dr Jekyll and Mr Hyde*. Even the bachelor lawyer Utterson, who never smiles, 'embarrassed in discourse; backward in sentiment; lean, long, dusty, dreary, and yet somehow lovable', is the younger brother of Mr Grewgious, and the parallel between the central characters of Mr Jasper and Dr Jekyll is even more evident. Jasper and Jekyll both in their different ways occupy a respected position in their societies, but both have an unknown, sinister side that is manifested in a separate personality. Mr Hyde is the embodiment of the vicious aspect of Dr Jekyll, just as The Murderer is the ruthless and violent part of Jasper. Both these baser personalities periodically take complete control, their emergence being accompanied by terrible birth pains: Mr Hyde is born with 'the most racking pangs' and deadly nausea, which pass off as quickly as the agonising fits that mark the advent of The Murderer. Both sinister personalities are killers, Hyde with an uncontrolled violence that is present, but more disciplined, in The Murderer. Finally in both stories these dual personalities are destined to die by their own hand.

The similarity is striking. Yet in comparison with *Drood*,

Stevenson's work is slighter both in size—it is a long short story which he wrote in three hectic days—and in subtlety. The chemical potion that enables Dr Jekyll to make the change to Hyde and back again is a somewhat clumsy piece of machinery, just as the physical change from the tall, portly doctor to the wizened figure of Hyde is more theatrical, but cruder, than the inward alteration in the outwardly unchanged Jasper. The choir-master, in whom knowledge of the desires and actions of his baser part are suppressed, is recognisable in modern psychological terms; there was no such amnesia in Jekyll/Hyde, whose 'two natures had memory in common'. It can now be seen that Dickens was engaged in making a much more profound psychological study than Stevenson. If he had lived to complete his design, we would not talk today of a 'Jekyll-and-Hyde character'. We would say instead that someone was 'doing a Jasper'.

The broad outline of *Edwin Drood* had now emerged. It was still only a framework. There remained numerous questions to be answered before this outline could be expanded into a detailed narrative. What was Jasper's background? Just how was he related to Edwin Drood? What had turned him into a dual personality? Why is there such emphasis on Cloisterham Tower if Drood is to be strangled? How exactly was the murder carried out and Drood's body disposed of? What was wrong with the body in the opium den vision? What is the role of the Opium Woman herself? In what way is the crime brought home to Jasper? How is the ring of diamonds and rubies found? What is the meaning of the scene on the cover with the man (usually taken to be Jasper) holding a lantern? Who is he staring at? Why in the pursuit scene up the spiral staircase is Crisparkle—as I take it to be from the clerical collar—looking so anxiously back *down* the stairs? What is the point of the shriek Durdles heard the previous Christmas? Why are we told that Helena dressed as a boy whenever the twins ran away from their stepfather? Does the telepathy between Helena and Neville have any part to play in the plot? And the question that has curiously obsessed some Droodists, particularly in the period before the First World War: who is Datchery? Is he a professional detective disguised with less than Holmesian efficiency, or is he one of the other characters in the story in disguise? Tartar? Helena Landless? Grewgious? Bazzard? Neville Landless?

My answers to these questions are included in the continuation of Dickens's story that follows in Part Two. It should be explained that Part Two does contain a page or two more of genuine Dickens. This was possible because of the so-called 'Sapsea Fragment', the five half-pages of manuscript about Sapsea and a new character called Poker, found by Forster among Dickens's papers; the beginning and the end of the episode were both missing (see above, p. 88 and note). It may have been rejected first draft for the introduction of Datchery, or perhaps an earlier unpublished piece from which Dickens lifted the character of Sapsea when he found he needed a 'solemn donkey' for his story. My chapter XXVI was already planned when I realised that the Sapsea Fragment would fit neatly into this context, so I incorporated it. For the rest, I did not try to imitate the Inimitable, but rather to find a style that would be acceptable to readers today and at the same time follow on the original narrative as smoothly as possible.

I believe that I have decoded Dickens's 'very curious and new idea'; but I make no claim that the evolution of the story or all the details of the solution are as the author himself would have developed them. Indeed, this would hardly be possible, if only because he still had to write a further five numbers, including a double one, and a modern continuation at such Victorian length would be excessive. My completion is only about half as long as this, necessarily compressing the final action and explanation. But within these limits I have aimed at a workmanlike solution to his mystery that is faithful to Dickens's text, and which as far as possible ties up the ends. I hope it is an honest piece of joinery, and I shall be content if the verdict on it is that of Robert Louis Stevenson on one of his own stories: 'Carpentry, of course, but not bad at that; and who else can carpenter in England, now that Wilkie Collins is played out?'

PART TWO

THE MYSTERY OF EDWIN DROOD

COMPLETED

CONTENTS

FOREWORD

I STRONGLY RECOMMEND reading Dickens's text before embarking on the following ending to his story. There is no substitute for Dickens himself.

For those unable to do so, however, it may be helpful to know that the first chapter of the continuation concerns a visit made by the mysterious Datchery to see the work of the surly stone-mason Durdles. This visit was foreshadowed earlier when Datchery encountered Mayor Sapsea and the street urchin Deputy who stones Durdles home when he is drunk:

Here, Deputy (preceded by a flying oyster-shell) appeared upon the scene, and requested to have the sum of threepence instantly 'chucked' to him by Mr Durdles, whom he had been vainly seeking up and down, as lawful wages overdue. While that gentleman, with his bundle under his arm, slowly found and counted out the money, Mr Sapsea informed the new settler of Durdles's habits, pursuits, abode, and reputation. "I suppose a curious stranger might come to see you, and your works, Mr Durdles, at any odd time?" said Mr Datchery upon that.

"Any gentleman is welcome to come and see me any evening if he brings liquor for two with him," returned Durdles, with a penny between his teeth and certain halfpence in his hands. "Or if he likes to make it twice two, he'll be double welcome."

"I shall come. Master Deputy, what do you owe me?"

"A job."

"Mind you pay me honestly with the job of showing me Mr Durdles's house when I want to go there."

(p. 167)

CHAPTER XXIV

A PAIR OF PROMISES

MR DATCHERY'S VISIT to Durdles and his works has finally been arranged without the necessity of further assistance from Deputy. Lounging in the Precincts one morning, hands in pockets, it happens that an idle fellow living on his means encounters the Stony One making his way in the opposite direction, and profits by the occasion to remind him of their earlier conversation on the subject.

"Durdles thought as you had gone and forgotten," growls that worthy, stopping and staring at him in a state of powderous suspicion, being always at his least genial in the morning hours when the effects of the previous day's potations are still upon him.

"Forgotten!" exclaims Datchery. "My dear fellow, our excursion is not merely a pleasure I have been long awaiting, but the thought of it alone has sustained me during some tedious business I have had to conduct in London. Now I am at your service!" He goes to remove his hat from his shock of grey hair, finds it under his other arm, and gives it a courtly flourish.

Durdles is mollified by this friendly civility and nods. "When do you want to come? This evening?" he asks.

"This evening?" responds Datchery judiciously. "I am sure the Cathedral is more romantic by night, but an elderly buffer could take a nasty fall"—stretching out a tentative leg that might be testing for an elusive step on a retreating spiral stair. "You would, I fancy, hardly wish to carry the elderly person with a broken limb down from the tower. I fear we must settle for a less romantic hour in the afternoon."

Durdles's enthusiasm for this proposal is muted, not so much because he has any notions of the romanticism of visiting the Cathedral by night—rather the reverse with his Tombatism—as that he fears Datchery may not consider the afternoon an appropriate time for that liquid refreshment which is his principal object in playing guide. He is therefore much relieved, on meeting Datchery at their rendezvous by the West Door later that afternoon, to observe two large flasks sticking their necks out of the capacious pockets of his coat.

It is Datchery's idea that they should mount the Tower while still fresh and enjoy the view over the town from its summit. They enter the Cathedral by the West Door. Durdles gets out his key that unlocks the iron gate to the stairway, re-locks it behind them, and they commence the long corkscrew ascent. They toil up stairs, along galleries high above the nave whence they can look down on the already unreal diminutive puppets below; then up further stairs and ladders, higher and still higher, until it seems as though they must have finally quitted the earth altogether and be ascending into heaven. Suddenly they emerge into the light and the cool air of the summit. Datchery survives the climb surprisingly well for his age, and is breathing less heavily than the mason who requires to be revived by recourse to the contents of one of the two flasks. He makes no comment on the quality, but the quantity that flows down his throat without any apparent let or hindrance, coupled with the smacking of the customer's lips when they are at length removed from the flask, testify to his satisfaction.

Meanwhile the visitor stands surveying the scene, hand clapped to his halo of grey hair. Below him lies a Cloisterham that reproduces in miniature the town they have just left: dolls' houses with little mossy roofs, on the tiny tiles of which stand minute chimney pots, some visibly leaning with age as they support almost microscopic birds; behind the houses scaled-down dusty yards with tiny rusty pumps and other debris; and through the houses stretches a High Street shrunken in its senility, empty but for a minuscule piebald horse pulling a no less lilliputian baker's cart. Beyond, the river is placid today, undisturbed by any conflict with the sea, and on its smooth surface the model barges with their brown sails are moving gently. Only the monastery ruin, its stark walls rising solid and severe by the river, refuses to convert itself into a toy.

When Durdles is refreshed and has recovered his breath, his interest does not lie in the prospect from the tower. His concern is to point out in detail all damage inflicted by the great storm of Christmas Eve. The visitor is required to inspect with interest every place where the ageing lead was stripped from the roof. The mason goes round the parapet particularising each venerable stone shifted by the gale, and then rehearsing the labours required by Durdles and his men to restore the fabric. The memory of such labour provokes further thirst, requiring further prolonged recourse to the flask. Throughout this tour of inspection Datchery follows his guide with a close and courteous attention to all that he is shown. It is only when, at Durdles's request, he looks straight down the cliff-like side of the tower to behold where the very hands of the clock itself had been torn away on that eventful day, that a vertigo paralyses him. The sheer abyss beneath him seems to numb and melt his limbs, while at the same time he is drawn towards that fatal drop as though by some powerful magnetic force and has to will himself to fight the force that would suck him down. Strange and terrifying form of gravity that operates more on the mind than upon the body! Trembling, he manages to draw himself back and to tear his eyes from the new clock hands beneath him that seem to be pointing the hour of his own fate. Durdles is not quick to perceive his predicament, but, once he has noticed the weakness of Datchery's limbs, goes to his support; and administers to him a draught of his own medicine. Fortified by the spirit, he is helped back down from the perilous place, leaning on Durdles or the wall as he shakily makes his way down the stairs again. At last they reach the ground level of the Cathedral in safety, but here a group of visitors is being marched around under the inferior and martial guidance of Mr Tope, so Durdles unlocks the door and they descend the further flight of steps to the quiet privacy of the crypt, where Datchery is not sorry to seat himself on a convenient block of stone.

After these supportive efforts Durdles has to refresh himself again.

"I am much obliged to you once again, Mr Durdles," says Datchery. "It did occur to me that you might have to help down a person with only one sound leg, but I had not foreseen that an elderly buffer with two sound legs might require your assistance in this way."

The recipient of these thanks has now succeeded in elevating his flask to the vertical, indicating that, whatever gravity may do to unaccustomed visitors to the roof, it cannot attract one more liquid drop from this particular vessel. Having made this scientific demonstration, his lips are free for speech again.

"Odd you were took like that," he observes pensively. "Durdles was very like that when he went up the tower with Mr Jarsper," he recalls.

"Indeed? And when was that?" Datchery is all courteous attention again.

"Just before the storm that was. One night the beginning of that week. Mr Jarsper wanted me to show him over the Cathedral by night."

"And you say you did not feel yourself at the top of the tower?"

"Proper strange I felt. Never felt like that before or since," rumbles the mason.

"Isn't that curious, seeing that it must have been dark and also that you are well accustomed to working at heights?"

"I don't know why it was. I did have a drink or two from a bottle he had."

Durdles falls silent and passes a hand across his lips. The old diplomatic hand soon interprets his silence. The second flask is proffered and as quickly accepted and broached. Refurbished by the contents, his reminiscence continues.

"Good stuff that was too, Mr Jarsper's. But I felt proper odd after it. It wasn't like this."

Datchery interprets the latter comment as referring not to the quality of his drink but to the strange effects of Jasper's.

"Fell asleep after it, I did, right where you are sitting now. Hours it must have been, judging by the moon. And yet I didn't seem properly asleep neither."

"Some hours, eh? That must have been a long wait for Mr Jasper. Was he there when you woke up?"

"He was. Mebbee he had a nap too. I don't know."

"Was he drinking with you?"

Durdles chuckles at the recollection. "Not a drop. Swilled his mouth round and spat it out. Waste o' good liquor. I suppose he thought it would do something to his singing. All the more for Durdles." With which philosophy he applies himself again to the other's flask.

"Probably went for a walk." He has the knack of resuming a conversation after imbibing his potations as though it has never

114

been interrupted. "I found the key o' the crypt on the floor beside me when I woke up. Reckon he took it."

"You must be a proper key ring, Mr Durdles," says the other smiling and idly stroking back his shock of hair, "with all the keys you have to carry about."

He is amused at the idea and chuckles again. "Ring. I ain't no ring. I keep 'em in my pocket." He delves into the great inner pocket in his invariable coarse flannel jacket and brings out his treasure trove. "That's the key to the doors to the crypt. That's the one to the gate to the tower. And this one's the Dean's tomb." A massy, old-fashioned key. "I didn't have that one the day I was with Mr Jarsper. I had the key of old Sapsea's tomb."

"What happened to that?" comes the idle question.

"I gave it back to Sapsea." The memory provokes a laugh in Durdles that is decidedly alcoholic. "Proper taken with them keys Mr Jarsper was when Sapsea give it to me. Clinked them together like they might have been his tuning forks. Reckon he thought he could start the choir off with them." With another chuckle at his wit, he applies himself to the flask again.

"I am told that your own ear is so finely tuned to sound that you can do what even the Choir Master cannot," Datchery observes respectfully.

"Ah," says Durdles as soon as he is free to articulate again. He is appreciative of the compliment but not sure of the reference, never having sung anything except an occasional drinking song.

"I believe your tuning fork can tell you where all the old bishops and monks are buried?"

"Ah, the Old Uns. Durdles knows how to find them! Tap-tap-tap. Nothing there. Tap-tap-tap. One buried there. Who is he? Tap-tap-tap. That's an Old Un with a crook. Durdles's hammer tells him."

"It must have taken you a lifetime of practice to reach such a degree of skill."

"You are a learned man." In his half-fuddled way the mason is paying tribute to the perceptiveness of his visitor. "But you couldn't learn it in ten years. Not in ten years you couldn't." He pauses to give ponderous emphasis to his statements. "Now take them journeymen of mine. They couldn't do it. Not in ten years,

115

not in twenty they couldn't do it. Why it took me a mort o' time to learn it."

The thought of the time he has spent in acquiring his arcane skill is enough to provoke a fresh thirst in the Stony One. As the flask is uplifted this time he tilts it upright and drains the last satisfying dregs from it. He smacks his lips and nods in appreciation. Then, as the object of the afternoon's excursion is now accomplished in his eyes, he starts to drift away up the crypt, brightly lit by the late afternoon sunshine pouring through the unglazed windows and encircling the waists of the heavy columns. Datchery regretfully realises that his time has expired with his drink, and wishes he had the conjurer's capacity for producing a third flask out of thin air or for pouring endless drink from an empty bottle. With reluctance he rises from his stone and strolls after Durdles, catching up with him at the top of the crypt steps where he is fumbling in his pocket to sort out the key of the door. He eventually finds it, and they emerge by the side door direct into the sunlight outside the Cathedral.

"Can you describe to an old buffer who could certainly never learn such a skill in a hundred years just how you manage to do it?' " he enquires, as he lounges easily along beside the rather unsteady figure of the mason.

They happen to be abreast of the Sapsea monument. Durdles stops, places his bundle on the ground, undoes it with fumbling fingers and extracts his hammer. Tap-tap-tap. "Space of five foot, then a coffin." Tap-tap-tap. "Rubbish left in the space by Durdles's men," he announces. Tap-tap-tap. "Coffin mostly empty. She was a poor wisp of a thing when she was living." He puts his hammer in the bundle, re-ties it with slow and careful concentration, and then looks at the other with hazy self-esteem.

"Remarkable!" exclaims Datchery with great animation, his hair seeming to start out all round his head in his enthusiasm. "Re-Mark-Able! I have been in many places on this Planet and can say that I have never seen the like. I would not have credited such a thing if a traveller from distant parts had told me he had seen it. Remarkable!"

Durdles shoulders his bundle again, walks slowly on with a kind of admiral's gait that bespeaks consciousness of his own genius, while Datchery walks beside him back to his yard. The two journeymen—who will never though they live twenty years learn the art of divining with a stone-mason's hammer—are still at work moving in and out of their sentry boxes with the mason's saw, which they do appear to have mastered. As they pick their way through the chunks of rough stone, dust and debris of the yard, Datchery is cautioned against treading in the lime heap, lest it eat his shoes, his toes and his very bones; and looking down at his elegantly shod feet that gentleman exercises particular caution. Having circumnavigated all hazards they eventually reach the door of Durdles's half-finished house. Here Datchery takes leave of him with a bow and highly civil thanks for a most instructive afternoon, and the hope that Mr Durdles will be able to spare the time for an equally enjoyable visit on another, future occasion.

As he leaves the stone-yard, Datchery turns and looks quizzically at Durdles. The journeymen are still moving steadily backwards and forwards, backwards and forwards, while the Stony One stands motionless on the spot where he left him. In the distance the unmoving white figure might, like Lot's wife, have turned into a pillar of salt—were it not that the amount of liquid he has absorbed must assuredly have dissolved him by internal deliquescence into a miniature Dead Sea. Datchery turns and walks slowly back, unconsciously jingling the money in his pocket as he walks. When he gets back to the white Sapsea tomb he stops to contemplate it and re-read the inscription. CANST THOU DO LIKEWISE? it asks him. "I wonder," says Datchery under his breath to himself. Rattling his money and reflecting deeply he returns to his vaulted chamber under John Jasper's Gate House.

At evening service in the Cathedral, the Choir Master is not in good voice. His face looks drawn; and as when he is under nervous tension, he takes the music too fast. The choir lose their tempo, become ragged. There is general relief when the service is over and they hastily pull off their soiled surplices. Jasper hurries home through the Precincts, oblivious to his surroundings. He is brought to the present by the crack of a stone against a near-by wall. There is no Wake-cock warning on this occasion. He turns instinctively towards the sound, but his assailant has learned from somewhere, or somebody, a new subtlety. The first stone is a decoy. As he turns in that direction, he exposes his rear to the hidden marksman and two missiles follow in quick succession.

The first knocks his tall hat to the ground. The second is a sharp flint that catches him square in the nape of the neck. From the Ambuscade comes a yelp of delight.

"Gotcha!"

Jasper stoops to retrieve his hat, then straightens up, his face working with fury. His opponent has little doubt as to his fate if caught. Having made good his promise to land a flint on the back of Jasper's head, Deputy is already in full retreat towards the shops of Cloisterham, which he knows in this age will afford him better sanctuary than the Church; so after running a few yards in hopeless pursuit, Jasper gives up.

"Baby-devil," he curses between his teeth, before turning and walking towards the Gate House. Aware for the first time as he is about to enter that his neck feels sticky, he puts up an investigatory hand, then glances down at it. There is blood on his hand.

CHAPTER XXV

DIVERS REACTIONS TO A NOTION

THE SUMMER IS past the dog-days, and the grittiness of London extends into the quiet quadrangles of Staple Inn. Canon Crisparkle has risen early in Cloisterham to get here, even forgoing his early morning plunge, but his step is springy. His mood this morning is an unusual blend of exhilaration and concern; and both have one source. He has received a letter the previous day earnestly requesting him to come to London at his earliest convenience on a matter closely affecting his pupil. Since the letter has come from his pupil's sister, his earliest convenience is by the first train the following morning, and he has an odd sensation of excitement and youthfulness at the same time. So as he comes in through the gateway of the Inn, past the porter in his lodge at the entrance, and into the quadrangle with its staircases and chambers grouped round it, he is reminded of his own college in Oxford: and of his own carefree days as an undergraduate. What a contrast with the fate of the student now studying in one of these attic rooms! Instead of the collegiate life around him, to be shut up in what was little better than a prison cell, cut off from the fellowship and the exercise in the fresh air that should be the prerogative of youth, with nothing but furtive night-time walks round the pavements of London. It could only be expected that neither mind nor body should be in a healthy state. Yet what could be the new problem that had evidently arisen to call forth this appeal? A mere question of his studies would not have carried that note of urgency. And Helena was too balanced, too self-disciplined herself to have written in this strain without good cause. The letter had given no indication of the nature of Neville's latest difficulty. The gravel scrunches grittily under Crisparkle's feet as he strides forward turning these thoughts in his head and rapidly mounts the stairs to Neville's attic.

As he opens the door he is aware of the heat of the room under the low sloping roof—no place for a boy to have spent his summer—and Tartar's flowers outside the window, which only serve as further sign that this room is shut off from the world as if by a curse. There are insects buzzing greedily round the flowers; yet none enters. These are but the thoughts of an instant, for at the moment of his entry Neville has jumped up from his books and greeted him. The young man's appearance is too evident a confirmation of the Canon's misgivings—a pallid face, dark circles underlining unnaturally bright eyes.

"Thank Heaven you have come, Mr Crisparkle, I did not sleep a wink last night," is the greeting. Then after wringing the Canon's hand warmly, he turns with the furious motion of an animal at bay, snatches a paper from beside his books on the table and hands it to Crisparkle with a quivering hand.

"Read this. It was pushed under Mr Tartar's door yesterday. He passed it to Helena to transmit to Mr Grewgious, and he asked her to write to you. Now read it."

The Canon takes the paper and reads it quickly with his sharp eyes:

Sir,

You should know for your own safety that the man whom you have befriended is of a violent and murderous character, and will answer for a capital crime to the law or to natural justice; and that he is paying his nocturnal addresses to a lady

destined by fate for another, who will ensure with his own life
that he will not succeed.

A FRIEND

Crisparkle reads it a second time with his eagle eyes. It is written
in carefully executed capital letters. "I cannot identify the author
for certain," he says, looking at his pupil.

"I would have known who it was from in any hand," exclaims
Neville, growing whiter and tense with anger. "No one could
have written that but John Jasper!" Crisparkle does not dissent.

"If he were man enough to come here instead of sending such
sneaking letters, I could ki . . ." he breaks out furiously, then
stops under the other's steady gaze. "I must not say it, I know."
He pauses to regain control of himself, and following Crisparkle's
eye unclenches his fists. "But I ask you to understand, Mr
Crisparkle, I have been living here like a prisoner, disciplining
myself, driving myself to work, while he hounds me in this way
even in my retreat, trying to drive away my friends, accusing me
of murder, of meeting Miss Rosa whom I never see, and making
threats against my life. It is more than I can support!"

The Canon lays a large sympathetic hand on the young man's
shoulder. "I know, Neville. I do understand. But listen to me."

Neville's chest still heaves and he answers half defiantly, "I will
do my best, sir."

"Good. Now do you not see that this is a letter written by a man
whose emotions are even more painful than your own, Neville?
This was not penned by a normal man. This comes from a lover
racked by jealousy, because he has had no word from the object of
his affection after his declaration of love has been rejected, and
does not even know where she has hidden herself. So he has
followed you—or had you followed—on your night walks, and in
his jealousy has persuaded himself that these are for the purpose of
secret meetings with her. This has inflamed his jealousy still
further, and driven him to this extraordinary composition."

Neville nods his head without speaking.

"Is it rational, Neville, to permit yourself to be provoked by a
person who is himself in a highly irrational state? Do you want to
become yourself like the man of whose conduct you complain?"

"Your arguments are always very strong when you put them to

me yourself, sir," answers the young man. "I acknowledge their justice and will endeavour to bear them constantly in mind. Yet when I am alone my feelings become stronger than my reason. I will do my best to control them." Then he bursts out with a rush: "But if I were to meet that gentleman face to face I know I could not answer for myself!" Next moment he hangs his head in shame. "I fear I am incorrigible, Mr Crisparkle."

"We are none of us incorrigible. Come, Neville, courage!" clapping him on the arm. "Remember that he is in worse shape than you! When you know that in the ring, even if your own head is singing, it gives you the strength to fight on. It is no different in life."

These words seem to touch Neville, who grasps the Canon's hand. "You do give me new courage, Mr Crisparkle. That is a lesson I will not forget."

"Bless you," says a woman's voice softly. It is Helena who has come upon them unheard, and now it is the Canon's turn to look embarrassed and his cheeks grow even more pink. "Miss Helena, forgive me . . . I have been carried away talking to Neville."

"I am more than grateful to you for it," she responds with cheeks to match his own. "I would not have interrupted you now, had not Mr Grewgious requested that you would come and see him on your arrival."

"I will go to him at once." Turning to Neville, "Then I will come back here and we will go through what you have read since my last visit, so you had better get your notes and your thoughts in order now."

While Neville is obediently opening his books, Helena accompanies him to the door of the chambers and speaks softly so that her brother cannot overhear. "Mr Grewgious asked me to join you both, but to leave Neville here. I will come shortly. It is better that we should not be seen going across the quadrangle together."

With a nod of comprehension he turns to go, raises her hand to his lips, and with light step descends the stairs towards the portal; old P.J.T., whose initials are inscribed there, would doubtless nod his sage wig that has seen young men and young women around 1747, when they were much as they are today.

Crisparkle finds Mr Grewgious in his chambers seated behind

his desk, several legal black boxes stacked neatly upon it. Compared with the healthful pink cheeks of his visitor, he looks so powder dry under his snuff-coloured tindery thatch that it is astonishing his life is not spent in a continual fit of sneezing, or that he does not carry a notice strictly prohibiting the lighting of fires in his vicinity. Perhaps those tin boxes on his desk are in the nature of a fire precaution, so should he be the victim of sudden instantaneous combustion, the papers in his trust would survive while he could go up in smoke with a clear conscience. Rising from behind his fire-break, he greets the Minor Canon:

"How do you do, reverend sir? May I offer you some refreshment after your journey?"—looking towards his hospitable closet. Crisparkle, whose inner refreshment at this moment disdains the merely physical, refuses politely, yet with the unspoken thought that a little liquid might be more appropriately applied to his host.

"And how do you find your pupil, reverend sir?"

Crisparkle relates his conversation with Neville, while the lawyer listens gravely, at the end of which the lithe figure of Helena slips in carrying a deceitful shopping basket. She is greeted with many attentions from Grewgious, and finally seated in the chair where Rosa once sat. At the end of these ceremonies, Grewgious turns to business.

"You have read the communication to Mr Tartar?" he asks in his expressionless voice, looking in the direction of Crisparkle, who indicates that he has.

"And do you both have an opinion as to its author?" he continues, anxious not to exclude the lady.

"I do," reply both Helena and Crisparkle simultaneously, a response which, for some reason that old P.J.T. might hazard a guess at, causes them both some confusion; with a mantling of blood in Helena's handsome cheeks and a deeper pink in Crisparkle's. If Grewgious has noticed the odd effect of his question, it is betrayed by nothing in his manner as he continues, turning towards her.

"And might I ask for your opinion?"

"It could have been written by only one man, John Jasper," she answers with a flash in her eyes, and a mixture of indignation and disdain that immediately replaces her embarrassment. "It is exactly as I foresaw. He is trying to isolate poor Neville from his friends and so destroy him. I said he would use Mr Tartar in this way, and he has."

"And what is Mr Tartar's view?"

"Contempt," is the fierce reply, "for the man and his work."

Mr Grewgious, smoothing his hair with his habitual action, turns towards Crisparkle.

"And you, reverend sir?"

"I fear this is the work of Jasper," answers the Canon, and feeling charitable today in particular, even towards Jasper, goes on: "Poor fellow. He must indeed be sadly jealous to be reduced to writing such stuff."

"Ump", is the only comment he gets.

"I think he genuinely believes that Neville's nightly walks serve as a diversion for secret assignations with Rosa."

"No doubt. You will also have noted that the missive refers to Neville answering for a capital crime to the law or to natural justice. May I ask how you understand natural justice and its operation, reverend sir?"

"I think he must have been intending to say Divine Justice," replies Crisparkle, a furrow wrinkling his forehead.

"But he does not say so," rebuts the lawyer. "And if you will permit me to say so to one of your cloth, I fear that the Divinity in this case is our local friend himself."

"You mean that it is a threat? Surely not in the sense that you mean!" exclaims the Canon. He turns to Helena for support, but she is looking at Mr Grewgious.

"And you will also have noted that our local friend says that he will ensure with his own life that Neville will not succeed. May I ask how you understand that he will ensure such an outcome with his own life?"

"He surely means that he will lay down his life on her behalf. He offered his life to her in the garden of the Nuns' House."

"But he does not say so," comes the dry response again. "He states that he will ensure with his own life that Neville will not succeed. May I ask how he will ensure this except by paying the capital penalty to the law for the violent removal of his rival?"

The good Minor Canon's face is a study. His candid features

radiate astonishment. "You cannot mean to imply that Jasper is—dangerous?"

The effect of this question on Grewgious is electric, as though the voice of Crisparkle has transmitted galvanic energy to his limbs. Leaping from his seat, he trots round the room in an access of energy, displaying his long shanks and white stockings at one extremity and brandishing his arms at the other.

"Do I think a hungry lion is dangerous? Do I think a starving tiger is dangerous? Do I think a rattlesnake is dangerous? Do I think a tarantula dangerous? Do I think a shark dangerous?" Then apparently calmed by the thought of this ferocious bestiary, he resumes his seat and his wooden look.

"Certainly what he has written is indefensible," urges Crisparkle, "and his expression is not well chosen. But one must make every allowance for him. He sincerely believes Neville to be responsible for the disappearance of his nephew, however mistaken he may be in such a view. He is also deeply, hopelessly, in love with your ward, and his jealousy of Neville has overcome his judgement. Is it surprising that he should react in such an irrational way, when he believes that the woman he is passionately in love with is being won from him by the very man he is convinced has murdered the nephew that he doted on?"

"Ump" is again the only comment he gets.

"Not being able to see your ward," continues the other, looking at Helena and warming sympathetically to his theme, "not even knowing where she might be, and when she might be secretly meeting Neville must have been the final straw that has driven him to this act of desperation."

Grewgious sits bolt upright in his chair, hands resting stiffly on his knees, unwaveringly watching Crisparkle as he puts the case for Jasper. Then he speaks with the same expressionless voice as ever, as though he has learned a lesson by rote and is repeating it aloud.

"Act of desperation. I would not altogether dissent from that view, reverend sir. But in the opinion of an unworldly old chip he will continue to perform acts of desperation, being not only a Fox but a Rabid Fox, sir.

"I will go further and say what I would not say outside these walls or to other ears than your own. I have kept silent, and would

124

have kept my silence now were it not for the danger that threatens. A danger, reverend sir, that you do not recognise.

"I consider it now my duty to tell you plainly that in my humble but convinced opinion our local friend is a Butcher, an Assassin and a Thug: in a word a Murderer."

"Murderer!" cries Crisparkle, aghast.

Grewgious rises slowly to his feet.

"A murderer who should be in court, where he belongs, and sentenced by the judge to be taken to a place of execution and there hanged by the neck until he be dead, which he richly deserves." Having concluded this denunciation, he resumes his seat and continues to look at the Canon, who is reduced to stunned silence.

Helena is not so affected. "How stupid I have been, Mr Grewgious," she breaks out. "I knew him to be evil the first day I met him. Even then I did not suspect. Now I understand it was all part of his plan to kill his nephew and lay the blame on my poor brother!" Both men look at Helena, in whose eyes a mixture of compassion and anger burns. "How that wretch deceived us! But now I see it as clear as day." She turns decisively towards Grewgious. "What are we going to do about him Mr Grewgious?"

"It was to discuss that very question that I asked you both to come here today," grinds out Grewgious.

Poor Crisparkle! His earlier euphoria has been slowly draining out of him. Now he is an unhappy man, a perplexed man. The very last thing on this earth that he wants to do is to disagree over anything with Helena Landless; and he also has great respect for the sagacity of Rosa's guardian. Yet here are both of them accepting an idea that profoundly shocks him, which he simply cannot believe to have a word of truth in it. He is in a situation where he needs every particle of that philosophy he has been expounding to Neville. Torn as he is, he does not hesitate. He is of the breed that three centuries earlier went to the stake for the truth as they saw it, and he would do the same if it were ever required of him. He has hardly been able to believe his ears, and the shock has deprived him of the ability to use his voice until this moment. Now he speaks.

"Do I rightly understand that you believe John Jasper murdered his nephew Edwin Drood?"

"That was precisely my meaning," is the answer he gets in the toneless voice of the lawyer.

"Jasper? Edwin Drood, his nephew? I simply cannot believe such a thing. I find it quite impossible even to contemplate the possibility that our Choir Master killed his nephew. Everything is against such an idea," maintains the bewildered Canon. "He was more energetic than anyone in pursuing the murderer. He swore an oath that he showed me recorded in his diary never to discuss the mystery until he held the clue to it in his hands, never to give up the search until he had fastened the crime upon the murderer. And he has been as good as his word ever since."

"An easy enough oath to swear, reverend sir, if you are the murderer and know your efforts will never find him."

"No! No! You have not known Jasper so closely as I have known him in Cloisterham. His nephew was the whole centre of Jasper's life, one might say its purpose. He thought of him when he was away, eagerly looked forward to his return. He doted on the boy, fussed over him like a mother hen."

"A curious relationship between uncle and nephew," suggests Grewgious.

"Certainly unusual. People did comment upon it. It was well known among the tradesmen, as Jasper was always buying little things for Drood. Even the Dean himself noticed and commented. But what attracted their comment was the unusual degree of affection that Jasper always showed for his nephew."

"And if a person should be a liar, a humbug, and a hypocrite?"

"His affection was shown in too many ways, over too long a period, to be explainable as mere hypocrisy. I have seen him daily in the Cathedral over a period of several years. A man cannot play-act every minute of the time. I have known him far more closely than you have done, or—forgive me—than you, Miss Helena. He is in some respects a strange man. But the one thing on which I entertain no doubt whatever is the utter sincerity of his affection and love for his nephew. Jasper is the very last man I could suspect of the crime. To me it is quite unbelievable! May I ask, Mr Grewgious, what has led you to your conclusion?"

"Evidence known only to me at the time of Drood's disappearance put the notion into my mind," replies the lawyer, remembering a certain contorted face and a certain heap of miry clothing lying upon a floor. "Later evidence has served to strengthen my earlier suspicion. On which subject permit me, reverend sir, to put a question to you."

"By all means."

"I understand the idea that Jasper is responsible for the crime is one that is repugnant to you, and you would not have entertained it had I not put the notion to you. But now it has been put to you, however inadequately, by an unimaginative old chip of a lawyer, is there nothing in the past that did not strike you at the time as suspicious, but which in the light of this notion might present itself in a different guise?"

Crisparkle reflects, while Grewgious sits and strokes his scant hair with deliberate movement. At first memory recalls nothing but the sight of Jasper clinging to the railings in Minor Canon Corner that Christmas morning. He is about to shake his head to the question when another memory, overlaid and well on the road to oblivion, is drawn up from the depths of his mind: he recalls a different image. Jasper sleeping on his couch before the fire in the Gate House, awakening with the cry "What is the matter? Who did it?" A furrow wrinkles the Canon's forehead, not unperceived by Grewgious. Who had done what? For was not this before the disappearance of Drood? The Canon had come to propose the reconciliation of the two young men. And had not a strange expression appeared on Jasper's face at this suggestion?

"I do remember one thing now," he admits, his honest face clouded with doubt. "But it could have many explanations. It is certainly not proof that Jasper is a murderer."

"None of the evidence we have is proof, in the sense that it would convince twelve honest men and a judge. I am not a criminal lawyer; but you may take the word of an old fogey of an attorney for that."

"But Mr Grewgious, can we do nothing for my poor brother?" exclaims Helena, distressed that the discovery of the villain—for such he still is in her eyes despite the Canon's advocacy, and for which she secretly respects him—is apparently in no way helping to improve Neville's lot.

"Patience, my dear young lady. The moves must come from our local friend. If we allow him enough rope, he will hang himself, and I beg to be understood literally!"

"Is there then nothing we can do?"

"For the moment there is nothing we can do to prove his guilt—or innocence," with a look at Crisparkle. "As the communication to Tartar shows, our local friend is under strain and under an inner compulsion to act. Sooner or later he will blunder and we will have him!" Saying which, Grewgious bangs his fist on his desk with a sudden crash that makes Crisparkle start.

Helena is for action, and Grewgious's waiting game does not suit her temperament, but she submits in the knowledge he is as convinced as herself that Jasper is the killer of Drood and that her brother is the victim of his plot.

"Meanwhile we must make sure our defences are strong against any attack he may make. It is for this reason that I have asked you to come here today. Miss Landless, your brother would be most ill-advised to continue to walk in the streets at night alone, or in your company, as he has been accustomed to do."

"I am sure Mr Tartar would be only too pleased to accompany him, despite the communication he has received," observes Helena with the faintest of smiles that gives no indication why she is so sure Mr Tartar would be happy to carry out this escort duty; though perhaps her mind may be on another young lady not so many miles away.

"Capital. I do not think our friend will wish to engage that ship of the line after his warning." Mr Grewgious makes a tick in the air with his finger and an air of satisfaction, and continues:

"Second. Miss Twinkleton has intimated to me that she has already remained with my ward for considerably longer than the month for which she originally contracted and, the season for the return of the young ladies to her establishment now approaching, her personal supervision and presence will shortly be required at the Nuns' House for many matters of detail, which she can not entrust to the otherwise excellent Mrs Tisher. Miss Rosa should not be left alone, and while we have no reason to believe our friend is likely to discover where she is to be found, it would be most imprudent, even for a short time, particularly in view of his communication to Mr Tartar."

"I will stay with her," volunteers Helena without a moment's hesitation. "I have no fear of Jasper."

"That would indeed be a most excellent arrangement, and one

that I am sure would give my ward much pleasure in having her friend to keep her company. But will not your brother miss you, Miss Helena?"

Helena gives a little laugh. "Neville was glad to see me when I came, but he will not be sorry to part with me for a little. We understand each other so well that we are not always good company for one another at such close quarters. Though he says nothing, and I say nothing, he feels my criticisms and resents them. Mr Tartar will be at hand if he needs company or there is danger."

Mr Grewgious makes a final tick in the air. "Then we have no more problems. I think that for their own safety Mr Tartar and Miss Rosa must be told we take the threat from Jasper very seriously. However, I am not sure whether it would be wise to risk upsetting your brother further. What would be your advice on this?"

"The question does not arise," replies Helena. "Neville will already know I believe Jasper to be the murderer; we always know what is in each other's mind. And it is better so, for it is a great comfort to him to know that the accuser is now the accused."

At this information it is Mr Grewgious's turn to show surprise, insofar as his features are capable of creaking into any emotional expression. Yet he keeps his counsel, and it is agreed that in two days Miss Twinkleton will leave Billickin's and Helena will join Rosa there, travelling by a circuitous route, in case she is followed, while Tartar will become the man-of-war patrolling round Neville. The plans being made, Helena slips out with her basket to the shops of Holborn, while a much preoccupied Canon returns to his pupil.

It is a matter for conjecture whether master or pupil has the greater difficulty this morning in addressing himself to his books.

So it comes about that Miss Twinkleton takes her departure from Billickin's, a departure that is a great deal smoother than her arrival. There has been only one set of bags to be packed and carried down, and so there is only one cab, and only one cab driver to be instructed. But the kernel of the matter is that all three ladies are secretly delighted by the change, though two of them feel obliged to perform the ritual of a tearful parting. Rosa has grown weary of her censored reading—that grows less and less like the original with every day that they spend at Billickin's—and is excited at the prospect of the arrival of her friend, with whom she can freely discuss her hopes and fears. Miss Twinkleton can scarce conceal her impatience to be mistress again in her own Nuns' House. The Billickin on her part seems to have lost some of her zest in the verbal exchanges, and is perhaps looking forward to a change of sparring partner with the arrival of Miss Landless later in the day: the name suggests a poor sort of governess who would not have the air of superiority even in defeat that is so galling to the susceptibilities of the Billickin. Whatever her reasons, she stays out of sight until the last moment, when she makes a languid appearance at the top of the steps, armoured in her shawl for a final joust.

"Would you inform an elderly person of your acquaintiance, Miss," she announces, "that if I had recognised her as being 'ere in the first place, she would have had my 'earty good wishes on her departure. And if she was here, she would be leaving healthier than when she come, and I am delighted to see it, though surprised I ham not, seeing as the nourishment she has been able to enjoy in London would have set her up after so many years of what I may only term a Hundermining Diet."

"Be so good, Rosa my dear, as to inform the person of the house that I am enjoying the best of health as I have always done, thanks to moderation and good manners, and that I wish her goodbye," responds Miss Twinkleton from the foot of the steps.

"Good manners don't fill the stomach, and sorry I am for them young ladies whose stomachs will be bloated out and their con-stitootions destroyed with good manners," retorts the Billickin with a sniff, drawing her shawl of state about her.

Miss Twinkleton colours, does not deign to transmit her final reply.

"Goodbye, Rosa my dear. I hope you will not have to remain long in this neighbourhood and will soon be able to return to your friends."

They embrace, Miss Twinkleton mounts the cab, and though she waves is soon gone, leaving Rosa with a small genuine tear in her eye, feeling very lonely. But not for long. Within the hour another cab is at the door. Helena springs out of it, and the bags are handed down, the driver is paid off without any ado, she has darted up the steps, and the two friends are in each other's arms and the cab off away down the road before the Billickin, keeping watch behind a muslin curtain at an upper window, can appear upon the scene. Being thus disadvantaged, she delays her appearance until the two young women are installed in their drawing room.

"Good evening, miss, I hope all is to your liking and as you'll be comfortable, though the bed *is* hard seeing as it was purchased for a party as could not sleep in a soft bed," says the Billickin with one of her bursts of candour.

"Thank you, I am sure I shall be very comfortable here," replies Helena agreeably yet firmly, turning her lustrous dark eyes on the Billickin. She is evidently no landless governess, nor yet a schoolteacher setting out to instruct, so there is no immediate cause for hostilities to break out. There is something too in her presence that tells the Billickin that this lithe figure would be formidable if aroused, and instinct counsels prudence.

"If there's anything you want, miss, subject to the rules of the house as Miss Rosa will favour you with, I'll be only too obliged, I'm sure." With which the Billickin and her shawl withdraw.

"Rosebud, my darling," says Helena, using the pet name by which Rosa is known at school, "there is something I must tell you at once. It will be a shock to you, but for your own sake you must know. Hold my hand, dear, while I tell you."

"Nothing has happened to Mr Tartar?" asks Rosa in great alarm.

"No, nothing like that. It is something you would never have imagined," answers Helena looking down compassionately at the innocent, youthful face of her friend.

"Perhaps you had better not tell me then," says Rosa dubiously.

"I must. It is something that very much concerns you. Now listen and hold my hand." Rosa obeys. "Mr Grewgious told Mr Crisparkle and myself that he believes John Jasper murdered Edwin!"

Rosa squeezes her friend's hand and reflects for a moment. "Thank you, Helena, it was kind of you to tell me so considerately. But it was not a shock to me."

"Then you have known all the time!"

"No . . . I have never put it into words as you have. I did wonder, except that there seemed no good reason why Mr Jasper should do such a dreadful thing, except . . ." She stops and her cheeks colour.

"It was your woman's instinct that told you," says Helena seeing a new Rosa for the first time, no longer the Rosebud of the Nuns' House, but a woman with power to divine. She releases her hand.

"How does Mr Grewgious know this?"

"He has some information, but did not tell us what it was. But I was to tell you so that you would know how dangerous that man is."

"I know already," answers Rosa with a shudder. Yet such is the unaccountability of human nature that her guardian's warning does not make her think of Jasper. It is Edwin whom she now remembers more fondly than she ever did when she thought him living. The memory of their last affectionate parting rises before her, the memory that will now for the rest of her life be her recollection of the man she might have married. "Poor Eddy." Tears fill her eyes. "Poor Eddy."

Helena comforts her, and then to raise her spirits imparts her other news.

"What do you think Mr Tartar is going to do? In a few days, when he has arranged for one of his men to guard Neville, he and Mr Crisparkle are coming to fetch us, and we are all going to spend the day at Mr Tartar's country estate in Hertfordshire!"

Rosa gives a wan smile. The news does please her, and at any other time she would have been able to think of nothing else. Today, strangely, it is Edwin that possesses her mind. She knows now for certain that his youthful honest figure will never be seen again in this world; and that makes his image more real, more tender.

That night she dreams of Edwin Drood.

CHAPTER XXVI

A PRIVATE SOLILOQUY BY A PUBLIC PERSON

MAYOR SAPSEA STANDS in his ground-floor sitting room, surveying himself in the mirror with satisfaction. The chain of office is not visible to mere human gaze: to the inward mayoral eye it is ever pendent about his neck, even when he is in his nightshirt. Since his elevation to the dignity of Mayor he is never unconscious of the invisible grace that has descended upon him, and has grown ever more stately in his address. He has not lost his old ecclesiastical dignity, but now embodies, as it were, the power spiritual and the power temporal. He blends his former pulpit style with that of the mayoral speech, and has become altogether so public a figure that even when alone in the privacy of his own home he has fallen into the habit of addressing himself aloud. Whereas he had, as he put it once to Jasper, wasted his evening conversation on the desert air, he has now become both orator and audience—for the greater the Jackass the more it enjoys hearing itself bray. So on this particular evening, being without other audience, he embarks on one of his discourses to himself:

"It is, I have no hesitation in asserting, a truth so self-evident that I stand in no danger of contradiction, that I am a Sociable man. I am, I may say, a Clubbable man, so long as I am not among Fools. For it is indisputable that a man is better off in his own company than in that of Idiots. Take for example the events of the other day.

*"Wishing to take the air, I proceeded by a circuitous route to the Club, it being our weekly night of meeting. I found that we mustered our full strength. We were enrolled under the denomination of The Eight Club. We were eight in number; we met at eight o'clock during eight months of the year; our annual subscription was eight shillings each; we played eight games of four-handed cribbage at eightpence the game; our frugal supper was composed of eight rolls, eight mutton chops, eight pork sausages, eight baked potatoes, eight marrow bones with eight toasts, and eight bottles of ale. There may or may not be a certain

* The following passage, ending on p. 137 with the words ' "Or if I was to deny . . ." ', is the so-called 'Sapsea Fragment', written by Dickens.

harmony of colour in the ruling idea of this (to adopt a phrase of our lively neighbours) reunion. It was a little idea of mine.

"A somewhat popular member of the Eight Club was a member by the name of Kimber. By profession dancing master. A commonplace hopeful sort of man, wholly destitute of dignity or knowledge of the world.

"As I entered the Club-room, Kimber was making the remark: 'And he still half believes him to be very high in the Church.'

"In the act of hanging up my hat on the Eighth peg by the door, I caught Kimber's visual ray. He lowered it, and passed a remark on the next change of the moon. I did not take particular notice of this at the moment, because the world was often pleased to be a little shy of Ecclesiastical topics in my presence. For I felt that I was picked out (though perhaps only through a coincidence) to a certain extent to represent what I call our glorious constitution in church and state. The phrase may be objected to by captious minds; but I own to it as mine. I threw it off in argument some little time back. I said, Our Glorious Constitution in Church and State.

"Another member of the Eight Club was Peartree, also member of the Royal College of Surgeons. Mr Peartree is not accountable to me for his opinions, and I say no more of them here than that he attends the poor gratis, whenever they want him, and is not the parish doctor. Mr Peartree may justify it to the grasp of *his* mind thus to do his republican utmost to bring an appointed officer into contempt. Suffice it that Mr Peartree can never justify it to the grasp of *mine*.

"Between Peartree and Kimber there was a sickly sort of feeble-minded alliance. It came under my particular notice when I sold off Kimber by auction. (Goods taken in execution.) He was a widower in a white under waistcoat and slight shoes with bows, and had two daughters not ill-looking. Indeed, the reverse. Both daughters taught dancing in Scholastic Establishments for Young Ladies—had done so at Mrs Sapsea's; nay, Twinkleton's—and both, in giving lessons, presented the unwomanly spectacle of having little fiddles tucked under their chins. In spite of which the younger one might, if I am correctly informed—I will raise the veil so far as to say I KNOW she might—have soared for life from this degrading taint, but for having the class of mind allotted to what I call the common herd, and being so incredibly devoid of veneration as to become painfully ludicrous.

"When I sold off Kimber without reserve, Peartree (as poor as he can hold together) had several prime household lots knocked down to him. *I* am not to be blinded, and of course it was as plain to me what he was going to do with them, as it was that he was a brown hulking sort of revolutionary subject who had been in India with the soldiers and ought (for the sake of society) to have his neck broke. I saw the lots shortly afterwards in Kimber's lodgings—through the windows—and I easily made out that there had been a sneaking pretence of lending them 'till better times'. A man with a smaller knowledge of the world than myself might have been led to suspect that Kimber had held back money from his creditors and fraudulently bought the goods. But besides that I knew for certain he had no money, I knew that this would involve a species of forethought not to be made compatible with the frivolity of a caperer, inoculating other people with capering, for his bread.

"As it was the first time I had seen either of those two since the Sale, I kept myself in what I call Abeyance. When selling him up, I had delivered a few remarks—shall I say a little homily? —concerning Kimber, which the world did regard as more than usually worth notice. I had come up into my pulpit, it was said, uncommonly like; and a murmur of recognition had repeated his (I will not name whose) title, before I spoke. I had then gone on to say that all present would find, in the first page of the Catalogue that was lying before them, in the last paragraph before the first lot, the following words: 'Sold in pursuance of a Writ of execution issued by a Creditor'. I had then proceeded to remind my Friends that however frivolous, not to say contemptible, the pursuits by which a man got his goods together, still his goods were as dear to him, and as cheap to society (if sold without reserve) as though his pursuits had been of a character that would bear serious contemplation. I had then divided my text (if I may be allowed so to call it) into three heads: firstly, Sold; secondly, In pursuance of a writ of execution; thirdly, Issued by a creditor; with a few moral reflections on each, and winding up with 'Now to the first lot' in a manner that was complimented when I afterwards mingled with my hearers.

135

"So not being certain on what terms I and Kimber stood, I was grave, I was chilling. Kimber, however, moving to me, I moved to Kimber. (I was the creditor who had issued the writ. Not that it matters.)

" 'I was alluding, Mr Sapsea,' said Kimber, 'when you came in, to a stranger who entered into conversation with me in the street as I came to the Club. He had been speaking to you just before, it seemed, by the churchyard; and though you had told him who you were, I could hardly persuade him that you were not high in the Church.'

" 'Idiot!' said Peartree.

" 'Ass!' said Kimber.

" 'Idiot and Ass!' said the other five members.

" 'Idiot and Ass, gentlemen,' I remonstrated, looking around me, 'are strong expressions to apply to a young man of good appearance and address.' My generosity was roused. I own it.

" 'You'll admit that he must be a Fool,' said Peartree.

" 'You can't deny that he must be a Blockhead,' said Kimber.

"Their tone of disgust amounted to being offensive. Why should the young man be so calumniated? What had he done? He had only made an innocent and natural mistake. I controlled my generous indignation, and said so.

" 'Natural,' repeated Kimber. '*He*'s a Natural!'

"The remaining six members of the Eight Club laughed unanimously. It stung me. It was a scornful laugh. My anger was roused on behalf of an absent friendless stranger. I rose (for I had been sitting down).

" 'Gentlemen,' I said with dignity, 'I will not remain one of this club allowing opprobrium to be cast on an unoffending person in his absence. I will not so violate what I call the sacred rites of hospitality. Gentlemen, until you know how to behave yourselves better, I leave you. Gentlemen, until then I withdraw from this place of meeting whatever personal qualifications I may have brought into it. Gentlemen, until then you cease to be the Eight Club, and must make the best you can of becoming the Seven.'

"I put on my hat and retired. As I went down the stairs I distinctly heard them give a suppressed cheer. Such is the power of demeanour and knowledge of mankind—I had forced it out of them.

"Whom should I meet in the street, within a few yards of the door of the inn where the Club was held, but the selfsame young man whose cause I had felt it my duty so warmly—and I will add so disinterestedly—to take up!

" 'Is it Mr Sapsea,' he said doubtfully, 'or is it—'

" 'It is Mr Sapsea,' I replied.

" 'Pardon me, Mr Sapsea; you appear warm, Sir.'

" 'I have been warm,' I said, 'and on your account.' Having stated the circumstances at some length (my generosity almost overpowered him), I asked him his name.

" 'Mr Sapsea,' he answered, looking down, 'your penetration is so acute, your glance into the souls of your fellow men is so penetrating, that if I was hardy enough to deny that my name is Poker, what would it avail me?'

"I don't know that I had quite exactly made out to a fraction that his name *was* Poker, but I dare say I had been pretty near doing it.

" 'Well, well,' said I, trying to put him at his ease by nodding my head, in a soothing way. 'Your name is Poker, and there is no harm in being named Poker.'

" 'Oh, Mr Sapsea!' cried the young man in a very well-behaved manner. 'Bless you for those words!' He then, as if ashamed of having given way to his feelings, looked down again.

" 'Come, Poker,' said I, 'let me hear more about you. Tell me. Where are you going to, Poker, and where do you come from?'

" 'Ah, Mr Sapsea!' exclaimed the young man. 'Disguise from you is impossible. You know already that I come from somewhere, and am going somewhere else. If I was to deny it, what would it avail me?'

" 'Then don't deny it,' was my remark.

" 'Or,' pursued Poker, in a kind of despondent rapture, 'or if I was to deny that I came to this town to see and hear you, Sir, what would it avail me? Or if I was to deny* that I had come to seek the distinguished Author of Cloisterham, I should not deceive you.'

" 'I certainly have a good deal of experience of books,' I admitted with due modesty, 'having sold not a few in my time,

*The 'Sapsea Fragment' ends here, in mid-sentence.

137

including unfoxed and bound in calf. I have not so far completed a work myself.'

" 'What need to have written a book,' cried the young man with reverential admiration, 'when you have achieved Immortality with a deathless page written in stone!'

"I was about to confess this little excursion of mine into authorship, and was not totally displeased to hear that this intelligent young man was already acquainted with my work. I admitted my Creation.

" 'What would it avail me if I were to deny that I have come to Cloisterham expressly to meet the author of a Ruby of English writing and to crave his permission to copy it in a book I am engaged upon?'

" 'As one author to another,' I replied without a moment's hesitation, 'you have my full authority to reproduce any small composition of mine. Provided, naturally, that full attribution of Authorship is made.'

"The young man almost wept from emotion. 'Bless you, Sir,' were all the words he could utter until he had mastered himself. 'Yet one thing amazes me,' he said as soon as he was able to speak, 'that a work from a mind so evidently imbued with Classical Learning should not have been composed by one of the clergy of this cathedral city. I would have declared by none less than—the Dean!'

" 'Young man, you are not wrong,' I felt bound to tell him. 'I am the Mayor of this city. By most of its inhabitants I am also considered to be, if I may coin a phrase, the Lay Dean of Cloisterham.'

" 'I knew I could not be wrong in this,' he declared with fervour.

" 'Seeing that I am Mayor, however, my little work is not to be found in the Cathedral, but on the tomb of my late reverential wife. I will conduct you to it,' was my answer, and while he ecstatically followed me, I was good enough to enquire into the nature of the book he was engaged in writing.

" 'How can I deny to you that I am compiling a work on the gems of English architecture, in order to bring them to the appreciation of the wider public,' said the young man with humility.

"We reached the churchyard. 'This,' I declared, indicating it

138

with an appropriate gesture of the hand, 'is the Monument of Mrs Sapsea.' I hope the young fellow may not have sustained permanent injury from the intensity of his emotion.

" 'This must be the Supreme Gem of my collection,' he cried at length. 'I cannot conceal from you that nothing less than the whole monument must occupy the frontispiece of my work. This Crown Jewel, the Inscription, must be seen in all the perfection of its setting.'

"After a becoming reflection my decision was made. 'I must make some sacrifice, and feeling for one's Dead must give way before the greater cause of Public Enlightenment. I give my consent.'

" 'Your feelings honour you,' he declared, wringing me respectfully by the hand, 'though I could have expected no less self-sacrifice from one who represents the Summit of Authority and of Moral Power in this city.'

" 'You are right again, Poker,' I said. 'A man in my position could act in no other way.'

" 'I shall not offend your tenderer feelings by making my sketches in your presence,' responded the sensitive young man. 'With your gracious permission I propose to carry out these painstaking but necessary preliminaries tomorrow. No care must be spared to render this perfection in every minute detail.'

"To this also I gave my assent. Seeing the young fellow still somewhat troubled, and suspecting with my knowledge of the world that there was still something on his mind, I encouraged him to speak.

"He appeared embarrassed, but I insisted in a kindly way that he should speak his mind. 'I cannot conceal from you,' said Poker hesitantly, 'that the world will not be content with less than the whole of this small miracle. I fear I must risk the further wounding of your feelings by requesting that I might also enter and record the Inner Sanctum of this sublime monument.'

" 'The coffin of the late Mrs Sapsea is of course of the finest seasoned oak, lead-lined, and with the brass fittings appropriate to her station,' I rejoined. 'But there is no Inscription within and little of note'—being also aware that some rubbish had been left inside by that lout Durdles and his oafs.

" 'Mr—Mayor—Dean Sapsea,' cried my young enthusiast.

'What would the world say if it were denied even a glimpse of the interior of this Taj Mahal in miniature! Would it not say that its Wonder is incomplete, its Homage mutilated, its Reverence diminished?'

" 'The world shall not lay this charge against me,' I affirmed. 'Come with me, and you shall have the key.'

" 'Naturally,' I said as we walked towards the house, 'you will find some oddments, some arisings or trifles appertaining to the work of the masons inside the tomb. These will be removed before it is available to the public, but in the meantime these will not appear, I presume, in any representation that you will wish to make for your frontispiece?'

" 'Would I dare to mar perfection by depicting any such temporary dross!' exclaimed Poker. 'Nothing but its Perfection shall be made visible!'

"Reassured, and deeply moved by the thought of future generations of pilgrims filing respectfully past the Sapsea Monument, I fell into silent contemplation until we reached the house, where I handed him the key.

" 'I receive the Key from St Peter,' said my young worshipper in a voice almost broken with tears. 'I cannot withhold from you that I will return it the moment my task is completed, as sure as my name is Poker.' "

Poker had indeed been as good as his word. The key lies again upon the table.

"Which shows," concludes Sapsea, "that a man does better to spend his time with one intelligent man than with seven fools."

Having thus concluded his soliloquy, he locks the key back in his iron safe, and, somewhat reluctantly, takes his candle upstairs to his empty double four-poster bed (Unsold at Auction).

CHAPTER XXVII

AGROUND

ON THE APPOINTED day a carriage and pair with Mr Tartar and Mr Crisparkle made its appearance before Billickin's. There was still a little autumnal haze, yet it did not need the sun to discern the well-turned-out equipage, the gloss of the horses' coats, the gleam of the brass, and the shine of the coachwork, as if it were attending an Admiral's inspection. The Billickin observing from an upper window was highly gratified with the impression created in the street as the ladies descended and were handed into the carriage by the gentlemen. The neighbours too thought the pretty girl at Billickin's had never looked so pretty, and if the younger ones were of the opinion that her new companion was a great improvement on her predecessor, while the elder ones were of just the reverse mind, both at least were agreed that the gentlemen were decidedly handsome. And one of them a clergyman! Wild speculation ran up the street that Rosa was eloping with Mr Tartar, that they were going to Gretna Green—though why this should be necessary with the clergyman in attendance nobody could explain. Amid such speculation behind many a curtain, the carriage moved off and the party started to make its way out of London.

By common—though unspoken—agreement the problems of Cloisterham were left behind them. The two girls sat side by side, and as the streets were soon as unfamiliar to Rosa as they were to Helena, they were fully occupied in observing and pointing out to each other the constantly changing scenes; though Rosa did find time for an occasional quick, shy glance at Tartar opposite her, while the lustrous eyes of Helena seemed to embrace the Minor Canon without effort. The men, better acquainted with the city, indicated to the ladies the places of interest, and between whiles returned to their own conversation. For it is one of the strangest things in the world to discover that a small boy one has known at school—and who remains eternally fixed at that age in the mind as though possessing the secret of eternal youth—has grown up and become a wholly adult and different person. So Tartar and Crisparkle were engaged in recalling to each other numbers of such spirits of small boys from the desks and inkwells of past classrooms, and constantly astounding one another with the revelations that these imps were now men, some already successful, others already failures, some with wives, and some with families. In this manner the journey passed quickly for all the party, the sun broke through, the horses went clipping along once they were out of London, and everyone was duly surprised when the carriage turned in between two brick pillars, each surmounted by a stone ball, up a short drive, and stopped in front of a delightful small country house.

"This is my flagship," said Tartar with a gesture of his sailor's hand towards the house. "Welcome aboard."

And there, as if to pipe them on board, was the sun-like visage of Mr Lobley beaming in greeting.

"I think, Captain," said Helena, after looking at the walls of mellow brick rising from the earth, "that you have run your ship aground."

"By intent," replied Tartar gallantly. "This being an offence under marine law known as barratry, I have happily been condemned to spend the remainder of my days in port." Rosa felt his eyes upon her as he spoke, and to hide her confusion she stood up.

The ladies were assisted from the carriage and entered the house. A smiling housekeeper in grey, with an assortment of bright keys hanging from her chatelaine and the round face and apple cheeks of a countrywoman, curtsied as the party came in and attended to the ladies.

Their host then showed them over the house, which was as perfect as it should be. It was neither too large nor too small, not too modern and not too old. It was a house with character that had grown and adapted itself to the numbers and humours of its owners, so that one was never quite sure where a corridor was going or what sort of room lay beyond the next doorway; and the furniture had the same character as the house and contrived to be both comfortable and pleasing. Everywhere was neat with the smell of polish and scent of herbs of a well-ordered home. Yet, thought Rosa, it felt a little untenanted, a little neglected in spirit. For it was a friendly house, too, that liked people—and there were not many people normally in it—and a house where families had lived, children had played and grown up—and there were no children. What a pleasure it would be to be mistress of such a house and bring life back into it! However quickly she pushed the thought down, up it came again like a cork, until, catching Helena's eye upon her in the delightful drawing room, she was unable to prevent a blush mounting her cheeks; and so looked the part even more.

The orderliness of the house aside, there was nothing to show the character of its present owner, until Tartar, as though reading the thought in the minds of his visitors, stopped on the upper floor at the foot of a very steep, very narrow, wooden staircase.

"Now for my own contribution. If you would be good enough to follow me," he announced with a twinkling eye. With that, he ascended the stairs as easily as a balloon, while the others followed him clinging to a wooden handrail. What a surprise rewarded them at the top! For in his chambers at Staple Inn they had been in the cabin of a vessel; here in the country they found themselves upon the deck!

Beneath their feet was the white holystoned planking, the ship's rails surrounded them, while in the centre rose a ship's mast with all its attendant cordage. There was a shining brass binnacle containing a compass, to show which way they were sailing; and a locker full of signal flags; and something mysterious under a canvas cover; and coils of rope like Catherine wheels on the deck; and fire buckets; and a life-buoy. And Rosa could even see in the distance the glint of sun on water that all but persuaded her that she was somehow magically afloat, sailing under Mr Tartar's command to unknown destinations in distant seas, and, as she moved forward towards the rails to catch sight of the ocean around her, a wisp of her hair floating in the breeze was caught fast by something, giving a tweak as sharp as jealousy. Tartar was instantly at her side, reassuring her that her hair had just been caught by a dead-eye in a shroud. This alarming intelligence turned out to mean that her lock had become entangled in a rope and block supporting the mast, and Tartar's large brown hands were soon at work with extraordinary delicacy disentangling the fine hair from the rough rope, until the silken threads somehow wrapped themselves round his fingers and she had to come to his assistance in disengaging himself. These exertions, or the unfamiliarity of her nautical surroundings, left Rosa with such a fluttering heart

143

that she did not know which way to turn. So when Tartar apologised for the accident and explained that the mast was only a jury rig, she looked up at this legal curiosity half expecting to find a judge in his wig on top about to pass sentence, and was afraid to move again lest her head be caught in some ropen noose and, like Jack Ketch the executioner, be hauled aloft by Mr Punch. But there was nothing on top except an object like a barrel, referred to by the sailor as a crow's-nest—evidently a very different kind of crow from those that haunted the Cathedral tower at Cloisterham, as Tartar mounted the rigging with the agility of a cat and in a trice was inside the crow's-nest going through a pantomime of scanning the horizon for danger. Then he clambered nimbly down and was beside them again.

"I have been accustomed to standing on deck where I could see all that was going on," he explained. "I found it impossible to overlook the estate from ground level. One is hardly better off on horseback, and besides I am no horseman. So I solved the problem by constructing my deck and lookout up here. Or rather Lobley and the local carpenter between them constructed it for me. So now I can exercise command over the estate from my own deck."

The broad sunburnt figure of Tartar stood between the two ladies, his keen blue eyes picking out the details in his fields.

"I can see almost all my land from one spot," he went on, waving his hand round the horizon. In all directions were trim fields, some already cleared of their golden crop, while in others small figures were at work harvesting. To complete the picture were some scattered woods, and one small lake from whose surface Rosa had caught the glint of the sun.

"If I need a closer look, science is at hand to help me." With a quick motion the canvas cover was whipped away, revealing a shining brass telescope on a stand that was swivelled round and focused on the reapers. Rosa was instructed how to apply her eye to the instrument. She had some difficulty in shutting the other eye, so Mr Tartar's large hand was delicately placed in front of the mutinous member. At once the distant reaper expanded into a man only a few yards away. She could see his features, his sinewy forearm, and the blade of the scythe cutting through the individual stalks.

"He looks dreadfully hot and thirsty," said Rosa, suddenly

seeing a toiling human being, where before the reaper had been no more than a picturesque piece of rural scenery.

"It is hot work and they certainly drink a good deal of beer that I provide," said Tartar with a smile. "Yet the day will come when men shall not have to labour so hard here to get in the fruits of the earth."

"Are you suggesting, Tartar, that you will be provided with manna on your estate like the children of Israel?" asked Crisparkle.

Tartar laughed heartily, showing his regular white teeth. "Or like you by your fag?" he riposted, before continuing more seriously. "But why should not progress come to the land? Steam power now operates our factories, the railways are covering the country with steam locomotives. I was trained under sail, yet our warships are now being fitted with steam engines. Any becalmed sailing vessel would be at the mercy of one with a steam engine. I even foresee the day when the warship of the future may have no sails at all!"

"No sails?" repeated Rosa, wide-eyed at the thought of the navy of Drake and Nelson without sails.

"So I believe," he went on, now in serious mood. "So why should steam not come to our aid in the countryside? Much of the work is of a mechanical nature, such as reaping, so why should it not be done by machines? My intention is to run my estate in the most modern way under my eye, and to introduce machinery to the operation of the farm wherever it may be possible."

Rosa looked at the peaceful country spread about her from her vantage point, and imagined it full of puffing monsters, tall chimneys, black smoke and clanking sounds. She was not at all sure that she liked the idea of the idyllic scene she had been surveying transformed in this way, and had opened her mouth to observe as much, when it occurred to her that it was not her business how Mr Tartar ran his estate; so she closed her red lips again and said nothing. But why was Helena looking at her with such amusement that she could feel the blood starting to mantle her cheeks again?

Meanwhile the second sun had been moving about beneath their feet—another way in which the world was turned topsy-turvy from the deck of this strange vessel—as the refulgent face of

145

Mr Lobley carried chairs, tables and dishes and set them out under the shade of a handsome beech in the garden. Some swift nautical communication must have passed unperceived between him and Tartar, as the latter now announced that luncheon was ready, and after a last reluctant look around from the deck, the party descended the companion ladder.

Lunch under the tree was all manner of delightful things from the garden and the estate, with a refreshing light wine made from grapes grown in the conservatory. Afterwards they strolled through the flower garden, the brick-walled kitchen garden that supplied all manner of fresh vegetables, the orchard where the apples hung heavy on the branches, and through a cool wood to a fence where they had a close view of sleek cattle switching at the flies with their tails.

"What is that?" asked Helena, pointing to a small structure where two men were at work.

"That is a small windmill I am having put up to pump water for the cattle."

"I thought a windmill would be too old-fashioned for you, and that you would want a steam pumping engine," said Rosa.

"Not at all. The wind is an old friend of mine and I should be foolish not to make use of him. Unfortunately he is not a very dependable friend," replied Tartar.

"Tell us of your encounters with the wind when you were in the Navy," suggested Rosa to get away from the subject of machinery.

As they strolled back to the house, Tartar recounted his experience of a fearful monsoon storm in Eastern waters when the masts were broken and the ship almost foundered in the mountainous seas. His hearers were silent as he told them of this terrifying adventure, and how none of the crew believed they would survive until they limped into Trincomalee harbour.

"Why, you know Ceylon" exclaimed Helena, her face lighting up.

"Quite well. I have been there a number of times."

"And all this time you have never admitted it. I was born and brought up there."

"I declare I had no idea you had any connection with that delightful island, though indeed I might have divined as much," declared Tartar gallantly.

It soon emerged that he had been to many of the places on the island known to Helena, so they had acquaintances there in common. Helena was delighted, and much moved, to find for the first time since her arrival in England someone other than her brother with whom she could talk of the country of her birth. Unhappy as her upbringing there had been, Ceylon remained the land of her childhood, full of exotic memories as well as miseries. Her natural eagerness soon carried her away into her past. Her adventures in Ceylon being not less interesting to Tartar than his were to her, their conversation was animated and lasted through tea, partaken under the same tree in the garden.

For Rosa tea was a less happy meal. A wasp, doubtless attracted by the delicious plum jam (from the plum trees in the orchard) on her plate, buzzed viciously around her until finally crushed by a blow from Tartar's fist. She also felt left out of the conversation about Ceylon, and engaged in desultory talk with Crisparkle, who was in the same case. Horrid thoughts began to buzz in her mind, worse than the wasp. Did not Helena have more in common with Tartar than she did? Was he not showing more interest in Helena than in herself? Would not Helena be a more effective mistress of this house? Was she not more practical, more sensible, more energetic? Would she not be a greater help to Tartar in running his estate than Rosa herself could ever be? Then Tartar would interrupt his conversation with Helena to smile at her, her fears would recede and her hopes rise, and she could once more imagine herself living in this idyllic setting surrounded by the fields and woods of the estate. Then, seeing him engrossed with Helena, the vision would change again to one of Helena installed here: but now the fields were trampled flat by herds of monstrous, noisy machines, there were factories in the pastures, and tall chimneys stuck up everywhere out of the ground pouring black greasy smoke across the fields, destroying the flocks like one of the murrains of Egypt.

After tea the carriage was summoned and the party prepared to return to London. All declared they had had a wonderful day; all felt the day had grown as fractious as a tired child. Tartar had found it interesting talking to Helena, yet he would have much preferred to talk to Rosa, but was conscious as host that he had to be polite to her friend; Helena was aware that she had monopolised Tartar too much, and had a feeling of guilt, not unmixed with satisfaction at his having paid so much attention to her in Rosa's company; while Crisparkle had been as frustrated as Tartar in his desire to talk to Helena, and the sight of his old friend's estate had given the good Canon a twinge of envy, that made him reflect whether he had been guilty of the sin of covetousness. So the party that returned in the carriage that evening was much more silent and thoughtful than the party that had set out in the morning—and the journey back seemed three times as long.

Next day Rosa and Helena did not have as much to say to each other as usual. Despite the departure of Miss Twinkleton, the old grittiness was there and worse than ever. The neighbours decided that the pretty girl at Billickin's had not got married after all.

CHAPTER XXVIII

A MARRIAGE PLAN

IN CLOISTERHAM THE Nuns' House was returning to life. For weeks it had been as empty as if King Henry the Eighth had just chased out the inhabitants of the convent, though there would scarcely have been anyone about to notice such an event in the deserted summer streets of the city. Now that the Prioress herself had returned, in the modern guise of Miss Twinkleton, preparations were in hand for the return of her scattered flock of novitiates. The maids were at work cleaning, sweeping and scrubbing, Mrs Tisher checking the linen, and the Prioress herself engaged in supervising them all, when she was not sending out instructions to parents and guardians. So the Old Beau of which the house-front reminded callers had visibly revived. During the holidays his eye-glass had acquired a sadly tarnished air, and through it he could hardly hope to espy a pretty girl should one walk past his nose; now it was brightly shining as ever in sly anticipation of the arrival of all those charming young ladies, who were the very reason for his being.

Miss Twinkleton herself was not less happy to be back. Life at Billickin's had been a kind of irregular warfare not suited to her temperament, so, sad as she had been at the separation from her favourite pupil, it was a sadness strongly diluted by the satisfaction of being mistress in her own house again. She ordered lunch and dinner for herself and Mrs Tisher with a satisfaction she had never derived before from this domestic activity, in the delightful certainty that no one would dare question the seasonableness, the appropriateness, or the nutritional value of her menu. Not even the tiresomeness of Miss Ferdinand in contracting the mumps, and so delaying her arrival for the start of the new term, nor the stupidity of the new maid, who could not replace any object in its place or the right way up, nor even the failure of two novice nuns to pay the fees for their instruction last term, were able to impair her new-found sense of freedom.

That she was still in another state of being from the Miss Twinkleton known to her charges had just been demonstrated by a small incident. Glancing out of an upper window, she had espied John Jasper coming up the street, casting, she was convinced, curious glances towards the house. In a sudden panic she turned to warn Rosa that the dark features she detested had tracked them down. The shock deprived her of speech, and, in the few moments before she recovered, she was able to apprehend that it was Mrs Tisher, not Rosa, who was now her companion: and that Jasper was passing along the street in Cloisterham upon his lawful occasions. He was, indeed, on his way to the house opposite for one of his regular convivial evenings of backgammon and conversation, on which Mayor Sapsea continued to set great store. For it was an odd fact that so few of his fellow citizens, who esteemed the Mayor in public, were inclined to spend their evenings with him in private, only Jasper continuing to frequent his house regularly for a game, supper, and the benefit of the Sapsea omniscience.

On this evening, having had the game, the cold supper, and being sated with Sapsea philosophy, Jasper was awaiting a suitable opportunity to withdraw, when he realised with a sinking sensation the Mayor was about to embark on a new subject.

"You were good enough, my friend, to give your approbation to a certain epistolary epitaph." Sapsea graciously inclined his form in the direction of Jasper, who responded with an inclination of the head and a polite grimace about the lips. "It will not be surprising to one of your discernment to know that a certain eminent scholar, one Dr Poker to designate him, is preparing a learned work on the architectural treasures of our great country." He paused to give a cough both portentous and modest. "It will, I understand from none other than the lips of the author himself, contain that small Composition in a place of honour, together with a representation of the Monument upon which it is inscribed."

There was a pause, and Jasper was understood to say that Dr Poker would do better to forget St Paul's than to make such a glaring omission.

"My reflections having been directed," continued Sapsea with complacent acceptance of this tribute, "by what I may term these external circumstances, to the lapidary commendation of my late wife, it has been borne upon me that more than eighteen months have now elapsed since I was deprived of the company of my reverential spouse. A loss not easily to be replaced." (Did the thought of the unreverential Miss Kimber cross his mind at this moment?) "She looked to me as few other women could look."

He looked in turn at the Choir Master to see whether he was following the drift of his discourse. Jasper contented himself with a nod of his dark head to indicate assent to whatever the proposition was.

"Yet I pose myself this question"—gazing past Jasper to an imaginary audience beyond. "Is there not something contrary to the course of nature itself in the spectacle of a solitary male? A Man who is lacking in the solace of Womankind?"

A shadow passed over the face of the music-master; but the question was too rhetorical for the speaker to notice the reaction of his listener.

"Now that what I may term the period of natural grief has expired, is there not even something culpable in a man of position, a man who, one might say, is looked to, who does not lend his support to the weaker sex?"

"Certainly it is not good for a man to be alone," agreed Jasper, conscious of having heard this sentiment before.

"And Finally," pursued Sapsea, seeming to become more clerical and to be reaching the climax of his sermon, "there is This Consideration.

"If a man be not only of Position, but is, as it were, the Personification of the Secular Power"—here the mayoral breast pouts towards his listener—"and if such a Man represents in addition the Secular Power in a city of Things Spiritual, would it not be his Bounden Duty to link and unite such Powers?

"I have not infrequently been taken for—a Certain Person," continued Sapsea, switching from the abstract to the personal without any apparent consciousness of change. "It is, I believe, hardly an error in those who have done so. On the contrary. It shows perception on their part. A man who can occupy one eminence may as easily occupy another. If I had taken Holy Orders, I venture to assert that I would have graced the pulpit of the Cathedral as well as I do my own. It is perhaps now a little late for me to contemplate the Cloth. It would not be becoming to one in my station to enter the ranks of the junior clergy. However, there is another solution. The marriage of Church and State may be accomplished in another fashion."

The phrase pleased Sapsea, for he repeated it, investing the word 'marriage' with heavy significance.

"The marriage of Church and State."

"The marriage of Church and State. Just so," repeated Jasper judicially, racking his brains to think of a suitable unattached lady who might be the object of such a union.

"Young man," returned the Mayor, "I have always remarked in you a maturity of judgement beyond your years. As representing the Cathedral, your approbation confirms my own views upon the path of duty that lies before me.

"In short, I have now decided to bestow my name upon—"

The moment of revelation was delayed by a loud banging on the front door. Sapsea, irritated at this interruption as if he were being heckled by some invisible individual, broke off and waited for some seconds for the disturbance to subside.

"I have decided to bestow my name upon," he repeated in measured tones, looking at Jasper—

"Miss Dean."

The thought of the Dean of Cloisterham having the auctioneer as son-in-law deprived Jasper of all speech. The twitching of muscles in his face alone indicated some strong interior emotion. Sapsea took his silence as awed approval.

"Miss Dean," he repeated, nodding his head. "She who is

accustomed to looking up to a father will revere a husband in the sublime union of Church and State."

Sapsea turned away towards the mirror the better to admire his portly figure that so gloriously blended the ingredients of the Constitution. Who but the Sovereign herself can thus unite them in One Person? The figure that gazed back at him from the mirror had already a viceregal air. The former vision, of a kneeling Sapsea being dubbed on the shoulder by a royal sword, has faded before a nobler: the spikes of a coronet have grown on his forehead. Nothing less could dignify an almost royal personage. He fell silent in the contemplation of his new majesty.

"Miss Dean. It could be no other," Jasper was able to pronounce at last.

The Mayor turned back to him, and inclined to him in a gracious bow of assent.

"It could be no other, It must be so. I shall pursue my suit without delay, so that the wedding may not be delayed."

Sapsea's wooing was instantly delayed by the serving maid entering to announce the arrival of Durdles.

"Let him enter," said Sapsea with lordly permission.

Durdles was shown in, looking far from pleased to find himself there. His coarse flannel suit was a shade less powdery than usual, as though the loose powder on its surface had been blown off, but lest this might be interpreted as acceptance of social convention on the Stony One's part, his boots in contrast were rimmed and splashed with white.

With his viceregal air still on him, Sapsea greeted Durdles without the offer of any liquid hospitality; which was perhaps as well, as Durdles was at his half-way house between drunkenness and sobriety.

"Ah, Durdles. I wanted a word with you about my tomb."

Durdles said nothing.

"My Tomb," continued the Mayor, investing it with all the significance of a Pharaoh's Pyramid, "My Tomb and its Inscription are to make their appearance before a wider public. They will have the place of honour in a book shortly to appear on the architectural gems of England by the well-known author Dr Poker"—who has this evening acquired the new status of a doctorate—"Dr Poker, who was pleased to call that small inscription a Ruby of English Prose."

He paused to allow Durdles an opportunity to show his appreciation. Durdles stayed dumb and motionless.

"We must shortly expect considerable numbers of visitors in Cloisterham, who will naturally wish to see it with their own eyes. Tope must be warned to make suitable preparations for their instruction and for guiding them" (this latter an aside rather in Jasper's direction). "Durdles, you will be good enough to attend to the cleaning of the tomb. The Gem must be seen in its full splendour by those who have come the length and breadth of England, and even from those foreign climes, with which I am not unfamiliar, to express their admiration."

"Durdles allus cleans his tombs," was the growling answer.

"This is no ordinary tomb. The purity of its stonework must distinguish it from—ordinary tombs." Sapsea looked severely at Durdles for having failed to understand that he was speaking of the specially sacrosanct. The latter did not deem it worth making any response.

"They will also wish to show their respect within the mausoleum. Was there not mention that you had seen some rubbish there?"

"Durdles don't need eyes. His hammer tells him."

"It must be cleared out. The interior must be as noble as the exterior."

The mason was not impressed by the regal command, or the vision of a small white gleaming gem in the churchyard.

"Durdles'll clear the rubbish," he growled, keeping to severely practical matters, "if you give him the key. You took it back."

The Mayor nodded gravely, and got out his safe key in preparation for opening the royal treasury.

"Why Mr Durdles, I haven't seen you for a long time," said Jasper as soon as Sapsea's back was turned, breaking into a broad grin that seemed to have nothing to do with the spectacle of the stone-mason. "You and I appreciated the tombs of Cloisterham before it became the fashion. We must spend another afternoon together before the visitors arrive."

"Any time that'll wash the dust out of Durdles's throat," rumbled the other, looking at Jasper with the suspicion that he was laughing at him.

Jasper still seemed to find life unusually comic. "Why Mr

153

Durdles," he exclaimed, clapping him on the shoulder, "you look as if you've been wading through your own quick-lime. It'll be eating the boots off your feet if you are not careful."

The Stony One did not even deign to look at them.

"It won't."

"Why not?"

" 'Cos that lot of lime was no good. There was some of the Old Uns' bones as had been put in it, and it didn't do nothing to them."

At that instant the vulpine look of amusement on Jasper's face vanished, as Sapsea turned round with the key and interrupted their conversation.

"Will you start tomorrow?" he demanded, as he handed over the large key to the tomb.

"Tomorrow?"

"Tomorrow. I'll see it's made worth your while," said Sapsea grandly.

A grunt that might be either agreement or dissent was his reply, as Durdles unbuttoned a capacious inner pocket, carefully placed the key inside and buttoned up the pocket again, then, evidently considering the interview at an end, turned to go.

"And you will clean the stonework inside, as well as outside?" pursued Sapsea.

"Can't clean it till the rubbish is out," pointed out Durdles.

"Then the sooner you start, the better," replied Sapsea, growing impatient with the mason's obduracy. "You will start work tomorrow?"

"Durdles'll do it in his time." Whether this was a promise, a compromise, or even refusal was still unclear. Sapsea, realising from past experience that nothing was to be done with Durdles in this frame of mind, decided to accept it as a promise and hope for the best.

"Very good. Tomorrow then."

Durdles was not disposed to argue further, and with a nod of agreement with something—either Sapsea's ideas or more probably his own—he started to move towards the door for the second time. Sapsea started to accompany him, gave a look in Jasper's direction expressive of the hopelessness of having to deal with idiots, and saw that Jasper was standing with his feet apart, swaying slightly.

"Are you feeling ill, Jasper?" asked Sapsea, in some alarm at the idea of having a sick man in his house.

The figure managed to motion towards an armchair. With Durdles on one side and Sapsea on the other, he was assisted to the chair, into which he half-collapsed, his eyes curiously glazed.

"Leave me. It will pass," he jerked out. Then his hands gripped the sides of the chair with agonised fingers, while mercuric drops stood out on his forehead. After a few moments the worst spasm passed, he relaxed, and his eyes slowly returned to their normal appearance.

"Forgive me. It is a constitutional weakness that afflicts me from time to time," he whispered.

"So I've heard," rumbled Durdles, looking fixedly at him.

"I shall be quite myself in a moment."

With some relief on his face, Sapsea poured a glass of wine and handed it to Durdles for the patient. Durdles awkwardly proffered it to Jasper, but the glass was waved away. After standing with it in his hand for some seconds, Durdles swallowed it by pure force of habit and rubbed the back of his hand across his lips.

Jasper rose from his chair with a faint smile. "I trust I did not alarm you. It is an old vertigo of mine that is severe while it lasts, but soon passes without permanent effect. However, I think I would like to take my leave, if Mr Durdles would be kind enough to escort me back to the Gate House. I am still a little shaky. Thank you, sir, for an entertaining and instructive evening."

Durdles assented, and accompanied the Choir Master back towards the Cathedral. A drink, Jasper maintained, would finally settle his disorder, and suggested that Durdles should join him. Durdles gave a doubting look at his companion, but habit was too strong again and he followed him up the stairs when they reached the Gate House. Durdles was immediately given a bottle, while Jasper busied himself with the special brew that was the sovereign remedy for his weakness, one that required some time in mixing and preparation. When it had been made, the two drank together.

The medicine was as effective as Jasper had maintained. After a short time he was completely restored and back in his earlier good humour. Soon he was leading Durdles in the singing of a drinking song, which he turned to perfection in a beautiful voice, while the mason accompanied him with some difficulty in a rumbling, wheezy bass. It was apparent after a time that Durdles had a greater difficulty than a lack of musical education, as he began to encounter problems in standing on his legs, and it became Jasper's role to support him in his turn. Eventually both legs and voice collapsed, Durdles having to be got down the winding stair. He accomplished part of this on his seat, and was left by Jasper propped up against the wall to revive in the cold night air.

Durdles's capacity for remaining in one place for a length of time was well known; he attracted no attention. Finally with a shake of the head as though to clear it, he started to lurch away, but was quite disoriented and stumbled in the wrong direction. He might have ended up in the river, if it was not for the intervention of his ballistic guide.

> "Widdy widdy wen!
> I—ket-ches-Im-out-ar-ter-ten,
> Widdy widdy wy!
> Then-E-don't-go-then-I-shy-
> Widdy Widdy Wake-cock warning!"

There followed a hail of pebbles, and by diligent stoning Deputy eventually succeeded in halting and then reversing Durdles's motion, starting him in the right direction. But things had such an erratic way of behaving that Durdles almost at once found himself trying to walk through a stone wall that had planted itself in his path.

"Sending-me-wrong," he accused thickly into the mildewed stone.

"Yer lie, I never," returned Deputy politely. "Yer wuz all wrong'n I put yer ter rights."

Another fusillade on the Stony One's left side got him moving again to his right. Yet such was his lack of equilibrium that he was next unaccountably attempting to make his way through a brick wall on the other side.

"Yer—can't—steer," declared Durdles.

"Yer Drunkenner Judge," retorted Deputy, executing a wild dance in the middle of the passage to relieve his feelings at the waywardness of his charge, and then hurling the final insult, "—and Worsenner Sheep!" As mere words had no effect on this sheep, the shepherd launched another barrage with a further cry of Widdy Widdy Wen! This finally got the errant sheep moving to his left, and so forward for a few paces, until he veered round with stumbling steps and ended back with his natural element, the stone wall.

So the process began over again, until, by degrees and accompanied by much expenditure of ammunition, Durdles was slowly shepherded on his wayward route back home. By the time midnight had struck, even the sound of Wake-cock warnings and the rattle of stones had died away.

Within the Gate House Jasper was still waiting. He waited until the Cathedral clock struck one. Then he donned his pea-jacket, opened a cupboard and took from it a lantern. From a drawer a jack-knife, a stout screwdriver. From the table he picked up an iron key. With this in his left hand, and the lantern in his right, he stole softly down the stairs.

CHAPTER XXIX

AN ENCOUNTER IN THE DARK

AT THE FOOT of the winding Gate House stairs, John Jasper pauses, cat-like, to accustom his eyes to the darkness before emerging. The night is neither very dark nor light. The moon is young, giving enough light to discern by, not enough to illuminate, appearing only fitfully between the clouds. There is a good deal of cloud moving quickly across the sky.

On such a night the old Cathedral is at its most strange. On a pitch-dark night it is invisible, a presence felt, yet not seen, while under a full moon it stands silvered, but solid as under the midday sun. Now it is neither. When the clouds are across the moon, there is just enough light to know that something is there, a mass of uncertain shape and being. It is some great stranded prehistoric monster, left behind by Time, whose life-cycle is measured in centuries and whose slow breathing is counted in days. A great immobile mountain of a beast, threatening by its very stillness, by the undefined nature of its menace. The awesome leviathan, digesting the unknown in its maw, lies in the midst of the

157

unwitting, sleeping town, save where the odd sleeper, disturbed in his rest by the presence, turns uneasily and moans in his bed. Then the clouds part. For a few moments the weak light of the moon reveals the outline of the Cathedral, all detail lost. The great tower is there, rising dim and prison fashion, true sister to the forbidding monastery ruin silhouetted blackly, not far off beside the secret waters of the river. The Cathedral then is pitiless, lacking aught of humanity, lacking even the comfort of religion. It might be the giant tomb of all the past dead of Cloisterham, not the living dead awaiting resurrection, but all who have mouldered to dust and sleep hopelessly for ever within its prison walls. The cloud passes again across the watery face of the moon, and the shapeless beast returns to fill the night with the age-old dread of the Nameless. It is not a time or place for a man with fancies in his head to be abroad.

Jasper appears armoured against such thoughts. Awaiting the moment when the moon is obscured once more, he slips out of his doorway into the Close. He moves soundlessly, always choosing the deeper dark, making his destination seem uncertain. Yet soon he is to be glimpsed among the tombs of the graveyard, a shadow that passes for a moment across the faintly glimmering faces of the newer gravestones, passing unseen before the older, lichen-encrusted stones that sag to one side. The shadow moves quickly, so that before the weakly moon is out again he is standing by the door to the Sapsea tomb. Here he places his unlit lantern on the ground while he fits the key into the lock. The door squeaks slightly as he pushes it open with care, and he freezes instantly and gives a long feline look into the darkness around before he takes up his lantern and slips inside. Only when the door has been cautiously closed again from the inside, and re-locked behind him, does he strike a light and apply it to the candle in his lantern.

In the warm light of the candle flame, this mournful spot is less chilling than the Cathedral. Before moving further into the tomb, he lifts the lantern and looks around with keen eyes that hold no trace of the film that was over them a few hours since. They see a low shelf against one wall of the mausoleum, resting on which is the coffin of the late Mrs Sapsea. The dulled brass of its handles is still able to catch the light of the flame. Above, at a higher level, is another similar shelf, this one untenanted, doubtless awaiting the auctioneer. On this shelf, and in the corners of the tomb, spiders have been at work; they have spared the coffin of Mrs Sapsea for some reason. Satisfied by this survey of the tomb from the door, he moves forward. A couple of blocks of stone—left deliberately no doubt by Durdles's journeymen, to save the trouble of removing them—half fill the passage between wall and coffin, but Jasper moves past them with the ease of a man negotiating a known obstacle.

Placing the lantern on the edge of the upper shelf, Jasper takes a chequered kerchief from his pocket and ties it across his nose and glossy side-whiskers. He adjusts the position of the lantern to throw the best light on the lid of the coffin beneath. Then, removing the screwdriver from his pocket, he leans over the lid and begins to undo the screws in the methodical manner of a man doing a job he knows. He makes his way round steadily, pocketing each screw in turn as it becomes free. So he works his way back to his starting point. Exchanging the screwdriver for the jack-knife, he prepares to lever the lid up, but finds the blade is unnecessary as the end of the lid comes up easily enough. Putting away the knife—he goes about the task with the regularity of a workman—he seizes the coffin lid by the centre, lifts it, swings it clear, and stands it upright against the wall. But at this moment the nervous tension in the man betrays itself. Turning abruptly from the lid outlined against the white wall, he snatches the lantern from its perch and holds it aloft above the opened coffin.

The dark casket responds sombrely to the rays. A whitish substance alone reflects back the light from the bottom of the coffin. No body, no skeleton, not even the frail bones of Mrs Sapsea remain. Jasper shows no surprise at the sight, though he runs his lantern round the inside of the coffin to make sure, and there is a look of slight puzzlement in his eyes. This expression is succeeded by a smile. After which he lays his head on the coffin and his body is shaken for a while by a fit of silent laughter.

After a couple of minutes his laughter ceases. He straightens up, removes the kerchief from his face, dabs at his eyes with it, and thrusts it back into a pocket. After a final look into the coffin to reassure himself, he places the lantern on the shelf again, and returns to being the methodical workman. There is a mouldering, charnel-house smell about the place that not even the odour of hot

159

metal and candle grease from the lantern can mask, yet Jasper gives no sign that he is conscious of it. Back goes the lid, in go the screws one by one. Each is carefully driven home and tightened until the circuit has been completed, and the lid is as the undertakers left it. Back into his pocket goes the screwdriver. He makes a final intent inspection of the outside of the coffin, and then of all the floor of the tomb, as though to satisfy himself that he is leaving no evidence of his visit. He stifles a sneeze brought on by the dust he has disturbed, and prepares to take his departure.

Only when his hand is inserting the key in the lock and he is about to extinguish the lantern, does he see for the first time a sheet of paper suspended from a nail on the inside of the door. With his alertness tonight for everything, he holds the light to it, half expecting it to be some record of work, repairs, or such trivia. Only five words are written in ink by a careless hand:

Meet me in the crypt.

He looks for a moment with little interest at this odd note of assignation. Then a start of recognition passes through his body. The lantern jerks in his hand. He seizes the paper and peers fiercely at it as though to wrest its secret from it by the intensity of his stare. After this keen perusal, it is carefully placed in an inner pocket, and he remains in deep thought, grim-faced. He stands thus motionless for a while before extinguishing the lantern and passing through the door.

Remembering to lock the door of the tomb behind him, he glances quickly around as he leaves; yet it is a symptom of his inner preoccupation that this time he does not wait for the feeble moon to be screened by cloud. He hurries straight back towards the red curtains of the Gate House. From the summit of the Cathedral he might be some venomous spider scuttling back to its lair.

Once inside he lights his lamp, pulls the paper from his pocket and studies it intently. He looks at the back—it is blank. Another thought. He dashes to a drawer, pulls out a packet of letters. Quick fingers undo the tape. He selects several letters, and constantly compares the writing with that on the sheet. The same under a powerful magnifying glass. Then he holds the letters and the sheet up to the light to compare the watermarks. At last he

puts them all down as his lips form a half-spoken word:
"Identical!"

Jasper's dark features have never looked so drawn, so set. For a full quarter of an hour he paces incessantly up and down the room: that same room where Edwin Drood and Neville Landless have quarrelled, where Mr Grewgious once broke certain news. Suddenly, his decision is made. He takes another, heavy key from a drawer, grasps his lantern again, creeps once more down the winding stairs. Now his caution is even greater than before. He stands long in the doorway before moving silently out into the darkness, where he remains motionless watching the Cathedral for a further five minutes before stealing to that side door, through which he entered the crypt in the company of Durdles on that earlier unaccountable expedition. He finds it without difficulty, quickly lets himself in, and once inside again stands motionless, watching and listening. There is utter silence until he strikes a light for his lantern. With this in his hand, he proceeds cautiously, step by step, down the worn stairs into the Cathedral crypt.

In the crypt is only the faintest luminescence from the pale moonlight outside. The columns are mysterious glimmering forms, a mere hint of phosphorescence such as might come from decaying bones. The whole place has a dolefully subterranean feel: the sheer weight of the massy old fabric above, and the great tower above that, seem relentlessly pressing on these pillars, driving all ever deeper and deeper into the earth to rejoin the dead even more ancient than those whose remains are within these walls.

Jasper has hardly entered the crypt before this small luminosity dies away. Total blackness now reigns, save where the tiny light of his candle throws its rays in a circle of a few feet around him.

He moves very slowly up the centre of the crypt with the same caution, holding the lantern advanced in front of himself to gain the maximum range of its light.

As he slowly advances and each pillar on either side comes within the orbit of his flickering flame, so the weak shadows that are cast by them change with little predatory movements. Catching these in the corner of his eye, Jasper instantly stops in his tracks with the look of a wary animal, half alarmed, half aware that his senses are cheating him.

After each stop, when he looks around and listens carefully, he puts another cautious foot forward again. Outside the little human circle of his light, the pillars and the blackness seem to stretch to eternity, through all space and time. He could be in one of those vast structures with the power of endless growth and reproduction, through which he has so often wandered in his opium visions.

At the next step he sees the thing he expects and fears. Standing, a few yards from him, hitherto concealed from view by a pillar, is the figure of Edwin Drood.

"Ned!" comes involuntarily from Jasper's lips. There is no mistaking that casually youthful nod of the head, nor the angle of the broad-brimmed hat on the long brown hair, nor the light moustache Drood cultivates on his upper lip, nor the stance of the body in the overcoat. Jasper stands confounded, not knowing if he is in the presence of a spirit, an opium dream, or a living man. Without moving any closer to Drood, he bends his body forward and concentrates on the face under the broad brim of the hat. The eyes glitter back at him; it is no ghost.

"But you are dead!" he cannot help saying in amazement.

A characteristic shake of Drood's head denies it.

"I swear you were dead when I put you in the coffin. I know it!"

Again the same, slightly pitying denial.

"Why don't you speak, Ned?"

Drood's hand points significantly to his throat.

"Ah . . . It was damaged. You still can't speak. But it was you that wrote the note?"

The other indicates that he did.

"Why do you want me here?"

Drood puts his left arm across his chest and reaches into an inner pocket. As his closed hand emerges, he stretches it out towards Jasper. The fingers uncurl. An object in the hand flashes softly in the lantern light. The hand moves slightly, the colour changes to the dull red glow of blood as a ruby catches the light.

Jasper makes no move to take the proffered ring, and looks at it in suspicious puzzlement. A ring? Drood had a shirt-pin, a watch and chain, never a ring.

"What do you want of me?"

162

The hand closes over the ring. With an enigmatic smile, Drood points with his forefinger first to his neck, then upwards in the air. Jasper is still uncertain what Drood is trying to communicate: a continuation of their dialogue above—or a gallows?

He has no opportunity to find out, for at this moment the overworked candle in his lantern gutters, the wick collapses and is extinguished in liquid fat. Total darkness returns to the crypt. Unable to see his hand before his face, Jasper grounds his lantern with an oath, hunts through his pockets, and eventually succeeds in striking a light.

Edwin Drood has vanished from the spot where he stood.

Jasper looks about him but can see nothing. Then thinking he hears a sound behind him, he turns towards the entrance to the crypt. Enlightenment suddenly floods into his face. With an ex-ultant cry he dashes to the Cathedral stairs:

"The Fellow-Traveller!"

CHAPTER XXX

THE TOWER

JASPER EMERGES FROM the crypt into the passage at the side of the chancel. The stained-glass window casts no lurid colours this night, just enough light for him to pick his way to the iron gate barring the staircase to the Tower. He finds it unlocked. It must be so!

Swiftly and silently he mounts the steps, seeming to know his way by instinct in the darkness up the narrow spiral staircase. When the staircase ends, he makes his way quickly along galleries and under low arches with the same sure touch, only once catch-ing his head on a projecting beam, which dizzies him but does not halt his progress. He mounts even narrower staircases, where cobwebs brush his face with faint fingers in the dark. Still he presses on, for there is no sign of the pursued ahead of him, and this time he must make no mistake. So he finally emerges at the summit of the tower.

The moon is covered. Pausing only to turn the key in the lock of the final door that gives access to the roof, he turns and peers into the surrounding blackness. He can discern nothing at first but the crenellations that surround the summit of the tower. So he advances again, slowly and warily as a beast of prey in search of a victim to assuage its appetite. Still he sees nothing, but his ear catches the hiss of quickly indrawn breath. Turning in the direction of the sound, he sees in black silhouette against the lighter dark of the sky the familiar outline of Drood's hat and coat.

Jasper gives a low laugh, and taking out his jack-knife clicks open the blade.

"I'll make a good job of you this time, I promise," he says in a steely voice, moving towards him.

The other does not speak or await Jasper's attack, but hurls himself ferociously on him. The sudden fury of the assault bears Jasper to the ground where he loses grip on his knife. The violence of his opponent wrestles Jasper on to his back, and clutches his throat with such hatred that Jasper's head swims and all seems lost. Only Jasper's groping fingers encountering the handle of his knife save him. With a convulsive effort he plunges the blade between his enemy's ribs. There is an agonised sound in his opponent's throat, and the fingers about his own relax. Shaking the other off, Jasper manages to scramble to his feet and suck in lungfuls of air.

Seeing his enemy on his feet again, too, Jasper tightens his grip on his knife and moves forward once more. This time his opponent makes no move, standing clutching one hand to his side. A strange bubbling voice issues from him, that would try to be saying *No, No!* Jasper listens to these gurglings with a smile of satisfaction, then throws down the knife that is no longer needed. Seizing his enemy with both hands, he presses him back to the parapet.

The dying man still resists to the utmost of his power, but it is draining from him. Jasper hoists him up and with a final supreme effort lifts him above his head, hurling him with all his strength from the tower.

The falling body gives out one long cry that fades until it ends abruptly with a sudden impact far below. Somewhere in the darkness of the town a dog raises a long dismal howl in sympathy.

Jasper leans against the parapet panting for some moments, until the moon returns. It reveals few signs of this struggle to the death: a knife with an ominously dulled blade, and Drood's hat that has fallen to the ground. He pays no attention to these, leaning over the parapet to see what has happened to his victim: he sees the body far beneath impaled on the railing below, a limb still twitching convulsively. Jasper straightens up. There is a serene look on his dark features as he turns away, murmuring to himself, "It is the vision. This is the reality."

A sound that could be a sob near by draws his attention for the first time to another figure on the roof with him. It is a small woman, well wrapped against the night cold, her hand over her mouth, staring at him with terrified eyes. He comes closer to identify her, peering into her face. She shrinks back as his features, streaked with blood and dirt, loom before her face.

"Rosa, my beloved."

Rosa has been witness of the violent scene on the tower, its sudden savagery leaving her paralysed, not knowing whether this is some phantasmagoria that will vanish as suddenly as it began.

"What else? Now that the journey is over, the delectable visions begin."

Poor Rosa stares at the terrifying face and the unintelligible things it is saying.

"How should you understand, my love? How were you to know? I have made the Journey up the Tower, to the summit above the abyss, hundreds, thousands, millions of times. Always accompanied by the fellow-traveller, my rival, my enemy. Here on the summit I outwit him, I crush him. He cries for mercy, but I hurl him from the tower so that his miserable body is impaled below like a Turkish robber."

She listens uncomprehending as the dark blood-smeared face, that might itself belong to an Eastern brigand, pours out its fantasy.

"I did it once before in the flesh. I planned it all so carefully, yet it was wrong. There was no resistance, no cries for mercy, no despair. He fell like a sack from the tower, broke his fall on the hands of the clock and wrenched them off. No writhing body on a spear. It wasn't worth the doing." He frowns at the memory. "It spoiled the vision too. Next time I saw it, it was wrong. Just a body, like a dead fly, at the foot of the tower. And then to find after all that he had lived and escaped me!—For the time."

The look of triumph returns, on the Oriental blood-streaked face in the moonlight. "Now I understand why. So that I should do it again—perfectly! This time it was right! He understood, he knew! He resisted me, fought back. I overcame him, ignored his cries, hurled him screaming from the tower. Now he is transfixed. Come, I will show you."

He tries to draw her to the parapet, but she shrinks back and refuses. He shrugs his shoulders. "No matter. *This* is the vision. It has been fulfilled at last."

Jasper stands for a minute savouring his triumph, before turning to Rosa with a smile about his lips that is more terrifying to her than the violence.

"The journey is over. The deed is done."

His glittering eyes rest upon her. "Now is the time when the great scenes begin . . . The Sultan and his escort, the countless attendants, the clashing cymbals, the flashing scimitars, the whirling dervishes, the swaying elephants arrayed in gorgeous colours . . . The thrice ten thousand dancing girls casting flowers, the entire Sultan's harem . . ." He leans forward and touches her as she shrinks back. "All the symbols of you, my beloved one!"

The sheer force of her revulsion from this madman gives her a new strength, and her lips are able to form the words.

"What do you mean?"

"Surely you understand that, my beloved? The enemy has been destroyed. Now comes the reward for the victor—your own delectable self!"

"No." The word is forced from her.

"It is your destiny. You cannot deny your fate." A fresh thought strikes him. "The ring! Of course. That was the challenge. The ring was for whoever won to give you. I should have taken it . . . No matter. I shall take it from his body now, and you, my dearest, shall wear it."

"You *are* mad," whispers Rosa more to herself than to Jasper.

"Only for love of you, my precious," he replies, catching her low words. "If I have killed a man, it was no more than the defence of my just right to you. It had to be one or other of us. It was a conflict that could have only one outcome."

Rosa stares back at him in silent horror.

"You will understand, and you will believe," enunciates Jasper

166

slowly, fixing her with his dark eyes. She is conscious that he is again endeavouring to impose his will upon her, to bring her under that hated influence he has attempted to exercise over her in the past during their music lessons, and even when he was far from her. Now she is in the dreadful physical presence of the man, and half paralysed by fear; yet she is no longer the schoolgirl that she was, and fights back with her own woman's will.

"You will understand," repeats Jasper, his hypnotic eyes upon her. Rosa can feel the power of the man's emanations focused upon her, when suddenly the spell is broken as Jasper comes to himself and glances quickly around in the darkness.

"I have no time to persuade you now," he says in a more normal voice. "There is work to be done. The thing below must be disposed of before morning. Come."

He seizes her by the wrist and starts to drag her towards the door to the stairs.

Even as they near the door, there is suddenly hammering on it from the other side. Jasper freezes in his tracks like an animal, listening. For a little there is silence, then the thud of a body throwing itself against the woodwork. The door is solid Cloisterham oak and does not yield. Pulling Rosa behind him to the tower parapet, Jasper looks down over the edge to the town below. Lights and figures are moving at the foot of the tower.

"We are discovered," he says grimly.

Rosa's heart has risen with the knowledge that her plight is known and that help is at hand. Yet what irony! It has come too soon. If only her rescuers had waited until Jasper had unlocked the door, and they were on their way down the tower. Then comes the thought—could she do it? Jasper seems lost in calculation, weighing his predicament. Profiting by this distraction of his, she breaks loose and runs for the door. Her hand is on the key by the time he catches her up and drags her away, pocketing the key as he does so.

"No you don't, my beauty."

Rosa responds by screaming for help at the top of her voice.

"Help! Help! Hel—"

Jasper's hand is clapped over her mouth, and she sinks her teeth in the flesh. His hand is drawn back sharply, and she is able to cry out once more.

"Help!"

With an oath Jasper hits her across the mouth. The blow dazes and silences her.

"Damn you, you've got spirit," says Jasper, torn between pain and admiration. "What a woman you are. And what a life we might have together, if we can get out of here."

Dragging her after him, he searches for another exit from the roof. There is none. After a fruitless search, Jasper acknowledges the fact.

"If we cannot live, at least we can die together," he says with a fanatical look, seizing Rosa up in his arms. She struggles and cries, but to no avail. Her physical resistance against the hated embrace is exhausted, and she feels her senses failing. The roof of the tower begins to spin about her, and she faints.

He looks down at the face of the little beauty lying senseless in his arms. "The vision was true. You are mine."

A regular assault is made on the door, as it begins to be battered down from the other side.

"They shall not separate us, my adorable." He bends his bloodied face to hers and kisses her cheek. "We shall stay together in death."

With Rosa in his arms he advances towards the parapet of the tower for the last time.

Even as he moves to the brink, a dismembered apparition appears before his eyes. First a single hand materialises from space on the stonework of the parapet. Then a second hand with a sinewy forearm attached does the same. Between the two a lone head appears, a head with a strangely white forehead, that might be a bandage in the moonlight. Then a powerful torso that wonderfully joins up these discrete parts into half a man. An instant later the whole man stands poised on the parapet, and leaps lightly down in the path of the amazed Jasper.

For once it is he who is at a disadvantage. Before he can disencumber himself of the woman in his arms, one brown fist has smashed into his face, knocking out a tooth. The other follows into his left eye, blinding it. The next catches him on the chin and drains all the strength from his legs, which start to buckle under him. He does not even see the *coup de grâce* under which he sinks senseless to the ground.

168

Tartar—for it is no other—immediately bends over the unconscious Rosa and reassures himself that she is unharmed. Lifting her in his arms he carries her to the door, where the woodwork is beginning to splinter, and shouts to those on the other side to desist. They do so, but the door cannot be opened. Guessing that the key is in Jasper's possession, he lays Rosa down again with the greatest gentleness, and searches Jasper's pockets until he finds it. As he unlocks the door, Crisparkle is the first to burst through. The Canon's face has lost its customary look, and there is anger upon it.

Jasper, on his hands and knees, struggles to get to his feet.

"Take him, Crisparkle," orders Tartar, his chest still heaving with the effort of scaling the tower.

In a trice Crisparkle has Jasper's arm in a lock that he has once applied gently to Neville Landless; tonight he is not so gentle. A constable following behind produces a pair of handcuffs, and the helpless Jasper is soon manacled, and being marched back down the stairs. Two pairs of eyes watch him closely to see he has no chance to repeat his attempt to throw himself from the tower.

Meanwhile Rosa is already being borne swiftly down before him. When her senses begin to return she is being carried along the street towards the Nuns' House. At first panic sweeps over her as she recalls what has happened. Is she still on the tower? Has he evaded the pursuers? She is on the point of crying out again, when something tells her that she is being carried home; that the arms around her are no longer fierce and cruel, but strong and gentle. Looking into the face of the man who is carrying her, she sees what her heart has already told her. Rosa relaxes back into the arms that once saved Crisparkle, and that she knows will never let her go.

CHAPTER XXXI

COUNCIL OF WAR

SEVERAL DAYS BEFORE the events on the Tower of Cloisterham Cathedral already narrated, Mr Grewgious had held a council of war at Staple Inn. The participants had been requested to arrive in ones and twos under cover of darkness in order not to advertise the gathering. In accordance with these instructions, they had passed conspiratorially through the lodge and made for Grewgious's chambers, knowing that the venerable P.J.T. above the doorway, like a night owl in a tree above their heads, was imparting to them his wise old warning that Perhaps Jasper's There. Now all were safely inside, and, with the assistance of some chairs fetched from neighbouring chambers, were seated in a circle about the round table. Mr Grewgious had already bustled about, convinced that the ladies must be starving and the gentlemen dying of thirst, and was at last persuaded, after some had taken a glass of his Madeira wine, that there was no more he could do for their bodily well-being.

Mr Grewgious sat at the table, his face expressionless as ever. Rosa sat on his right, serious, yet blooming too, a fact that might be attributable to the apparent accident that her neighbour was Mr Tartar. On the lawyer's left was Helena Landless, whose observant eye did not miss Rosa's beauty, and next to her sat her brother Neville, looking the more pallid and nervy in contrast with the robust solidity of Tartar opposite. The group was completed by a solemn Minor Canon awaiting what Grewgious had to say.

"Thank you all for coming tonight," began Grewgious in his usual reciting manner, though none of his listeners doubted that he was in serious mood. "I apologise again for the inadequacy of my chambers. You must forgive them as the working quarters of an Angular bachelor, who rarely has the pleasure of entertaining ladies and gentlemen." He may have noticed an encouraging little smile from Rosa telling him that he was being a foolish old fellow—if so, he continued without showing it. "I took the liberty of asking you to visit me here as I was aware that our local friend, who is friend to none of us, would not be likely to disturb our meeting. Nevertheless I asked you to take precautions, as I have information concerning that quarter which it is my duty to impart to you." He paused for a moment in a silence of expectancy.

"First," he continued, lifting one hand from his knee and extending a bony forefinger, "A person by name of Datchery has for some time been employed by me in the capacity of detective. Not a *police* detective, but if one with as little sense of imagination as myself may be permitted to coin a phrase, a *private* detective.

"He recently reported to me that our local friend had gone on several expeditions with Durdles the mason round the Cathedral and the tombs. He would have seen in Durdles's yard a pile of quick-lime so potent that it would consume human bones. Just before the disappearance of Edwin Drood he accompanied Durdles on a night expedition. Durdles was made so drunk—or drugged with some additive to his drink supplied by our friend who took good care not to consume any himself—that he was scarcely able to ascend the tower, and on his return to the crypt with our friend was so overcome that he slept for hours. Yet he was not so drugged that he did not suspect that the key to the crypt—and possibly of the Sapsea tomb—was abstracted from him and returned before he awoke."

"The Sapsea . . .?" The Minor Canon appeared to wish to ask a question, only to be silenced by Grewgious's hand being up-raised.

"Allow me," grated the lawyer. "My narrative may answer your questions.

"Second. At my instigation an individual by the name of Poker ingratiated himself with Mayor Sapsea, and by means of a stratagem obtained the key of the Sapsea tomb." Grewgious coughed slightly as though apologising in advance for what he was about to say. "He succeeded in persuading Mayor Sapsea that his tomb and its inscription were of such merit that they would receive a place of prominence in a book he was writing, and that in consequence numerous persons would soon be visiting Cloisterham expressly to see the tomb, both outside and inside." His audience was too rapt to smile, and the lawyer went on.

"Third," ticking off three fingers. "Durdles has in consequence been summoned to Mayor Sapsea's house. There is little doubt that the Mayor will instruct him to renovate the tomb in anticipation of these visitors. Durdles, who is no friend to Sapsea, has not responded, and will do nothing until told by Datchery, who has a good understanding with him."

"Fourth." He looked round the table for a moment as though reluctant to continue. When he resumed his voice was unchanged, but Rosa realised that it had sunk a little in register. "On obtaining the key, Poker entered the tomb. He opened the coffin of the late

Mrs Sapsea with all due reverence"—this in the direction of the Minor Canon—"and found inside no skeleton. Only lime and some fragments of bone that were not identifiable."

"Fifth. Many years ago I was given a solemn trust. A ring of diamonds and rubies, which had been taken from the finger of Miss Rosa's dead mother, was entrusted to me to give to Edwin Drood before his marriage."

The eyes in his dried face suddenly became a little moist, as though the sap that had always run through the core of the man had at last penetrated that exterior of seasoned timber the world saw. With sudden understanding, Rosa put one of her hands over his in a quick movement of sympathy. Not allowing himself to be deflected from his task by any sign of weakness, her guardian continued:

"I carried out that trust and handed the ring in my care to Edwin Drood in the presence of my clerk Bazzard. Drood placed it in an inner pocket. I told him that he was going to make the final arrangements for the wedding, that if he placed it on Miss Rosa's finger it would be a solemn seal upon their undertaking. I also charged him, by the living and by the dead, that if there were anything amiss between himself and Miss Rosa, to return the ring to me . . . . As you know the two young people freely agreed to go their own way in life . . . I did not see Drood again, and the ring disappeared with him."

A tear slowly trickled down Rosa's face. Helena's impulse was to run and comfort her friend, yet something held her back.

"This," said Grewgious, putting a forefinger and thumb in his waistcoat pocket, "is the ring."

He placed the ring on the table in front of them. Under the light of the table lamp its diamonds flashed as brilliantly—and as heartlessly—as they had on the finger of the dead woman.

"This ring was found in the coffin of Mrs Sapsea."

There was a silence and no one spoke the thought that was in everyone's mind, until Grewgious finally did so.

"I fear we must conclude that the body of Edwin Drood was placed in the coffin of Mrs Sapsea with a corrosive substance that has destroyed all trace of the body, but which the ring in his pocket alone has resisted."

A sob escaped from Rosa as the tears began to flow down her

cheeks. Helena jumped up, put her arms round her and held her close. "So horrible . . .," sobbed Rosa. "I knew he was dead but . . ."

"Don't think about it any more, darling," urged Helena.

"I . . . I teased him . . . about being b-buried . . . in the . . . P-Pyramids . . . and B-Bel-Belzoni . . . choking to . . . death in a tomb . . . . That's . . . s-so horrible. I . . . I . . . didn't . . . m-mean it."

"Of course you didn't. How could you possibly have known?"

Rosa was eventually comforted and sat dabbing at her eyes, miserable for herself, for Eddy, and for her spoiled complexion.

Crisparkle, embarrassed at Rosa's distress, spoke to distract attention from her.

"You think that the jewellery I found at the weir had been taken from the body before it was put in the coffin, and then planted by the murderer?"

Now that his deposition had been made the lawyer sat watching, methodically stroking his sandy thatch. "My information from my *private* detective"—Mr Grewgious appeared to have taken a fancy to this unimaginative notion of his—"is that our local friend had an exact inventory of every piece of jewellery possessed by Edwin Drood. He would have had no difficulty in removing these pieces and planting them at the weir, I presume, reverend sir."

Neville Landless leaped excitedly from his chair. "But he would have known nothing of this ring, so he would have overlooked it when removing the jewellery he knew of from the body."

"Exactly so."

"Then the wretch has betrayed himself! If I could lay my hands on him!"

"One moment, Neville," interposed Crisparkle, quietening his pupil with a steady look, as well as with the tone of his voice. "Our task is not to punish the murderer. We must leave that to the law when the evidence of his guilt has been found. As I understand Mr Grewgious, we may be sure that we have found the last resting place of poor young Drood. Yet we have no firm proof that his uncle was the one responsible for his murder. Anyone could have removed his obvious jewellery, yet missed the ring in an inner pocket."

"That is precisely the legal position," assented the lawyer, inclining his head towards the Minor Canon, as if offering him a better view of his bad imitation of a wig.

"If this rogue Jasper can be scared into thinking there is something wrong in the tomb, he will go there to see what has happened. As only the murderer will know where the body was hidden, surely that would count heavily against him?" It was the practical sense of the sailor. Tartar spoke for the first time in a quiet voice that commanded attention.

"A good idea, Tartar," exclaimed his old master, seeing an opportunity to put the presumed guilt of Jasper to a test. "But how is it to be done?"

"Durdles the mason is likely to be told to inspect the tomb, I think you said, sir? If Jasper could be present when these instructions are given, this might suffice."

"The very idea that was in my own old head," replied Grewgious. "Our local friend regularly spends evenings with Sapsea to keep him in his pocket. Datchery shall arrange that Durdles will call at Sapsea's house during their next session. Our friend shall hear every word."

"One more point," said Tartar, his mind moving on practical detail. "If Jasper put Drood in Mrs Sapsea's coffin, what happened to her remains?"

"I have been able to obtain no definite information on this question." Mr Grewgious smoothed his head as he launched into the dangerous waters of speculation. "If I were to venture a supposition"—which called for an extra smoothing—"and of course this could only be a supposition without any evidence in support"—further smoothing—"it would be that when our friend removed the lime from the yard to destroy the body of Drood, he buried her remains in the heap so that they too would be speedily destroyed. In which case we must assume that no evidence will now remain."

"Suppose then," continued Tartar, "the mason can let drop that this batch of lime was defective. That should put Jasper in a panic that her remains have not yet been destroyed, and worse still, the body of Drood may still be recognisable in the coffin. That should send him under full sail to the tomb to find out."

Grewgious banged his fist on the table, so that the ring jumped and sparkled with a new life of its own.

174

"Capital!" he said.

"It may be for Jasper," replied the sailor.

"Supposing Jasper does go to the tomb," objected Crisparkle, who with his customary fairness had had second thoughts during this conversation. "It will still not prove that he is the murderer. He may say that he has just heard that the tomb is of great interest and that he wished to look at it first, before Durdles and the visitors."

"Certainly, he could say this, and it could be believed by some members of a jury." Grewgious's reply suggested that, as a lawyer, he was aware there were no limits to human credulity.

Neville Landless had been growing increasingly impatient with the arguments about legal proof, seeing his own ambiguous position stretching out into an unendurable future, while a succession of bewigged lawyers argued in a succession of dusty courts and never arrived at any final conclusion. "What we need is a confession," he burst out with nervous agitation. "That is the only way to show the world he is the murderer!"

"But how, Neville?" This time Crisparkle's question and steadying gaze have no effect.

"I have an idea." He jumped to his feet. "Look, I am much the same height and age as Drood. I know his characteristics well! I can disguise and dress myself to look like him. I will appear in the tomb when he goes to look at the coffin. He will think me either a ghost, or that Drood somehow escaped and is still alive. In either case it will be such a terrible shock he will probably break down and admit the deed!"

"He would see you at once in the tomb. There is no room for concealment," commented the Minor Canon.

"Then in the crypt of the Cathedral," cried Neville, so far from being deterred by the objection that he grew more excited as his ideas expanded. "There is plenty of space for concealment there. He can be lured there by a message left in the tomb. It could apparently be written by Drood himself. I could do that. I am good at copying writing. That will fill him with doubt and fear. Let him have a taste of his own medicine. Let the fear work on him. He must go to the crypt, if only to find out if Drood is living. Then Drood will appear before him. At that moment he will surely make some admission from his own lips!"

There was silence. The idea was appealing: to settle the matter beyond doubt by getting Jasper to confess the crime himself. Yet in every other mind rose the countervailing doubts whether Neville had the skill and the coolness of head to carry it off. Could he deceive Jasper? Would he not spoil all by some characteristic impetuous action? Could he be trusted not to fall on his hated enemy?

The silence was broken by his sister.

"It is a good idea of yours, Neville," said Helena with authority. "We should do all we can to trap this monster. But you and he are enemies too bitter for you to play the part. It falls to me."

"You!" exclaimed Crisparkle, his face portraying a mixture of surprise and admiration.

"Why not? Have you forgotten that I have lived in a more dangerous country than this disguised as a man? Do you think I have not studied the man who was to have married my friend and who quarrelled with my own twin brother? I am as tall as Neville. With the clothes, a wig, and those aids to appearance known to a woman, Jasper will believe in the darkness of the crypt that he is seeing his nephew."

"Bravo," applauded Tartar with enthusiasm. Such was Helena's quiet confidence that no one doubted her ability to do as she had said.

"The risk will be great," said Crisparkle, displaying some agitation.

"I have no fear of Jasper," responded Helena disdainfully.

"Suppose he tries to kill you?"

"Then, Canon, I hope you will be there to protect me," replied the lady, smiling at him. How could he deny such a request? A little pinker than usual in the cheeks, the Minor Canon subsided.

"On condition that your old fag is there to keep an eye on his master," declared Tartar, grinning at Crisparkle, who shook him warmly by the hand.

"What shall you do if he speaks to you?" asked Rosa, mindful of her ordeal with Jasper in the garden of the Nuns' House.

"I cannot speak with a man's voice, so I must remain silent," answered Helena. "But I can mime. I could suggest the rope to him." Her hand slowly pointed to her neck and upwards to an imaginary gallows. Her gaze dropping to the responsive stones on

176

the table, she continued: "And I can show him the ring. *He* will understand it was the ring Edwin was to place on Rosa's finger, and remained in his possession after their engagement was broken." With a quick movement—conveying withal the air of huntress—she picked it up. "Still better, I shall place it in his hand." Turning again to Crisparkle: "You told us, Canon, that he recorded in his diary an oath never to discuss the mystery until he held the clue to it in his hand. Then let the murderous hypocrite hold it and recall his own words!" Remembering that the ring was not hers to take, she added apologetically to the lawyer: "That is, if I may, Mr Grewgious?"

"If it will help to trap our friend, you may certainly have it, my dear," responded Grewgious in his usual voice, giving no indication that he was parting once again with the object which he held most precious in the world—or perhaps now second most precious? "On two conditions only. One, that Miss Rosa does not object to her mother's ring being so employed. Second, that I may be present as witness to our friend's reactions in the crypt." To which Mr Grewgious uttered under his breath a legal aside that sounded uncommonly like "Damn him".

Miss Rosa has no objections. The ring held nothing but morbid associations for her, and she felt something sinister had been removed when the bright circlet was taken from the table. And now that she had recovered from the first shock of seeing the visible proof of Eddy's death, his figure rose as powerfully and affectionately before her as on the day when Helena had broken to her the news of the lawyer's suspicions. She saw again her poor brother—for so Eddy seemed now in their long relationship—and she knew it was her bounden duty to be present when his presumed murderer was put to the test. The feeling was even stronger than her instinctive revulsion at the thought of Jasper: and surely there could be no danger with Mr Tartar in attendance. So she too put in her claim to be present.

Mr Grewgious was quite firm that Miss Rosa must not be in any position of risk, or add to the dangers that might be run by Helena. On her side Rosa was just as firm—in the prettiest way, as befitted an indulged and petted orphan from the Nuns' House. Yet if his heart was touched by her pleas, the head of her guardian remained as hard as its surface, and he was obdurate.

177

Neville, frustrated in his plan to play the part of Drood, then demanded that he should at least be present in the crypt with his sister. Yet the more excitedly he pressed his claim, the more he defeated his purpose. The silent consensus of the meeting was that he was too volatile, too undisciplined, too unreliable to be trusted even as a watcher in the crypt. So Mr Grewgious made a diplomatic suggestion: it might just be possible, all other circumstances being favourable, for Miss Rosa to be at the Cathedral in a safe observation post, say at the summit of the tower, whence a bird's-eye view might be obtained of the movements of the quarry below; but this would of course be quite out of the question unless Mr Neville would be good enough to act as her escort and protector, and join her as aerial observer. Neville could not refuse this proposal without appearing churlish. In this manner Rosa's wish was met without apparent risk, while her presence would ensure that Neville would remain on the tower, so that all would not be marred by some impetuous action on his part.

At any other time Neville would have been delighted to have Rosa as his companion, but now he was inwardly furious at thus being exiled from the scene of the drama he had himself devised. Unable to express his feelings openly, he made an immediate mental reservation. From the subtle telepathy that existed between himself and his twin sister he would know what was happening in the crypt almost as though he were playing the role himself. So he would don a hat and coat like Drood's, and play the part despite them all!

The council of war, having decided its strategy, sat long working out details of the plan. Then its members, all but one not displeased with the night's work, dispersed as unobtrusively as they had assembled. The last figure melted away under the observation of only old P.J.T., leaving Grewgious at last alone in his chambers. He gave a deep sigh—perhaps from relief that the discussion was over, perhaps for another reason. He went to a window and pushed it open, standing for a while gazing at the night sky, where the twinkling of the bright stars reminded him of something else, something he had twice possessed and twice handed to another. Grewgious closed the window, and his thoughts came back to the present and the plans that had been agreed upon that evening. He was not to know that the fateful decision of the evening was one that had remained unspoken.

CHAPTER XXXII

A LESSON AT THE WEIR

ON A BRIGHT afternoon two figures were to be seen taking Canon Crisparkle's favourite walk to Cloisterham Weir. The sun was shining from a sky with few clouds, and from time to time the wind moved odd fallen leaves from their path as if it were some invisible crossing sweeper clearing a passage for them. There was sufficient strength in that same invisible sweeper to raise up little wavelets on the water, such as those round Crisparkle's head when he went swimming in the morning. That afternoon the pair were too engrossed in their own thoughts to be paying heed to the antics of nature. The man, in clerical dress, was walking with his hands behind his back, his tall hat bending forward on his bowed head, seeing none of the sweeper's activities, and it was not until they were close that his features could be discerned as those of Crisparkle himself in this uncharacteristic pose. It became apparent from what he was saying to his companion that they were discussing the events in Cloisterham Cathedral for the first time since their occurrence.

". . . and I hold myself very much to blame, Miss Helena," he was saying to her.

"How can you say that, Canon?" was her spirited rejoinder. "We knew there must be risks in dealing with such a man, but we all agreed voluntarily to accept them in order to bring the wretch to justice. Poor Neville was the one who paid the price. It could have been any one of us."

He shook his head, still staring down at the ground.

"No, no! That is not the point. We all took a certain risk. The point is that the rest of you played your parts magnificently, while my actions caused the disaster."

"You must not look at it in this light," she answered with sympathy in her eyes.

"I fear I must, because it is the truth," continued Crisparkle. "Tartar was heroic, as I should have expected of him. How he climbed the outside of the tower when he realised that Rosa was in danger, using only the iron footholds left by the masons and the lightning conductor, only he and Heaven can know. It looks impossible by daylight. One slip in the dark and he would have been dashed to pieces."

"No one but a sailor could have done it. It was Providence that sent him."

"*You*, of course, were superb too. When the light from Jasper's lantern fell on you in the crypt, I give you my word I caught my breath. Even Jasper could not believe you were not his nephew, and you got the admission from him that he had put Drood in the coffin. You were Edwin Drood—to the life!"

"In life I did not think kindly of him," said Helena regretfully.

"You more than made amends for any lack of charity . . . And Neville could have done no more than he did. He not only died defending Rosa, he would have taken Jasper alive single-handed if he had not been stabbed."

"Poor Neville," said Helena softly. Then she turned her gypsy face to Crisparkle, so that he was forced to give up his stubborn inspection of the ground. "But, Canon, would not you have also defended me, if Jasper had attacked me in the crypt?"

"If only I might have had that honour," responded Crisparkle fervently.

Her lustrous eyes looked into his. "I know that, Canon," she said gently. "Thank God you did not have to. But had it been required of you, you would have done the same."

"Would . . . would . . . would," repeated her companion with some bitterness. "All I did in reality was to make the mistake that led to the tragedy . . . When Jasper shouted and dashed from the crypt, I followed him. Not being as familiar with the place as he was, I lost ground and he got ahead of me in the dark. I thought he was running from the building in panic, and I made for the Cathedral door. The others followed me, so Jasper got up the tower unobserved. That was my terrible error." He sighed deeply.

"It was only natural you should have thought and acted so," she replied firmly. "Jasper should not have been able to get up the tower."

He was not to be persuaded, his mind still filled with vivid images. "I shall never, never forget what happened then. You, still in Drood's clothes, following from the crypt into the chancel, crying out that something terrible was happening on the tower,

180

that Neville and Jasper were fighting to the death. Then clutching your side in pain . . ."

Her face went pale. "I felt the knife in Neville's side."

". . . and a few seconds later you gave a fearful scream . . ."

"I was falling with Neville from the tower."

". . . you collapsed to the ground, your limbs jerked convulsively and finally you passed into a profound swoon." Crisparkle's healthful face was haggard as he re-lived the memory.

"That was the impact and the final agony."

Both were silent for some seconds before he continued in a low voice. "As soon as we had brought you back to consciousness, you started up, ran from the Cathedral . . . We found him there . . ."

Almost at the Weir now, they walked on without speaking, until he spoke again. "I felt I should not leave you, yet my duty lay elsewhere. With what feelings I cannot tell you, I left you and ran to the top of the tower. I arrived at the moment everything was over. Tartar unlocked the door as I reached it. Jasper was on the ground. All I had to do was to secure him until the police handcuffed him . . . These scenes are seared upon my memory for ever. I shall never, never forget them."

Helena stopped walking, and Crisparkle followed suit. Turning to face him, she placed her gloved right hand upon his left sleeve and looked into his eyes as she spoke:

"These are memories we all share, that none of us will forget. You must not dwell on them and continue to reproach yourself because you think you were responsible.

"You made one small mistake. It would not have mattered had not other far worse mistakes been made. Neville had been told by Mr Tartar to lock the gate to the tower stairs and the door at the summit after him when he and Rosa went up. In his excitement poor Neville forgot, and so let Jasper up the tower. But that is not all . . . The worst mistake was mine—a much more culpable mistake, as I had the time to reflect and you did not. I knew what was in Neville's mind. I knew he would want to play the part of Drood on the tower, would want to dress like me. I did nothing to stop him. I thought it would be harmless, that it would be some compensation to him for not being allowed to play the part himself in the crypt. So I did nothing. It was a tragic error. It was that which cost my poor brother his life."

181

Crisparkle looked aghast. "I never thought of that. My poor Helena. How dreadful for you. But you acted in all good faith. You must not reproach yourself."

"I do not." She looked up at him seriously." There is something else I must say to you, even though it may seem callous and cruel." He nodded. "Neville and I knew and understood each other's feelings and thoughts. But our natures were not the same. Though I was the woman and he the man, he was the more emotional. You of all men know only too well the violence of his feelings. Under your tutelage, and I shall be eternally grateful to you for it, he did make great efforts to discipline himself. Yet the old Neville kept breaking through. Despite all your help and guidance my brother would never have settled into society."

"Never is a strong word."

"I use it advisedly. If he could have been taught to master himself, it would have been by you. Yet at heart he remained the same Neville. His life would have been one of outbursts, quarrels, friction with those about him in his ungoverned moments."

Crisparkle shook his head. "It distresses me to hear you speak so."

"It is the truth, whether we like it or no. Listen to me. I *know* because I felt it all here." She raised her hand and touched her breast. "Don't you understand, there were two people in me, not one. Since Neville died, there has been a terrible gap inside me. You cannot imagine what it is like to lose half of yourself. It must be what a devoted husband or wife feels when the other dies."

Crisparkle opened his mouth to speak, thought better of it, and stayed silent.

"Yet despite this sense that I am only half myself, for the first time in my life I know peace. That other half was turbulent, unhappy, frustrated, doomed to disappointment—and all of this was echoed in me. I could never be happy while Neville lived, and nor could he. Now he is at peace . . . and I am also."

She looked earnestly into his face to see how he received her confession. He stood pensive, his face betraying nothing.

"If it was the will of Providence that my poor brother should be given peace, is it our place to question it? And if we were in some measure the instruments of that Will, what need have we to reproach ourselves?"

The Minor Canon stood silent for a few moments. Then he raised Helena's hand to his lips.

"I may once have been your teacher and Neville's," he said with humility. "Now you have become mine. You have lifted a great burden from my shoulders."

Side by side they walked on towards the Weir, her arm on his. When they reached it, they stood together and watched the water pouring over. It seemed to the Minor Canon that the sense of guilt he had felt since the death of Neville Landless was flowing over the Weir with the water, away to the sea. If he were partly responsible, he shared that responsibility now with Helena, and that brought them closer together. And if, as she had said, it was a greater Design, of which he was one part, what could he as a clergyman do but accept it thankfully?

As he watched the water, it seemed very long ago that he had swum here, searching for Drood's body—when all the time it had lain so close to his own Cathedral. Truth was indeed strange! He knew now that John Jasper was a murderer who had killed Edwin Drood and Neville Landless. Yet he also knew that he was a devoted uncle whose life had revolved around his nephew and who had doted on him. The mystery remained as profound as ever, as inexplicable as the existence of Evil in God's world.

CHAPTER XXXIII

THE SECRETS OF THE PRISON-HOUSE

JOHN JASPER WAS condemned to death at the Assize for the wilful murder of Neville Landless. The prisoner continued to deny any responsibility for the death of Edwin Drood, and claimed to have acted only in self-defence against Landless. Since he plainly had killed Landless by hurling him from the Cathedral tower, he now sat in the condemned cell in Maidstone jail awaiting his determined day of execution, two weeks hence.

Canon Crisparkle had felt it his duty to offer such solace as he could to the former Choir Master; his offer had been refused. Then a letter had come from the prison chaplain to say that Jasper had asked to see him. Crisparkle had responded at once, and so had been conducted along gloomy echoing passages, permeated with the unmistakable smell of prison, with heavy studded doors at intervals. At the end of a long passage on an upper floor the silent jailer stopped before the final door, unlocked it, and motioned him to pass inside. Not without a slight hesitation, Crisparkle went alone into the condemned cell. He was expecting to find a dark and fearful place, for so he had imagined the last stopping place for a succession of murderers before the grave must be—he found himself in a low and narrow cell bright with white walls and ceiling.

The whiteness was so striking, so clean, that walls and ceiling must have been newly lime-washed. Perhaps such redecoration was needed for a new tenant, even upon such a short lease, to cover up the despairing scribblings of the last tenant whose lease had expired? Light flooded in from a long barred window high in the wall touching the white ceiling, that in turn reflected it pitilessly down into the small cell. The simple furniture was ranged against one wall: a wooden bed, a deal table, a plain chair. A heavy black Bible was placed exactly in the centre of the table. There was no place for concealment, even for a mouse. Here all was revealed, even the dreadful knowledge which the rest of mankind is mercifully spared of the exact moment and manner of death.

Coming from the gloom of the corridor, Crisparkle blinked as he entered and did not immediately perceive the man in prison clothing lying on the bed in an uneasy doze, until he started as the cell door clanged shut and rose to his feet.

"I am sorry, Crisparkle . . . I fear I was day-dreaming. There is little else to do here . . . ."

"Thank you for coming. The chaplain said he would be good enough to write to you. Pray take the chair."

The prisoner's hair had been cropped close, giving a convict air that added to the gauntness of his face. His cheeks were sunken, with rings beneath the haunted eyes as though he slept little in this place. Yet there was an irony about the mouth and in his manner.

Crisparkle did as he was bidden, while the other seated himself on the bed.

"It seems very bare here. Is there anything I can obtain for your comfort?" asked the visitor.

"I fear your chair is the only kind that the prison authorities provide," said the prisoner with a wry twist of his full lips. "In answer to your kind enquiry, yes, there is one thing. I prefer to make that request of you later. In general, I lack for nothing. I am accustomed to prison. All my life has been spent in a prison. The only difference here is to know that I shall soon be leaving the prison-house for ever."

The dark, gaunt face looked at Crisparkle with a humourless smile. "I have not asked you here today, Canon, to obtain the consolation of religion, nor to make a confession. Yet I need some other being to share with me the burden of the past. Are you willing to take an apple from the tree of knowledge?"

"I will hear all you have to say," replied Crisparkle.

The prisoner shot him a quizzical look, then settled his back against the wall, and began his story.

"You will know well from your classical studies that Egyptian jasper was a stone much used in ancient art. I have read somewhere the description of the stone—'The jasper is somewhat green, yet specked with bloody spots.' It is not inapt." Again the humourless smile. "It is also said to be a word of Oriental origin . . . in Arabic it is *yashb*. Again not inapt, for John Jasper was born in Cairo of an Egyptian mother."

Crisparkle gave a start of surprise which the prisoner noted with silent, inward amusement, then continued his narrative. He spoke of Jasper as though he were another man, with complete detachment.

"Jasper's father was an Englishman who was born at the turn of the century. He was training to be a civil engineer, and as a young man went to Paris at the time when it became fashionable to go to the Continent again at the end of the Napoleonic wars. Here he happened to meet some of the men of science who had accompanied Napoleon on his expedition to Egypt. Their accounts of this exotic, and in England still little-known, country, filled the young man with the resolve to go there. He arrived at a time when the energetic ruler Mehemet Ali was just beginning to introduce Western knowledge to his country. So the young man remained to do engineering work and eventually to found an engineering firm there. His name was John Drood.

"Egypt then was still strictly governed by Muslim codes of

conduct. As a bachelor, John Drood could not obtain quarters at first except in a merchants' warehouse. He was an easy-going young man—much as his son Edwin was later to become—in a hot country among a sensual people. The women looked doubly attractive to him with their eyes enhanced by kohl and the veils across their faces. A few doors away from him lived a pretty young widow in search of another husband, who allowed him to catch sight of her unveiled face several times, a clear invitation to him. No formalities were required, no ceremony, documents, or even witnesses were essential for a marriage. A single sentence uttered by the woman made her a man's wife. So John Drood drifted easily into acquiring an Egyptian wife, as his son almost drifted into marriage a generation later. In due course a son was born, and named John after his father. By some whim his mother nicknamed him Jasper.

"His mother pampered him, not only from her natural love for her child, but, divorce being so easy under Muslim law, he represented the Egyptian woman's chief hold over her husband. No other children were born, rendering this son especially precious. He was normally confined to the house, and not allowed to mix with other children, so he grew up a lonely, spoilt child. With his father he learned to speak English, but as John Drood was often away for long periods at engineering sites outside the capital, the child spent much of his time with his mother, speaking Arabic. His great delight was to be allowed to accompany her about the streets of Cairo, where the houses had overhanging upper stories and latticed windows—behind which the water jars would cool in summer—and open-fronted shops sold goods of all kinds. His favourites were the sellers of sweetmeats, especially the delicious *lokum*, Turkish delight, containing nuts, and the street conjurers that would sometimes be found performing their miracles among the colourful crowds and bustle of the capital. Camels might wend their way among the people, bringing goods in convoy from distant places, or the surviving pilgrims, safely returned from the hazardous journey to Mecca. There were beggars, merchants, holy men, the strange Copts, dervishes, the veiled women—all the busy life and excitement of Cairo. On these expeditions his mother would be veiled and well dressed, while he walked beside her in ragged and filthy clothes. It was not neglect on her part, rather the reverse. For it would be unlucky if the child were admired, risking the Evil Eye, so in public it was the custom for children to appear thus in rags. Poor woman—she tried to avert misfortune and the Evil Eye and did not succeed for herself, or for her son.

"As her husband was a Frank and a Christian, she decided that she must be a Christian too. She had little real understanding of that religion, and she could not attend a church—the first chanting ever heard by John Jasper was that of Muslim children learning the Koran! Her husband did not approve of her using henna to dye her hands and to ornament her feet, as was the local fashion, so she had tattooed in blue on her arm the Christian cross—more perhaps a talisman to secure her husband's love than a religious sign. One day at the public baths—as much a place for ladies to gather and amuse themselves as a bathing place—one of her jealous former friends saw the blue cross on her bare arm and denounced her as an apostate from the faith of Islam. She was seized, taken before a court and sentenced, while John Drood was away working on the construction of a new canal. She was mounted on the high saddled ass that ladies usually rode, attended by soldiers and surrounded by a rabble reviling her. (The Cairo mob was ever volatile—and there is no more vicious mob than one inspired by religious fanaticism!) She was taken in a boat to the middle of the Nile, stripped nearly naked, half strangled and then thrown into the water. A song was even composed about her fate, and became very popular in Cairo at the time. Such were the people and customs where John Jasper was born and spent his early years!

"Drood heard of his wife's arrest at his distant canal site. He instantly began the journey back by camel. It took several days. He was too late. He was attached to his exotic wife, and at first was almost distracted with grief. He thought of leaving the country for good, and did return to England for a time, leaving the child in the care of his wife's relatives. Once in England he was soon attracted by another, and married an Englishwoman as his second wife. With this new responsibility he decided to return to Egypt, where he had already started to carve out a successful career. He did not admit his previous marriage to an Egyptian: while his first marriage was valid by local custom and law, there was no documentary proof that it had ever existed, and he chose to ignore it. The new Mrs Drood loathed Egypt. She soon returned to England for the birth of her son, Edwin—named after her husband's father—and never went back to Cairo. Being of a somewhat sickly disposition, she had no more children and concentrated her affections on young Edwin while her husband continued to work in Egypt. After enjoying ill-health for a number of years she finally died without ever learning of her husband's previous marriage. He for his part had some qualms of conscience over leaving his first son to be brought up as a young Egyptian, and on next visit to England brought the boy with him. He was placed with foster parents under the name of John Jasper.

"Have you any notion of the feelings of that child?" demanded the narrator fiercely, suddenly losing the impersonal tone in which he had recounted the story of John Drood. "Can you understand the feelings of that solitary child in Cairo, loved by his parents and especially pampered and protected by his mother, having her taken from him in circumstances of public shame that, small as he was, he was still old enough to understand? Then to be left with relatives who cared little for him, to whom he was an embarrassment, the child of an apostate? Can you understand how that child felt utterly abandoned by both his parents, lost and unloved? The sense of desolation, of neglect, the utter hopelessness? . . . No I think you cannot. None but a child who has had such an experience can know what it means. . . . And after that to be taken from the country that he knew and placed with foster parents—honest folk who took their money and fed and clothed the child, but quite without imagination or any understanding of what went on inside his mind: transported suddenly into a world that was alien in customs, climate, clothing, food, outlook—everything. He might have died and been translated from the warm world he once knew to some cold spirit world. Indeed, it felt to him like death." The narrator was silent for a while, staring with fixed, sightless gaze at his listener, as though re-living past scenes and emotions from that childhood. Then he resumed his story in his previous manner.

"In England John Jasper was a lonely, and at first a backward, child. He sang to console himself, and being found by the local parson to have a good voice, a place was found for him in a choir school. Here the masters were kindly, sorry for the strange boy—his fellow pupils were not so kind. His darkness of skin, foreign ways, and indifferent knowledge of English made him an outsider, the natural butt of their jokes. By nature warm-hearted and emotional, he grew introverted, learning to conceal his emotions. So he never made any close friends at school. He remained apart from his fellows for the rest of his schooldays . . . and for the rest of his life. At school he was known as The Sphinx, on the schoolboy grounds that he came from Egypt, yet the name was so appropriate that it stuck with him until he left. The schooling he received there was not particularly good, except for music, a principal study in which the grounding was thorough, and music was also something into which his frustrated emotions could be poured so that he passed beyond mere mechanical excellence to becoming an accomplished singer and musician.

"Whenever he came to England John Drood paid a secret visit to his elder son, bringing him presents from Egypt that would remind him of his native country. After the death of his second wife—Drood never remarried—he was able to introduce the two boys to each other. John Jasper inevitably knew the truth, while Edwin Drood always accepted him without question as a maternal uncle. So too in time did everyone: Durdles little dreamed that when showing Jasper the sarcophagus of 'your own brother-in-law', he was pointing out to him the grave of his father!

"For John Jasper, after his years of loneliness, to acquire a younger brother was a gift beyond price. Here at last was someone on whom his natural affection could be lavished. His desire to have roots, belong somewhere, to love and be loved, all found their object in Edwin Drood. His 'nephew' became the focus of his life. The boy eventually went to a public school, and in his own way became quite fond of his 'Uncle', often staying with him in the holidays. Jasper on his side never became reconciled to being addressed as 'Uncle', for this suggested an artificial gap between them, and he was invariably jealous of anything divisive in their relationship. For this reason, too, he knew that the secret of their real bond must for ever remain locked in his own breast: true marriage as his mother's to John Drood had been under Muslim law, it would have no recognition in Christian England, and he

189

was only too well aware that revelation of the truth would unspeakably shock the conventional young man that Edwin was growing into at his public school. So John Jasper remained silent; hungry, watchful and exacting in his affection. His Egyptian blood gave a warmth that to the Anglo-Saxon Edwin was sometimes irksome, even womanish; his education made Edwin despise as molly-coddling the fussy attentions that John Jasper had received from his mother and now instinctively lavished on his young kinsman. Yet despite the petty irritations caused by their differences in temperament and upbringing, the bond of affection was genuine enough on Edwin's side, even though he was not subtle enough to sense its full depths on Jasper's.

"John Drood had been a robust enough man when he first went to Egypt. His exertions there, combined with the climate, began to affect his health after some years, and on the advice of doctors he returned and spent a year in England to recruit his strength. He arrived to find that an old college friend, Henry Bud, had just lost his wife through drowning. With natural sympathy for a man whose fate was so like his own, he did his best to comfort him: Bud having a pretty young daughter, Rosa, the idea grew up between them that she and Edwin might one day marry. Under the shock of his wife's death Bud went into a decline that ended in his own death a year later, and it was more to comfort the dying man than from any strong conviction on his own side that Drood drew up the betrothal plan. After Bud's death he returned to Egypt and built up his engineering firm. Eventually he contracted a disease, thought to be from the water, and returned to England for the last time, now a dying man himself. He decided to spend his last days in the quiet of Cloisterham.

"He was gratified to learn that such a good understanding now existed between his two sons, aged twenty-one and fifteen respectively, and with a dying man's desire to settle family affairs, and in some measure to make amends to Jasper for not being acknowledged as the elder son, left him a small legacy and in his will made him the guardian of Edwin; the bulk of his capital lay in the engineering partnership in Egypt, which it was arranged Edwin should take over as soon as he qualified. Several years after the death of John Drood, John Jasper, who on leaving school had obtained a musical post, and enjoyed a growing reputation for such a young man, was appointed Lay Precentor and Choir Master of Cloisterham Cathedral.

"Jasper soon began to teach those pupils at the local schools who required special tuition in music, so Rosa, for whom nothing was too good, naturally became one of his pupils. The combination of her dark eyes and her fair-skinned beauty, even as a schoolgirl, transfixed Jasper as so many fair Circassian slaves had captivated their masters in Cairo. At first he worshipped her from a distance, for was she not destined to marry Edwin? Slowly the casual, patronising attitude of Drood himself towards the girl transformed Jasper's distant adoration into a burning passion to possess her himself. So too his thinking changed. He and Rosa shared a common history that could not be mere chance: her mother had died young, so had his; Rosa's had been drowned in a river, such had been the fate of his own; both were in effect orphans without a home of their own. The parallel course of their destinies proved to him beyond question that their fates were foreordained, that Rosa Bud was destined to be his.

"The physical closeness of their music lessons then became a torment to him. He remained loyal to Drood in observing the outward proprieties, while he was unable to resist endeavouring to implant in Rosa the passion that was consuming him. He had discovered while at school that under emotional stress he had some abnormal power of reading the thoughts of others and implanting his own in their minds—perhaps some gift inherited in his mother's blood from the famous sorcerers of Egypt?—and this faculty had been useful to him as teacher and Choir Master. His experiments at school were only sometimes successful, and, even when they were, the practical result had unhappily been to increase his reputation for oddity, giving 'The Sphinx' a sinister as much as a humorous meaning. So too for his fair pupil. The feminine sensitivity of Rosa made her more perceptive of his emanations than his schoolfellows had been, and in the same proportion increased her aversion to him. What he interpreted at first as maidenly shrinking, or even a feminine wile, was, as he finally could not disguise from himself, repugnance on the part of Rosa. Yet he could not bring himself to desist, even when his efforts caused his beloved to faint in the Crisparkles' drawing room, and the only result of this secret wooing was mounting frustration.

"During this time his equally deeply rooted affection for Edwin Drood remained to all appearance unaffected. That too was part of his being, his own response to the loneliness, uncertainties and emotional starvation of his own childhood. Yet deep within him, unformulated and unacknowledged, a profound resentment against Drood was building up. It began with frustration over the woman he so passionately desired with all his ardent Eastern blood. Drood's casual attitude towards her could only be salt in the wounds of his rejected rival. It was bad enough that Drood should be able to possess the woman Jasper wanted so easily, without effort—even without will; that he should belittle her in the bargain was almost unbearable. His water-colour of her that hung in the Gate House was the shrine of Jasper's goddess, and was at the same time a constant outrage in its parody of her looks. Yet this was not all. Was he not the legitimate elder son of John Drood, and so the rightful fiancé of Rosa Bud? It was *he* who should have the right to her in marriage! His claim was in every way stronger than that of Drood.

"Jasper's need for his nephew was too great for such resentment even to take shape within his conscious thoughts. His constant jealous watch on their relationship would censor them deep down in the mines of the mind. Even so, they were not destroyed, remaining as a poison carried by underground streams through these great subterranean caverns, leading to new areas of deep bitterness. For if Drood as the younger son had no right to Rosa, what right had he to the other benefits he had received at his elder brother's expense? To the superior education at one of England's great schools, while Jasper had had to sing for the paltry schooling he had received? To the professional education that would enable him to live comfortably for the rest of his life, while Jasper could never aspire to rise higher than mere music-master? To a way of life that would enable him to marry in ease, while Jasper's resources were hardly more than sufficient for one? To the inheritance of the family business when Jasper had only a petty legacy? In every way Edwin Drood had robbed his elder brother of his birthright. He became the thief of another's property, the supplanter, the enemy.

"In Jasper's conscious thoughts Edwin Drood still remained his beloved 'nephew', the centre of his life and being, whom he was always eager to see and welcome at Cloisterham. In reality the two people he loved most in the world, Edwin and Rosa, were inwardly tearing him apart. This unresolved inner conflict brought terrible depressions, then despair, upon Jasper. Not understanding their origin, he attributed them to unrequited love, so refuelling his own inner tension. He began to despair of his sanity, to avoid the company of his fellows. He sought distraction in low haunts, and would probably have taken to the bottle if a sailor he met in such a place had not talked to him of opium. He knew it was used as a solace in the East, so he followed the sailor's instructions and made his way to the den of the opium woman in the East End of London.

"At first the opium pipe brought wonderful relief. Under its influence all the forbidden thoughts that were tormenting him welled up into immensely satisfying visions. To begin with the repressed hatred of Drood made him the victim of the dreamer. Always they travelled together mysteriously up the great Tower of Cloisterham Cathedral, Jasper with the unsuspecting Drood as fellow-traveller. There were awful abysses on every side, past which they finally reached the summit. Here the interloper was half-strangled, just as Jasper's mother had been strangled, and despite his abject pleas for mercy tossed still living and screaming from the Tower to be impaled below, like the thief he was, Eastern-fashion upon a spear. Then would follow the splendid colourful processions recalling the scenes of his childhood mingled with the Arabian Nights, and voluptuous houris, all in the likeness of Rosa. In this opium paradise, he would sing melodiously. After, he would hurry back to Cloisterham, purged of his torment for the time, remembering nothing of his murderous vision.

These respites grew shorter and less effective. As he could not always absent himself to reach the den in London, he obtained some opium and took to smoking a pipe in secret in his own quarters. He even tried laudanum—opium in alcohol—counting the red drops into a wine glass. The results were never as satisfying as the pipes of the opium woman, so from time to time he hurried back to her. Yet even her skill could not prevent the drug from losing some of its effect, nor, worse still, the growing symptoms of his addiction: the terrifying dreams that haunted his sleep in which he wandered through empty nightmare palaces and sinister landscapes. At times he would go into waking dreams in the daytime. Hallucinations would seize him in the Cathedral in the course of the service, when all about him acquired a fearful unreality. So eventually the opium that had begun as a comfort ended by adding to his torments. Opium can be a good friend—it is a friendship for which a usurious price is finally exacted!

"He now reached the brink of insanity. What saved him from Bedlam was his very weakness. He had always been divided from his birth: by blood he belonged half to North Africa and half to England; his most impressionable years were spent in the Muslim world of Cairo, his education was in England. He had no firm roots, no real family. Profoundly divided by background and by blood, he was additionally torn apart within himself, one half of him hating the man whom the other half clung to with an obsessive, almost maternal feeling. Under what had become intolerable tensions, his personality finally ruptured. He broke into two halves as his conflicting emotions polarised into two individuals . . . It happened in that very opium den that had ceased to bring its old relief. On emerging from an opium dream, he was looking at the woman, wondering what comfort she got from the drug, when a seizure compelled him to sit in her chair, clinging to its arms. It was the birth pangs of the second personality, uninhibited by the old restraints on Jasper, revengeful, violent. The new man fell at once on a sleeping Chinaman, starting to strangle him, then on a Lascar who tried to draw a knife— violent from the very start! He could not even see a knife, in the company of Edwin Drood, without the temptation to plunge it in him. So let us call this personality The Murderer. But the other personality, whom we may continue to call John Jasper, remained the possessive and affectionate 'uncle' that he always had been, tenderly and fussily watching over the welfare of Edwin Drood. As each personality was utterly incompatible with the other, each had to take its turn in possession of the physical body.

"The change from one master to the other was a physical agony. As one personality emerged to take command and drove the other back, a short but fierce struggle took place within the body, accompanied by a rigor, an unwholesome sweat, and a glazing of the eyes; a passing weakness followed. These fits bore little resemblance to opium day-dreams. Strange they should have been seen by others, yet never recognised for what they were! And the consequence of those fits should have been clear. Even Drood noticed dimly that after his paroxysm on *her* birthday, his uncle was 'very unlike' his usual self. He was right: a different man was inhabiting the Choir Master's body. The affectionate fussing uncle who had welcomed him, and whose face always expressed hungry, watchful affection when addressed in his direction, was not the man emerging from the fit—controlled, bitter, insincere, yet sinister with warning. Drood thought, poor fool, that his uncle was sacrificing himself. He little thought *he* was to be the sacrifice! Yet why blame the young man? Even that damned sharp lawyer didn't suspect that the Jasper exhausted by hunting for his nephew was not the man who recovered from the fainting fit. *That* was The Murderer, voracious and plausible, deceiving you too, if I remember correctly Crisparkle?"

"Yes," assented Crisparkle, though in a daze. He did not know whether he was dreaming, but he did know that what he had heard offered a solution, bizarre as it was, to the paradox that had so puzzled him.

"If I understand you aright," he went on, "there are two quite different personalities that take turns in control of the body."

"Yes," replied the gaunt man without expression.

"Then what decides which one is in control at any time?"

"Normally John Jasper is in control. The Murderer takes over if action or planning for his own ends is required."

"So in a crisis The Murderer returns?"

"Of course . . . As when Grewgious announced that the engagement had been broken; or the news that the tomb was to be inspected and that the lime used to destroy Drood's body might not have done its work."

"And the occasion on Rosa's birthday to which you referred?"

"That was a critical moment also. It was Drood's last chance to renounce her before the plans for his death were put in motion."

Crisparkle frowned. "Surely, though, each personality must be aware of the actions performed by the other?"

"By no means. These personalities are two different states of being, and what is done in one state of being is not necessarily known in another. So if you should get drunk and lose your watch—something I am sure you have never done, Canon, but this is a scientific fact—" the prisoner gave one of his mirthless grins at Crisparkle—"you may not be able to recall what you have done with it when you are sober, and only remember when you are drunk again."

"Do you mean that neither Jasper nor The Murderer is aware of the actions that have been performed by the other?"

"Not entirely. The Murderer knows everything. He rises from a deeper level, below that of normal consciousness, so he is aware of all, while Jasper has no suspicion of his existence or of his murderous actions."

"So Jasper has no knowledge of the murder of Drood?"

"None."

"Surely he must have had some inklings, some suspicions?"

"No. If anything reaches his consciousness, he believes it to be no more than the fantasy of an opium dream."

"So Jasper's pursuit of the murderer was quite sincere?"

"Wholly sincere." The prisoner gave his mouth a wry twist. "He little realised he was pursuing himself."

"And his professions to Rosa in the garden of the Nuns' House were also genuine?"

"Entirely genuine. He truly believed he was being disloyal to his dear boy in offering to abandon his search for the murderer in return for her love. When he spoke of his labours in the cause of a just vengeance for six toiling months, he spoke no more than the exact truth as he knew it. He was offering the greatest sacrifice he could make to win her."

A fresh thought struck into Crisparkle's soul at these words. Courageous a man as he was, he felt a sudden chill as if a deathly hand had been laid upon him.

"You know everything," he said. "So you must be . . ."

"Yes," said the prisoner. "I am The Murderer."

CHAPTER XXXIV

SPECKED WITH BLOODY SPOTS

"I AM THE Murderer," repeated the prisoner. "Only I can tell you how Drood died.

"I did not have to plan his murder—all I had to do was to turn the vision into reality."

The man's coolly ironic gaze held Crisparkle's eyes as he continued his story in the hard light of the white cell.

"Yet one thing the vision did not show me: how to dispose of the body. As though by fate, the solution presented itself when Durdles was given the key of the Sapsea tomb in my presence. I relieved him of it in the churchyard when opening his bundle to give him his hammer! With it I was able to carry out a reconnaissance of the tomb and assure myself that I could open the coffin and get Drood's body inside. I took a wax impression of the key, so that a locksmith in London who asks no questions could make me a duplicate, and I was able to slip the original back in Durdles's house. He never knew it had been out of his possession. I had my own keys to the Cathedral and the Tower, and I could now go wherever needful for the murder.

"It only remained to prepare the tomb. That I did the night Durdles took me up the tower. I gave him opium in his drink, and while he slept I took his key and locked him in the crypt to make doubly sure. I opened the coffin and buried the remains of Mrs Sapsea in the heap of quick-lime so they would never be found. I put quick-lime in the coffin, with more in the tomb ready to cover Drood's body—if anyone had chanced to find it, it would have been thought rubbish left by Durdles's men! The sot slept through it all."

Crisparkle's eyes remained on the man with the features of Edwin Drood's uncle, that over-affectionate uncle who had been so wrapped up in his nephew that his life had revolved about him. The dark drawn face was the same, even though the hair, cut short in prison gave a different look to him; yet the face itself was not so different as the expression and those cold eyes while he unemotionally recounted his preparations for killing the young man! Crisparkle had earlier experienced shock and horror as the story of Jasper had unfolded, but as his mind had comprehended the full enormity of this dual being it seemed as though he had passed beyond the point of emotion and, like the narrator himself, had become void of all feeling. He was drained alike of emotion and of strength, almost paralysed. He looked at the other fascinated, as a rabbit might watch a stoat, and had The Murderer now fallen upon him he would scarce have been able to move a muscle in that athletic frame in his own defence. But the mind of The Murderer was on another quarry.

"There was a risk that someone might hear the cry of the falling body, or find it before I could descend from the tower—but not a grave risk. I knew that few people cared to walk in the Precincts late at night. I learned from Durdles the chance was even less at Christmas. The Christmas before, Jasper had let out a shriek of despair there in his torment. Only Durdles and a dog had heard. So I had to make sure that Durdles had drink enough to make him sleep through the Last Trump. My chief concern was that accursed Deputy. But Christmas kept him off the street, while Durdles was too drunk to go out, let alone be stoned home.

"Another stroke of fate. The arrival of Landless gave me the perfect suspect." The Murderer indulged in brief silent laughter at the memory. "I read Landless like a book. He had a mixture of hot blood in his veins, the same deprived upbringing as myself, the same resentments—I knew him like my own hand. I could play any tune on him I wished. To make him and Drood quarrel would have been absurdly easy, even without the inflammatory drink I gave them. All I needed to do then was spread the news of the quarrel. As for bringing them together at the time of the murder, it was you who so thoughtfully arranged that, Crisparkle!

"The murder itself I had accomplished a million times. I knew what needed to be done."

As he began to speak of the murder, it seemed to Crisparkle that his voice became deeper. The ironic smile disappeared from his mouth, his eyes no longer looked at Crisparkle but saw another scene. He continued in melodious tones as though deep within him was the desire to sing, and yet withal there was a note of sadness as if the song were disappointing to the singer.

"When Drood came back from his walk by the river with Landless that night," he went on mellifluously, "he seemed depressed,

198

even edgy. I know the reason now, but then I did not know of his parting from Rosa. So while I had to get him up the Tower, he wanted to go to bed. Normally I would have had little trouble in persuading 'my dear boy' to do as I wished. That night he was stubborn. At last the storm enabled me to persuade him that it must be seen from the vantage point of the Tower. As we made our way in the teeth of the storm to the Cathedral, the wind got under the brim of his hat and sent it sailing into the graveyard, where it was lost among the tombs. In the darkness we searched for it in vain. After this he wanted to change his mind again. It needed all my power of persuasion to cajole him into the Cathedral and up the Tower.

"On the summit the wind was so fierce we clung to the stonework to keep our footing. It was impossible to speak there, so I had no chance to tell him the things that were in my heart, why I was killing him, or to listen to his pleas. Deeds had to take the place of the words I had ready. As he watched the play of distant lightning on the sea, I slipped my silk scarf over his head and started to garrot him. He began to struggle and then, quite suddenly his struggles ceased, though I knew him to be still conscious. The will to resist, to live, had died before his body. It puzzled me then. Now I understand that too. His rejection by Rosa had hurt him more than he would admit. When he realised that the only other person in his life, his uncle, had turned on him also, something broke in that spoilt young man, who never had a real problem in his life. He was dead in spirit before I killed him. There was no more satisfaction than in strangling a corpse. Nor could I even hurl him from the tower, when the wind was another invisible killer trying to dislodge us both from the summit. As I released my grip and hung on to the parapet, he fell across the stonework, slid limply over, and dropped down the side of the tower without a sound—or any that could be heard above the storm. He broke his fall on the hands of the tower clock and tore them off. Then he became a minute spot visible only in the lightning, lying at the foot of the tower . . . .

"The rest you will know. The body was soon conveyed to the tomb near by. I removed his jewellery—except that ring I knew nothing of—put him in the coffin covered with the corrosive layer and resealed it. It took me as long to find his hat as to do the rest. I

199

dared not leave that until daylight, in case it should be discovered as proof that Drood had returned alive from his walk by the river with Landless. Eventually I did find it, caught on a gravestone. I cut it in pieces and burned them in the grate. . . . The watch that Drood had inherited from his grandfather Edwin through his father, and that still had the initials E.D. on it, together with his distinctive pin, I kept."

He gave Crisparkle a curious look before he went on with his story. His voice had returned to its normal tone.

"I had only one fear of discovery," he said, "that Durdles's hammer might detect the new body in the Sapsea tomb before the quick-lime had done its work. Jasper had already served me well in organising the search for his dear boy along the river, well away from the graveyard. When Grewgious told him that the engagement had been broken off between Drood and Rosa—and I had to take over again in a devil of a hurry!—I saw the chance to do even better. I decided to propound the view to Grewgious, and to you too when you came in, Crisparkle, that the young man had left Cloisterham of his own free will to avoid the embarrassment of his new situation.

"I think I convinced you, did I not? It suited me well, for the search for him in Cloisterham would have been called off altogether. . . . It was *you* who kindly changed my mind for me, Crisparkle."

"I?"

"Yes. You were good enough to inform us that Neville Landless believed himself to be in love with Rosa. For aught I knew he was the real reason for the breaking of the engagement. Do you not understand? I had removed one rival from my path, when you told me I had another!"

His cold eyes looked straight at the Canon.

"So I had to destroy him too. He had to be cast in the role of Drood's murderer again. But I could hardly alter my views on Drood's disappearance so quickly to you and Grewgious, and I employed a small stratagem." With his ironic smile, he asked, "Do you know why you went to the Weir that day?"

"I am not sure that I do. It is a favourite walk of mine. I simply found myself there."

"Wondering how you got there, and suddenly thinking of Drood and whether his body might be trapped against the timbers?"

"Why, yes." Crisparkle recalled how the name of Drood had formed in his mind as he listened to the falling water.

"It was I who willed that thought and your walk to the Weir."

"You willed it!" exclaimed the good Canon in disbelief, yet chilling at the thought that he might have been the unknowing accessory of this fratricide.

"You may choose to disbelieve in animal magnetism," answered the other. "You cannot deny you went to the Weir and found the jewellery I had planted there. So my plan was completed. I had destroyed my enemy, and my other rival Landless was the suspect. Jasper, I knew, would continue to hound him as the murderer of his nephew."

The ironic, bitter look was now etched deeply in the gaunt face.

"Yet I was left with a sense of failure," he said. "It was not as it had been promised in the vision. The reality was different. I know now that things do not happen in life as they do in visions. That was something I had not foreseen. There was little in the killing to relish in the memory, and I had done it without achieving my great object—Rosa. So in the end I had to go back to the opium woman to get the satisfaction of the vision." He laughed wryly to himself. "Satisfaction? There was no longer satisfaction even in the vision. It was a poor thing compared to what it had once been. The reality had corrupted the vision itself. The killing was too quick, too easy, the body was not impaled below, was no more than a black beetle on the ground. So even the vision failed me.

"Until that last time . . . When I opened the coffin I was surprised to find nothing—I had not expected every part of the body to be so completely dissolved. So when I read the message and then saw the figure in the crypt, I thought it might be Drood somehow come back from the dead to confront me for the last time. The ring puzzled me—it meant nothing. But then the hand pointed upwards, and I saw it as a challenge to the final decisive conflict on the tower."

For the first time a look of satisfaction, of rapture, appeared on the dark features. "That was as the vision should be. The resistance . . . the cries . . . the flying body . . . the impaled figure below . . . the final convulsions . . . then the reward . . . *She* was there . . .

"That was the reality at last!"

The ecstasy died from his face as memory moved on to the outcome of his supreme moment, and how all had turned to ashes.

"It was all delusion," he said in a bitter voice. "In the end the vision was a lie. The vision cheated me, as it did Macbeth. Now, like him, I too await death."

The Murderer fell silent. He appeared exhausted and passed a trembling hand across his eyes.

"It will ease your spirit now you have confessed," said Crisparkle at last.

"Confessed? I have made no confession. I have given you the facts. I have no remorse—I would do all again in the same circumstances."

Crisparkle remembered his request. "You said there was something I could do for you?"

"Yes. Send the opium woman to me."

"The opium woman!"

"I do not expect you to understand. It isn't the vision I want, that is finished. But I am tortured here, not by remorse for what I have done—I have told you I would do it again—but for want of opium!"

The control the man had exercised over himself during their talk began to fail, and he held out shaking hands towards the Canon in supplication.

"Without opium I suffer tortures no words can describe, a hell on earth you cannot conceive, you of all people. To me the slightest sounds are agony, yet voices whisper in my ears incessantly, clocks tick with sledge-hammer blows. Time is endless, infinite. Yet I cannot sleep. Endless visions haunt me asleep and awake. While you are here you keep them at bay. The moment you are gone, these walls will crack, vile things will creep from them and eat my flesh. . . . "

He pressed his hands against his eyes, as though sheer force might drive away the dreadful creations of his addiction. Crisparkle felt a fresh horror. He understood now the gaunt face and the dark rings beneath the haunted eyes.

"All this because I am without opium. These horrors are because it is withdrawn from me here. I am given food and water, but I need it more. Those I can if need be do without. But this is a starvation that destroys the sanity, not the body. I have only two weeks to live, but before then I shall be mad! For pity's sake, Crisparkle, send me the opium woman!"

There was the sound of a key in the lock and the cell door swung open to reveal the jailer. In his presence the prisoner instantly fell silent while his haunted eyes pleaded with Crisparkle. The Canon, not knowing how to respond, stood up without speaking and made his way from the cell. As he passed through the doorway, he heard a final plea behind him:

"For God's sake!"

With these agonised words still ringing in his ears, Crisparkle walked back down the echoing corridor.

CHAPTER XXXV

THE TURN OF THE CIRCLE

THREE DAYS AFTER Crisparkle, John Jasper has a visitor.

The man in the condemned cell is sitting at the deal table. From an unclouded sky outside the afternoon sunshine is streaming through the long barred window high up in the wall, so that light fills every corner of the white-walled cell, penetrating each crack and crevice as though it has a being of its own and is some bright liquid pouring into the narrow container. The dark head of Jasper is bowed over the Bible in front of him, oblivious in his concentration of any discomfort from the hardness of his chair. The sensuous lips in the gaunt, swarthy face move slightly as they form the words of the prophet Isaiah, which from his expression would seem to yield him some profound inward satisfaction:

For the day of vengeance is in mine heart,
and the year of my redeemed is come.
    And I looked, and there was none to help;
and I wondered that there was none to uphold:
therefore mine own arm brought salvation unto
me; and my fury, it upheld me.

John Jasper does not break off reading at the sound of the key in the lock, and merely turns his head with some irritation as the door opens and his visitor passes inside. It is the opium woman. A strange apparition from the slums, her dirty shapeless clothing silhouetted against the clinical walls! As the jailer closes the door she stands looking around her nervously, her lizard eyes flicking round the cell as though to see if there is any other way of escape. As she stands there, the prisoner himself does not show immediate recognition, until with a quick intake of breath he hisses: "It's you!"

She nods and says nothing, her eyes still warily taking in the scene.

"Have you brought opium?" he asks with a sudden note of hope in his voice, rising from his chair.

An opportune fit of coughing now catches her breath. She clutches with claw-like fingers at the ragged shawl about her chest, a choking thing sucking in gasps of air between the convulsive paroxysms that rack her. Rocking her body, her eyes become sightless; she has in all appearance not heard the question.

"Poor me, poor me," she gasps at last. "I've nigh on caught my death on that coach. Oh my lungs is so bad."

"Have you brought opium?" The question is repeated impatiently.

"I brought it, deary."

"Make me a pipe. Quick."

"I said I brought it. I didn't say as I'd got it, did I?"

"What do you mean?" fiercely.

"Like I said, I brought it. But those two women turnkeys searched me something shameful, didn't they?" Another fit of coughing delays her explanation. "Took me pipe and opium from me," she whines. "How am I to get me living now, without me pipe, and opium that dreffle dear?"

"Could you conceal nothing?"

"Not from those two, deary. Worse than the excise they are."

"Not even laudanum?" with a last hope.

"That's poor stuff as does you no good. Never have nothing to do with laudanum," she wheezes back with automatic professional pride.

He turns on her with sudden fury, so that she shrinks back

towards the cell door. "Anything will serve when you suffer as I do from lack of it!" The rage just as quickly passes and he slumps back in dejection on his chair.

"Next time I'll bring you some hidden so cunning they'll never find it," she promises ingratiatingly.

"Next time, next time," he mutters unbelievingly. Then with sudden suspicion, "Why did you come?"

"A gennelman come and said. An old customer of yours wants you bad in Maidstone jail he said. So here I come," she wheezes. "Me that has given you so many a pipe o' comfort when you was low before and had the all-overs, didn't I poppet?" She falls naturally into that tone of coaxing that works on her bemused clients. "So I come to give what comfort I could to me old customer, didn't I, deary?"

The prisoner is not so malleable now as when he has smoked one or two of her pipes.

"How did you know it was me?" he questions under beetling brows.

"Everyone knows. Everyone in England knows about the murders in Cloisterham. It's in the papers, they say. How you was on the tower with Miss Rosa. And didn't I nurse her and her mother when they was no more than babbies?"

"You?" in astonishment.

She nods. "Afore I married a Jack and went to live in the docks didn't I look after her mother as a babby? And when Miss Rosa was born I come and looked after her too, didn't I? After, her poor mother got drowned, just like my Jack, and she was sent off to school poor mite." She fumbles in the recesses of the clothing under her shawl, and then the talons offer him some small object in their grip. "Here."

He ignores her. "You knew both Rosa and her mother as babies then?"

"Haven't I told you? And alike as two peas they was, the pretty little things. Here." Again the proffered talons.

He stares at her and shakes his head, not in refusal of her offer but in pursuance of his own thoughts. "And to think that you knew her all the time."

"Here. Take it," she wheezes, thinking that he is refusing her. "Here's the very ring she had on her finger when she fell in the river, poor love."

He takes it, his thoughts still on the strange coincidence of their fates, and glances carelessly at it, turning the metal circle in his hand. In the diffused light of the cell the white stones are colourless, the others a dull redness, as though the life had now gone from them. He passes it back to her without great interest: it had not been Rosa's ring.

The haggard woman receives it from him, and, with a secret smile, restores it to its hiding place under her layers of garments. Then she sits down on the bed, as if in hope that he will follow her example and relax on it as of old. Still he is not to be cajoled; and her revelation, the first surprise now over, has awakened suspicion in his mind again.

"How did you know I came from Cloisterham?" he demands, fixing his gaunt gaze on her.

Her gutter-rat intelligence senses a trap and evades it. "When I heard of the murder there, I knew as it must be you," she croaks, giving him a sly look.

"Murder? That was no murder, whatever they may say," retorted Jasper. "It was self-defence against a murderer, Neville Landless. I should be rewarded for ridding the world of a homicidal maniac, instead of sitting here." He strode up the cell and back again.

She watches his every movement with her reptilian eyes, before she replies in a voice that is hardly above a whisper.

"Not that murder, deary. The other one."

Jasper stops in his tracks and stares hard at her. "I see now. You are one of them. I should have known."

"One of who?"

"The gang who would like to pin the death of my dear boy on me, instead of on Neville Landless. The conspiracy to hang me for ridding the world of a violent murderer. It was Grewgious who sent you, wasn't it?"

"Never heard of him," she croaks back, never taking her gaze from the gaunt man.

"You will tell the truth before you leave here," is his reply in a threatening voice.

Another paroxysm of coughing is his answer, so he stands back and watches her closely as she slowly recovers her breath. "Oh me lungs is dreffle bad, dreffle bad. All wore away they are, like a string bag." Her choking finally subsides.

He waits until there is silence and then continues inexorably. "You haven't answered me yet. I will have the truth."

"Truth don't bring no comfort in this life, lovey," comes back the wheezy warning.

"I will have the truth," he repeats.

She peers at him, and with a smirk that may be malice or senility, delivers her answer. "If you wants the truth, ye shall have it. But it won't taste so sweet as a pipe of opium, deary."

"Go on!"

She settles herself on the bed—it lacks the comfortable angle of her own broken-legged furniture—pokes her head forward, tortoise-fashion, and so watches him as she speaks. "From the first time you come to me," she croaks, "you had a vision afore you saw the sights. Always the same. You went a journey. Somewhere high up where a slip would mean death. Like it might be a high tower."

She stops to see the effect of her words. He says nothing.

"And always a fellow-traveller that went with you. A fellow-traveller as never knew the fate awaiting him." She waits again, then continues. "A fellow-traveller as has a sweetheart and must die for it on the tower."

Again she pauses and looks at him. Jasper runs his tongue over his lips, and says hoarsely: "What are these fantasies to me?"

Her voice is almost a whisper, and her statement almost a question. "A fellow-traveller as is named Ned."

"Ned!" Jasper starts and his pallid face goes even whiter. "You're lying."

"If his name was truly Ned, how should I know but from your lips?"

There is a silence. "Opium dreams," says John Jasper hoarsely. "What have such imaginings to do with life?"

"Plenty, I should say, deary, plenty . . . For I talked with Ned myself."

"Impossible!"

"I talked with him in Cloisterham on Christmas Eve, and he give me three and sixpence for opium . . . And I told him Ned was a terrible threatened name, if he had a sweetheart."

Jasper gives a forced laugh. "Now I know you are romancing. First nurse to Rosa and her mother, now meeting Ned in

Cloisterham the day he disappeared. You have had too many of your own pipes, old woman." He looks down at the straggly locks of the crone on the bed. "How could you ever have been in Cloisterham and met Ned?"

"Becos I followed ye there, didn't I?" she replies viciously, angered at his mockery. "Only I lost you, and while I was sitting by the gate he comes along and speaks to me, kindly. He says his name is Edwin, but he hadn't no sweetheart, and I tells him to be thankful his name ain't Ned, such a threatened name as it is. I thought then as he wasn't Ned. Now I knows better. He was Ned."

"Then what did he look like?"

She describes Edwin Drood, his clothes and his appearance, down to the very spot he had on his cheek that day. It cannot be doubted that she saw Drood on Christmas Eve.

"Why did you follow me to Cloisterham?"

She leers back at him. "Suppose a gennelman like you as had secrets might like to help an old woman."

"Blackmail!" in a tone of disgust. "A common blackmailer."

"Just a word, deary. And is helping people to keep alive worse than a-killing them?" she wheezes venomously.

"I shall not talk with you any more about this matter. It serves no purpose."

"I thought ye wanted the truth, deary. So you said."

Jasper turns away from her. "I have sworn a solemn oath," he replies in a tone of finality, "never to discuss the mystery with any human creature until I hold the clue to it in my hand."

The crone rocks her body backwards and forwards on the bed with a convulsive shaking that may be another coughing fit or suppressed laughter.

"No need to worry about your oath, deary," she splutters.

"What do you mean?"

"Becos it ain't binding on you no more."

"Why not?"

"You've held the clue to it in your hand, haven't you?"

"I don't understand you. When? What clue?"

"The ring. You held that in your hand. You don't think you imagined that?"

"Rosa's mother's ring. What has that got to do with it?"

"Everything, deary, everything. That was the very same ring the murderer left on Edwin Drood's body when he put him to rot in the coffin. The ring that was all that was left when they opened the coffin."

"So?"

"The murderer knew all his other jewellery and took it off him, didn't he? But he didn't know of the ring, so it was found. And who but his dear relation knew all his jewellery and not his ring?"

"It's not true," says Jasper, whose hoarseness is suddenly afflicting him again in that tender organ the throat, which is so affected by his mood. "Neville Landless killed him."

"So you say now. It's not what you said afore your visions."

"Opium pipe-dreams. No more."

"And not what you said after neither . . .."

"What do you mean, after . . .?" hoarsely.

"After it happened. Last time you come and had a pipe to comfort you, you talked . . .."

"Unintelligible . . . "

"Not when ye had had a pipe or two to relax you as I knows how to make."

"Pipe-dreams."

"Some was, deary. Millions and billions of times you said you done it. That was the dreams. But you says, 'When it was *really* done . . .' that was what you says, 'When it was *really* done . . .' "

"Yes. What?" His voice is now almost as hoarse as the old woman's.

"You says, 'When it was really done, it seemed not worth the doing, it was done so soon . . . not worth the doing, it was done so soon,' you says."

"When it was really done, it seemed not worth the doing, it was done so soon," Jasper repeats in a mechanical, strangled voice.

The opium woman falls silent, sensing that no more needs be said. John Jasper stands rigid in the centre of the cell, not speaking, his face a mask. Yet she knows that within him some of her words—she does not know which—have started up some great irresistible movement: as a pebble trickling from the summit of a mountain will gather others and still more until a mighty avalanche of rock is thundering down the mountainside.

Such an overwhelming force, she knows, is sweeping through the silent, motionless man. She watches, saying nothing.

At last he speaks in a hoarse, terrible voice that is not his own.

"It was so. It was not worth the doing. It was no better than killing a corpse . . . .

"Ne . . . e . . . e . . . d!!!" The last is an appalling shriek, scarce recognisable as a word, that breaks from Jasper's lips. He reels to the wall of the cell and leans panting against it. Mere animal sounds emerge from his singer's throat. Then with unseeing eyes he staggers drunkenly and falls across the bed, where he lies unmoving, his head clutched in his hands.

The woman gets up from the bed and looks down at her old customer, lying across the bed without any sign of life but for the occasional convulsive twitch, as she has so often seen him in the past.

She shakes her fist at him. "Ye've killed two good men and would have killed my little Rosa. Good riddance to ye!" is her parting malediction.

The jailer, summoned by the cry, unlocks the cell door. The opium woman, after a final basilisk look at Jasper from the threshold, brushes past another figure outside the door, and scuttles away up the echoing corridor. Having reassured himself that no harm has come to his prisoner, the jailer locks the cell again. When he returns with the evening meal, the prisoner is still lying motionless in the same position on the bed. So he remains.

In the morning the jailer comes with the prisoner's breakfast. He unlocks the door—and the plate falls from his hand and rolls across the floor. In all his life he has never seen such a sight in the condemned cell. Every previous occupant's last hope has been to escape the hangman: John Jasper alone has taken that office upon himself.

The bars in the long cell window have served as the gallows; strips torn from his bedding have improvised the hemp; the wooden chair, now kicked away, has been the drop. The scarf-like rope is around his neck, he too has died of strangulation. The body hangs upon the lime-washed wall, black hair and whiskers silhouetted against the pure whiteness. The dark eyes remain wide open, blank now of vision and of visions alike.

The Bible still lies open on the table at the same page, the light of

210

the new day falling on the words of the prophet: 'For the day of vengeance is in mine heart . . . therefore mine own arm brought salvation unto me; and my fury, it upheld me.'

At last the Avenger had found The Murderer.

CHAPTER XXXVI

VESPERS

FOR THE LIVING, life went on as it does; even if not quite as before. In the Cathedral a new Choir Master directed the white-robed choir. Their singing acquired a more workmanlike, every-day sound. The congregation may miss those inspired moments when John Jasper was in good voice, raising the whole choir with him, but the fevered and the unpredictable has gone too. The whole Cathedral has become less brooding, less introspective, and has acquired again the solid Englishness of the Anglican Church, that durable compromise of Church and State. But alas for the Cloisterham champion of the Constitution! Mr Sapsea's suit with Miss Dean did not prosper, indeed was greeted with such frigidity that whenever the Dean and Sapsea met, whatever the season of the year, an east wind blew straight down the street. The mayoralty passed on to one of his despised rivals, none other than a Cloisterham butcher, a mere purveyor of tripes and intestines. To those unwise enough to be button-holed by Sapsea he would expatiate at great length on the unworthiness of the new mayor, how he had always seen through Jasper and had kept a pret-ty close eye on him; but somehow he found it more and more difficult to acquire an audience.

Minor Canon Crisparkle, on the other hand, did not take long to recover his customary spirits, aided by mortification of the flesh in icy rivers and furious swimming. His recovery was also aided by Miss Helena Landless, who, as soon as the period of mourning for her brother was over, became Mrs Canon Crisparkle (and in the fulness of time Mrs Dean Crisparkle too). They set up house in Minor Canon Corner where the china shepherdess was as delighted with her new daughter as she had been implacably hostile to the brother. So all was harmony in the household, and Cloisterham rumour ran that Crisparkle had even hung up his boxing gloves.

There was another wedding too, with Crisparkle himself officiating. What a twittering there was in the Nuns' House before this event! When Rosa appeared to pay a call on Miss Twinkleton in the company of her Jack, who had climbed the Beanstalk and slain the Giant at the top for her, every feminine eye was at the windows. Had the Nuns' House been afloat it must infallibly have turned turtle and sunk! Let Rosebud hang on to the arm of her sailor, for there are willing hands aplenty to rescue him should he show the slightest need! And what a ferment of excitement reigns after their departure until the wedding, so that Miss Twinkleton —hardly less excited than her charges—has the greatest difficulty in maintaining scholastic discipline and ladylike deportment, Miss Ferdinand being quite out of hand and impervious to punishments of writing out the fables of Monsieur La Fontaine, only being brought to order by the ultimate sanction of threatened exclusion from the ceremony.

On the day itself few Cloisterham citizens were not to be seen in or near the church. Even Stony Durdles was there, wearing his—presumably only—suit with horn buttons, but without a speck of dust to be seen from the soles of his boots to the crown of his head. How this was achieved was never known, it being commonly surmised that his journeymen had laid him over a line and applied themselves to work with carpet beaters in place of the usual stone saw. In one respect Durdles had not changed, and proposed to drink the health of the happy couple as many times as he could manage that evening, special escort arrangements having been made to that end with Deputy. The Billickin was also present, seated in the church in her best finery, torn between satisfaction at being invited to the wedding by her former tenant and a metropolitan contempt for the ways of the provinces. Her old enemy Miss Twinkleton with her girls having been seated well away from her, she had no opportunity to resume their verbal duel, so contented herself with an occasional telling look in that direction contriving to convey her surprise that the young ladies had succeeded in remaining alive on such blood-thinning diet. The Billickin was also diverted by a genteel shock-headed elderly gentleman seated near her, who made himself very agreeable; she had the feeling she had seen him in London; but could not quite remember where.

It was Mr Grewgious himself who gave away the Bride, without assistance from dancing masters. He had a splendid new suit for the occasion, but nature still defeated the tailor, for such was the shape of Mr Grewgious's shanks that his new trousers *would* work their way upwards in defiance of gravity and expose his stocking. But who cared? He had delivered the Bride, never so pretty as today, blushing in her mother's wedding dress. The best man, a sailor almost as handsome as Tartar and the new focus of interest for the young ladies, produced the bridegroom and the ring. (Not *the* ring: that Rosa declared she would never wear, and requested Mr Grewgious to retain in his keeping in memory of her mother, which he was very ready to do.) So all having been made ready, Crisparkle made no mistake in tying the lovers' knot.

One day, not long after, when sitting in the garden of that half-nautical country estate where he was now a frequent and welcome visitor, Rosa put a question to Mr Grewgious. He looked the same, yet with a subtle difference: while his features were as cork-like as ever, the sap of life now seemed to run through this old tree with such vigour that it would not have surprised anyone to see fresh green leaves starting to burgeon from his fingers or the birds of the air coming down to nest in the tindery thatch. Rosa, who had been examining her own fingers and rings, suddenly looked up and said, "Grew!"—for such was the affectionate name by which he was now known to her and to Tartar, and would be to their children too—"Grew, how did my old nurse get the ring? You have never told me the whole story."

"Well, my dear," he replied seriously (for the woman had not long survived Jasper), "it is a sad story, and I did not wish to mar the happiness that should attend a wedding, but now it is right that you should know.

"When Mr Crisparkle was asked by Jasper to send her to the condemned cell, he came to ask my advice. We decided to go and see her together. You may imagine my surprise at finding she was the very woman who had been nurse to both your mother and yourself as babies! It seems she was a very poor and distant relative of your mother's family. When your mother was about four years old, she had left to marry a sailor. She had a hard life, for he soon drowned at sea, leaving her in poverty. I fear she drank to forget her sorrows for the next sixteen years—but sorrows do not drown so easily as men. Then you were born, my dear. Your mother found out where she was, and sent for her to be your nurse too. Such was the influence you and your mother exercised over her that she never touched a drop of drink during that time."

Rosa put a handkerchief to her eyes; though it was long ago, she had been fond of her nurse in a childish way.

"She was deeply attached to you both. You see, my dear, she had no family or children of her own. She thought of you and your mother as *her* babies. She told us how very much alike you were at that age. And not only at that age!" added Mr Grewgious, as though with a sudden access of kindred feeling for the woman.

"So she was very sad when you in your turn ceased to be a baby and the time for parting came. Your mother gave her as a memento a ring resembling her own diamond and ruby ring that she had always much admired. She was so attached to this ring that she prized it and kept it even in her darkest days."

Grewgious paused for a moment, at the thought, perhaps, of another who had done the same.

"When she left you both, she returned to the docks. Ill-health led her to opium, and to dependence upon it, as it has others. Ill-health and poverty, so she took to selling it to the likes of herself as a means of livelihood.

"She was not an evil person, my dear," he added gently. "She recognised the evil in Jasper and did her best to thwart his designs. For she gradually came to realise from odd words her customer let fall under the influence of the drug that he had murderous designs upon some unknown person he called Ned. Ned also had a sweetheart who called him Eddy. But these were not the only names he uttered. His murderous imaginings would be followed by colourful visions, when he would often in his ecstasy call out the name of Rosa."

Despite the warmth of the autumn day, a shiver passed through the small figure.

"At first she thought the name Rosa mere coincidence. Then one day he muttered Rosebud. The notion came to her that the object of his passions was none other than Rosa Bud, *her* baby, HER Rosa!! The conviction grew ever more strong within her. The thought that you might unknowingly marry a murderer began to haunt her. She grew dark with hatred for him, determined to frustrate his schemes. Yet there was little she could do without more knowledge. She did not know who he was, or where he came from. She would have warned you, but she had no idea where you were, not even where you had been sent to school after your mother's death. She attempted to learn all she could from him while he was under the influence of the drug, experimenting with the mixture to make him talk more. To her deep disappointment, despite these efforts, he never divulged as much as she needed to know. Her only other resource was to follow him, as she did to Cloisterham.

"On the first occasion, Christmas Eve, she encountered Edwin, and would have warned him of his fate if she had known his identity. While she thought he seemed to recognise her that day, Edwin had changed so much since they had last seen one another—she was your nurse and he only a small boy—that *she* did not recognise *him*. He told her that his name was Edwin and denied he had a sweetheart, so she had no reason to believe that he was the intended victim."

"Poor Eddy!" thought Rosa. "So close to safety, yet so far!"

"On her second visit she was more successful," he continued, "discovering from Datchery Jasper's name, and where he lived and worked. It also enabled Datchery to trace her, through Deputy, to her den in London, but when he went to see her there to discover what she knew of Jasper, she mistrusted him. Knowing him to live beneath Jasper's Gate House, she suspected him of being an ally sent to find out the extent of her knowledge, and gave him no answer to his questions.

"So you see, my dear, when Mr Crisparkle and I appeared and told her that Jasper had murdered Edwin as well as Neville, and had also attempted to kill *you* on the Tower, she had an even bigger score to settle with him, and readily agreed to the visit. We hoped that she might be able to induce him to repeat his admission to the murder of Edwin. For being an interested party in clearing the name of Helena's brother, Mr Crisparkle felt that his own position would be less delicate if the murderer confessed before an independent witness. So I myself was in attendance for this eventuality, but, as you know, his confession took . . . another form."

"Then Jasper never really held the clue in his hand. There were a pair of rings, and he had the imitation one," said Rosa wonderingly.

"Just so, my dear," answered Grewgious. "Our friend never could distinguish the true and the false."

Rosa, after a thoughtful pause, asked another question. "Grew, who is Mr Datchery? He was at the wedding, but I haven't seen him since then, and I did want to thank him for all the work he did."

"I am sure, my dear," responded Mr Grewgious with a twinkle, "that Mr Datchery would be much displeased if I were to describe him as being anyone other than Mr Datchery, for that is who he is."

"Don't be tiresome and lawyerish, Grew. You know perfectly well what I mean," rejoined Rosa, pouting her little red mouth at him.

"Well, if you had framed your question in a different way, my dear, it would have made it easier for me to answer. Suppose you had asked who *was* Mr Datchery, I should have been able to give you the kind of answer you seem to want."

Rosa jumped up from her chair, brushed a fly away from his forehead and kissed him lightly. "Very well, who *was* Mr Datchery?"

"Mr Datchery *was* Mr Bazzard," creaked Grewgious, getting as close to a smile as his face would ever permit.

"That sulky clerk of yours?"

"Yes, poor fellow. He had a very frustrating time being my clerk. So when I wanted some detective work doing on our friend, I sent him to Cloisterham. He got a wig and things from his theatrical circle and became Mr Datchery. And Mr Poker too, of course, only that was himself without the wig! When he found the ring in the coffin, he recognised it at once, having been the witness when I gave it to Edwin. But he preferred being Mr Datchery so much that he decided to remain Mr Datchery for good, and changed his name by deed poll."

"And is he happier now, Grew?"

"Of course he is. The Thorn of Anxiety has come out at last. I think we can safely say that it has been Completely Extracted."

"I'm not sure I understand," said Rosa, wrinkling her forehead.

216

"Mr Bazzard, being dissatisfied with being Mr Bazzard, attempted to remedy the situation by writing a play, *The Thorn of Anxiety*. Unfortunately nobody ever has, nor I fear ever will, produce this play upon the stage. So Mr Bazzard has found an even better remedy. He has been able to transform himself into another personality, Mr Datchery, that suits him very well in every way, being, as you might say, custom-made for him to his own design. So now he proposes to remain that individual for the rest of his life."

"Is he going to remain your clerk too?"

"Bless me, no. I already have another clerk, and between ourselves, a much better clerk. Datchery so much liked the work on which I employed him in Cloisterham, that he has decided to continue this line on his own account. He is now a private detective."

"Is he good at that?"

"Very competent. Much better than he ever was as my clerk. You see it requires some knowledge of the law—which he has. Tick that off. Ability to act a part to acquire information—which he has. Tick that off. Curiosity about other people's business. Tick that off."

"And he hated taking orders from you," chimed in Rosa, "and now he can work for anyone he wants to, and needn't work for anyone he doesn't want to."

"Tick that off!" exclaimed Grewgious with enthusiasm.

"And he has found a profession that suits him perfectly, and so he will live happily ever after like us," she concluded. Then with scant concern for logic, "And if he doesn't like being Datchery any more, then he can just become somebody else. What a perfect idea!"

"I hope you won't want to become somebody else. I should not like it if you were to become somebody else, my dear."

"Of course I won't, you silly Grew," retorted Rosa, jumping up and kissing him again. "I'm much too happy as I am." Then more seriously, "Do you think Mr Ba-tchery will be successful?"

"I see no reason why Mr Batchery should not be a great success," said Mr Grewgious solemnly.

"You're teasing. It's a serious question, Grew."

"With a serious answer, my dear. He already has several other clients, and has taken on as an assistant the boy Deputy, who is very useful in finding out information for him, as he was in tracking down your nurse."

"So you think being a *private* detective, as you call it, is a serious profession?"

"In the view of an Angular and unimaginative old fellow," said Mr Grewgious judicially, "the *Private* Detective has a promising future. Yes, I think I can confidently say, a promising future."

AFTERWORD

WRITING THIS BOOK has posed a dilemma. I wanted to explain the reasons for my solution, yet I did not want to undermine the interest in my ending by revealing all its details in advance. So, in Part One, I concentrated on the central problem of *Edwin Drood*, that of John Jasper, and largely ignored the secondary problems of the story, in particular the role of Helena Landless and the identity of Datchery. It may now fairly be asked why I chose the solutions to these conundrums embodied in my ending in Part Two.

The key episode is the dramatic scene at the bottom of the monthly cover, where a man holding a lantern is staring at a second figure standing upright in the darkness, wearing a hat and coat. Collins's original sketch for the cover is more useful than Fildes's final version. Collins's Edwin at the top of the cover, where he is emerging from the Cathedral with Rosa on his arm, has a pronounced, rather drooping moustache—which disappeared in Fildes's version—and so has the standing figure in the lantern scene. This makes it virtually certain that the figure was intended to represent Edwin Drood. Since Drood is dead before this scene takes place, it has to be an impersonation. Dickens appears to have been grooming Helena Landless to undertake some male role, with the information that she ran away four times from her stepfather in Ceylon 'dressed as a boy'. A case has been made for Helena as the detective Datchery, but it is surely stretching the credulity of the reader to accept that a young lady who is known in Cloisterham could get away with posing in broad daylight as a retired male diplomat. These objections would not apply if she were to appear on one occasion only, to be seen in the darkness by the light of a lantern, without speaking. The earlier impersonations of Edwin Drood by a pupil of Miss Twinkleton have already been pointed out (see above p. 88). There is also another allusion that has not. As I did not wish to reveal my dénouement prematurely, I quoted (at pp. 84–5) only half of

219

the passage Dickens first wrote as one paragraph. For just as he encapsulated the role of Jasper in the whimsical closet paragraphs at the beginning of the third number, so at the start of the fourth number he outlined the fate of Edwin Drood under the guise of the end-of-term activities at the Nuns' House. After the suffocation of Miss Ferdinand, the passage continues:

> Nor were these the only tokens of dispersal. Boxes appeared in the bedrooms (where they were capital at other times), and a surprising amount of packing took place, out of all proportion to the amount packed. Largesse, in the form of odds and ends of cold cream and pomatum, and also of hairpins, was freely distributed among the attendants. On charges of inviolable secrecy, confidences were interchanged respecting golden youth of England expected to call, "at home," on the first opportunity. Miss Giggles (deficient in sentiment) did indeed profess that she, for her part, acknowledged such homage by making faces at the golden youth; but this young lady was outvoted by an immense majority.
>
> On the last night before a recess, it was always expressly made a point of honour that nobody should go to sleep, and that ghosts should be encouraged by all possible means. This compact invariably broke down, and all the young ladies went to sleep very soon, and got up very early.

> (p.112)

In this context box may be equated with coffin, which since it contains a murdered body would be 'capital' (in the same sense as capital punishment). There is packing out of all proportion to the amount to be packed: quick-lime has to be packed round the corpse. Personal possessions are distributed, as Drood's will be at the Weir, including a specific mention of hairpins, the feminine equivalent of Drood's shirt-pin which Crisparkle would find in the mud. The golden youth refers to the wealthy Tartar who will eventually replace Edwin in Rosa's affections. Lastly, there is the rather laboured introduction of ghosts, coupled with hint that the business will not be a success. This is surely an allusion to the impersonation of Drood and his final, unreal appearance in the scene on the cover. It is the part for which Dickens seems to have been preparing Helena Landless.

I have no evidence that the author had in mind a double false Drood. Yet it seemed in accordance with the spirit of the story that the other twin should also play the part in his own way. According to Forster, Neville Landless would die in the attempt to seize the murderer, and I thought it appropriate that his death should take the form of The Murderer's fantasy killing of Edwin Drood.

If Helena is to act the part of Edwin Drood, who then is Dick Datchery? One of the remaining characters, or a professional detective? Bazzard, so conveniently absent from his duties after his master Grewgious has been thinking about keeping an eye on Jasper, must start as favourite. The surly, laconic Bazzard is admittedly almost as unlike the courtly, mellifluous Datchery as it is possible to imagine; but Felix Aylmer put the authority of his own distinguished career in the theatre in support of Bazzard, pointing out that it is typical of the character actor to be disappointingly ordinary off stage, unrecognisably different from the characters he portrays on stage. Dickens would have been aware of this fact from his own acting experience, and the transformation of Bazzard into Datchery becomes quite credible from this point of view. Dickens was perhaps giving a hint of such a transformation when he compared Bazzard to a 'fabulous Familiar' called into existence by a magic spell—the same magic may translate him. So Bazzard, dissatisfied with his lot as a farmer's son and then a lawyer's clerk, finds his satisfaction in being transformed into the completely contrasting personality of the retired diplomat Dick Datchery. Seen in these terms, I found Bazzard not only acceptable but inevitable as the choice for Datchery, even before I realised that this sudden jump from one personality to a totally contrasting one was another reflection of the Jasper personalities. I kept the revelation of Datchery's identity to the very end of my continuation, as the final example of the duality theme. I even went one step further than Dickens may have intended, in suggesting that Bazzard was so enamoured of both his new personality and his new occupation that he intended to retain them permanently by turning private detective with Deputy as his assistant. So the choice between another character or a professional detective being Datchery was resolved—the character becomes the professional detective!

I have re-read *Edwin Drood* many times in the course of this work, and such is the richness of the text, that each time I have found something new. The idea of duality extends far beyond the mechanics of the plot, it is something that penetrates the whole of Dickens's last novel; the examples that have been quoted are by no means exhaustive. The idea seems to be at the very root of his creative inspiration in writing his final work. Perhaps it is linked with the sad, elegiac note that pervades *Edwin Drood*. For Dickens knew in his heart that his time was running out, and that he might not live to complete his story. He was himself one of those former Cloisterham children he described, for whom 'the rustling sounds and fresh scents of their earliest impressions revived when the circle of their lives was very nearly traced, and the beginning and the end were drawing together' (p. 120). Decaying, autumnal Cloisterham in which the story opens is like some reflection in the water of his own fast-ageing body. In *The Mystery of Edwin Drood* was Dickens the artist really writing a parable on the mysterious dualism of the mortal human body and of the human spirit?

The meaning of his novel I must leave to the scholars and critics. My concern is with the mystery story, and I hope I have offered a readable solution to it and thrown some light on its structure. If my analysis is correct, Dickens's place in the history of the crime story is due for reassessment. At present he is credited with having introduced the first detective into modern English fiction, Inspector Bucket in *Bleak House*. I suggest we now need to acknowledge that in *The Mystery of Edwin Drood* Dickens was also engaged in writing the first great psychological crime story in our literature.